INVESTIGATIVE REPORTING AND EDITING

PAUL N. WILLIAMS

Ohio State University

PRENTICE-HALL, INC., Englewood Cliffs, New Jersey 07632

Library of Congress Cataloging in Publication Data

WILLIAMS, PAUL N. (date)
   Investigative reporting and editing.

   Bibliography: p.
   Includes index.
     1. Reporters and reporting.   I. Title.
PN4781.W63 1978   070.4'3   77-4855
ISBN 0-13-504662-9

*To Pat, Patty, John, Nina and Jan—
my family, who endured living with a journalist
looking for trouble.*

Printed in the United States of America

10 9 8 7 6 5 4 3 2

Prentice-Hall International, Inc., *London*
Prentice-Hall of Australia Pty. Limited, *Sydney*
Prentice-Hall of Canada, Ltd., *Toronto*
Prentice-Hall of India Private Limited, *New Delhi*
Prentice-Hall of Japan, Inc., *Tokyo*
Prentice-Hall of Southeast Asia Pte. Ltd., *Singapore*
Whitehall Books Limited, *Wellington, New Zealand*

Contents

(handwritten margin notes: Paper trails · Interviews · observation · Computers · Writing · Organizing · Example)

Foreword

I FIRST met Paul Williams the summer of 1976 at the founding convention of *Investigative Reporters and Editors* at Indianapolis. He surprised me. I had admired him from a distance for his original journalistic work, including his leadership in exposing corruption in one of the most conventionally revered charities in the country. But even though I have been a reporter my whole life and have known hundreds of other reporters and should have known better, I still half-expected that Paul Williams, indefatigable investigator, would match the stereotype of the swaggering tough guy. Of course, he wasn't. He was a gentle and modest man of intelligence, the kind of person you would like and respect even if you knew nothing of his work. Four months later Paul Williams died suddenly of a heart attack. He was 54 years old.

Paul represented a conventional and unimportant tradition in journalism, which is not so unusual. But he also personified a new and significant reality.

He met the old convention of the proper reporter and editor. He had once been a paperboy, a "little merchant." One summer he even worked in a paper mill. He had been a copyboy doing odd jobs inside a newspaper office, all before he became a professional reporter and editor. This is the old-fashioned idea of a "real newspaperman," the mythical creature who somehow had ink in his veins from birth.

He met that tradition and would have been declared a good old boy in the trade solely on that Horatio Alger version of how newspapermen are created—and in the old tradition it was always a male. The world of journalism is full of people with that kind of background and among them are some of the best and some of the worst practitioners of our trade. Another way of saying this is that it really doesn't make any difference whether you delivered papers as a kid.

But Paul Williams was not just a good old boy. He represented something new and different in modern American journalism. He knew that the mechanical and technical skills were important, that you must get details accurately in hand, and that you must be capable of fast work. But he also knew something far more important: You need a sense of morality about your society and you need to accept personal responsibility for your role in that society.

In his last years he demonstrated that all the proven power of the press and of individual reporters when given support and freedom is not terribly significant if this power is turned against petty targets. The ills of American and world society do not arise from overtime parkers or welfare mothers but from negligence and crimes of large, prestigious organizations. Paul understood that. Not enough journalists and journalistic organizations shared his profound insight.

In this book, Paul records the question we are frequently asked: "What's the difference between investigative reporting and just good reporting?"

His appropriate answer is: "No difference . . . and a lot of difference." A good reporter always has to discover enough about his or her subject to test the validity of information that is printed. But the big difference that gives new meaning to "investigative reporting" is, as he has written, "a gradual shift from the old style of reporting on spectacular single incidents and personal crimes to more original and conscientious reporting on the systematic operations of American society."

Paul led teams of reporters who used careful and intelligent analysis of the masses of data by which modern organizations do business. He demonstrated that the individual reporter working on complex stories is still important but there are some stories like complex corporate and governmental crime that are best done by coordinated research by a team of disciplined journalists.

It was typical of Paul Williams, both as a scholar and a journalist, that at the end of his life he was one of the founders of Investigative Reporters and Editors. Within that group he led the organization's initial project to establish an archive of validated research information unearthed by others so that journalists "reporting on the systematic operations of American society" will begin to have at least one small instrument—previously proven information—in their unequal contest with malefactors of great power.

Paul Williams' career, particularly his last Pulitzer-prize-winning investigation (the first for reporting ever to be given to a weekly paper), his work as a university teacher, and this book are memorials to a decent and dedicated man who personified the best in American journalism.

BEN H. BAGDIKIAN
University of California, Berkeley

Introduction

THIS BOOK is the personal effort of one editor and reporter to explore and chart the world of investigative reporting—both as it has been and as it can be.

The surge of interest that developed in the 1970s, largely as a result of Watergate, generated much argument about investigative reporting. To some it seemed that an exotic new media form had been created, and that its application represented a daring and dangerous extension of the journalist's constitutional franchise.

Not so. Call it muckraking, exposé, whatever you wish, investigative reporting has been part of American journalistic tradition since the early eighteenth-century days of John Peter Zenger. It helped break up the Tweed Ring in New York City more than a century ago. It was Nellie Bly's tool when she posed as a mental patient in order to get inside an insane asylum. It burgeoned in the era of the muckrakers—Steffens, Tarbell, Sinclair, Spargo—and stimulated important changes in national policy. Theodore Roosevelt tried to squelch it before Richard Nixon and Spiro Agnew were born. Investigative reporting helped expose the perpetrators of Teapot Dome in the 1920s and clean up the labor-union movement in the 1950s. Its renewed strength in the 1970s emphasizes its fundamental nature.

One of my oldest newspaper friends wrote to me after he heard I was teaching investigative reporting and asked: "What's the difference between investigative reporting and just good reporting?" I was to hear a dozen variations of his question as I worked on this book, and I learned to answer it in two parts: "No difference" and "A lot of difference." No difference because good reporting assumes an investigative attitude and investigative methods; a lot of difference because investigative reporting in its more recent manifestations has begun to change the definitions of news values. Essentially, the big difference is a gradual shift from the old style of reporting on spectacular single incidents and personal crimes to more original and conscientious reporting on the systematic operations of American society.

Today's investigative reporter doesn't always wait for things to happen. He or she is not geared to events. In interviews with more than 100 reporters and editors, I was struck by the regularity with which they volunteered phrases like these:

"People need to know how things really work."

"You have to keep looking for patterns."

"The job is to try to pull things together for the reader."

For too long, too much of journalism has been organized into locational beats, like the police station, the city clerk's office, the courthouse. The beat system encourages the reporter to accept the official version of events. It restricts his movements. It does not motivate him to find out, for example, what happened in the years before an industrial-safety problem grew into a lawsuit on his court beat. Pressures of time, space, tradition, training, even commercial constraints, keep him from asking the essential question: "Why?"

The modern investigative reporter inverts tradition. He resists daily deadlines. He cuts across beat lines to pursue trouble wherever it originates. His main question *is* the essential question: "Why?"

Conscious aversion to the accepted way is perhaps the most important attribute of today's investigative reporter. His choice of story subjects forces new thinking about standard definitions of news and of the role of the newspaper. He is not content to score a scoop saying that a public figure is under official investigation. He is searching instead for the problems that officialdom ignores. He wants to know, for instance, why one class of citizens virtually escapes prosecution for income-tax evasion while another class faces swift retribution. He is, in short, concerned about the equitable operation of the entire social system. The job of every newspaper, in fact, is to examine and report on all the institutions of society.

The perceptive reporter sees many examples of institutional leadership that has lost sight of its original goals and its clients' needs. As he filters these observations into his experience, he wonders if there may be something more to say about why such remissness occurs so often. He also begins to challenge a tenet of old-style journalism, the one that says: "You can't fight city hall." That tenet was based on the belief that people couldn't know how city hall (the system) really worked—and shouldn't try. The investigative reporter believes they can—and should.

The best reporters, therefore, try to go beyond catching criminals or unmasking single incidents of corporate cynicism. They try to define not only what is operationally unsuccessful but also what is conceptually false. To undertake such a role, of course, smacks of impudence. Persistent questioning of accepted mythology upsets the high priests. The investigative reporter consciously chooses to get in harm's way, and his reward is about equal parts of pain and pleasure. He is practicing what David Kraslow calls "high-risk" journalism. He is raising moral issues. He is pointing out conflicts and contradictions.

The risks, the pain, and the pleasure are exemplified in the storm of Watergate and the tidal waves it will cause to sweep back and forth through our society for decades to come. There were strong, traditional arguments against reporters' probing into banking transactions and the tax records of public persons. There was the serious question of using unnamed sources to report that a Vice President was under suspicion of illegal fund-raising. There were strong arguments against suggesting, without documentary evidence or direct, quotable testimony, that the United States Attorney General had knowledge of the criminal cover-up. Only gradually were these reservations overruled in most editors' minds by public interest in possible (and, as it developed, actual) interference with American judicial and legal processes. In retrospect, the painful and dangerous individual and collective decisions of reporters, editors, and publishers were, for the most part, justified.

The Watergate storm, however, jarred the American system to its foundations. New waves of reaction rushed in: tighter rules for campaign financing, efforts to codify and sanctify official secrecy, increased attention to the law of privacy, mixed fates in many states for sunshine laws and shield laws.

And in hundreds of American towns, the storm also induced a sudden jump in attempts at investigative reporting, much of it ill conceived and poorly executed. Watergate was to make hometown editors and reporters realize that investigative reporting carries heavier burdens when it deals with real people than when it deals with remote, symbolic figures. The reporter for the hometown newspaper must live with the knowledge that his big story will bring opprobrium and grief to the family of his subjects; that it may close an industrial plant and wipe out hundreds of jobs; that it can queer a deal for a proposed new factory whose payrolls, it will be argued vehemently, will far outweigh a few thousand dollars of insiders' profit for a few city officials. The aggressive hometown reporter of business news or consumer interests will also find himself at odds with the newspaper's business manager—and perhaps with its publisher.

To cope with these dilemmas requires a certain amount of missionary zeal, or what Bill Lambert calls "a low threshold of indignation." This book cannot create that zeal nor define that threshold. Its aim is to help students of journalism and practicing reporters develop investigative concepts, problem-solving methods, and fact-finding skills.

I have written this book for people who want to use such zeal for the betterment of some of the 1,700 hometown daily newspapers in the United States. It is a book for advanced students and working journeymen who want to write thorough, perceptive, responsible reports on how things really work right around home. It is not a book for beginning journalists—and it offers no easy ways for the novice investigative reporter to get his feet wet.

Investigative reporting is unavoidably complex. That does not mean, however, that it cannot be accomplished successfully by the determined tyro. But a word of precaution: investigative reporting is high-risk journalism on any level.

However complex and however fraught with risks, investigative reporting is without question an essential part of American journalism. My goal here is twofold: to help reporters define and refine story concepts and apply professional techniques to solving operational problems, and to help students, reporters, and editors think carefully about whether the investigative approach is right for them and their audiences. Should the book meet its objective, I can then hope that its readers will resolve not just to perform the tricks of the trade, but to maintain and advance investigative reporting as an honorable form of journalism—one that truly serves the public interest.

PAUL N. WILLIAMS

The Cast of Characters

"Acknowledgments" just wouldn't work as a heading for this section.

In my research, of course, I read many books and articles, as well as several hundred columns of newspaper stories that purported to qualify as investigative reporting. I also carried on extensive correspondence with reporters, editors, and academics.

But to give a feeling for the state and future of the art of investigative reporting in actual practice, I traveled some 10,000 miles over a two-year period to visit working journalists in their newsrooms. As I did so, I came to view them as major characters in the drama of investigative journalism that is being played every day before the American audience. To accord them greater identity, I have chosen to sketch the background of each of my interviewees in a sort of playbill. In general, the professional affiliations shown are those held in early 1977.

Len Ackland, business reporter for the *Des Moines Register*, formerly with Dispatch News Service International and the *Rocky Mountain Journal*. Books: *Credibility Gap: A Digest of the Pentagon Papers* (compiler, 1972) and *Why Are We Still in Vietnam*? (editor, 1970).

Andrew Alexander, political writer, onetime investigative reporter teamed with Keith McKnight for the *Dayton Journal-Herald*. An overseas reporter in Australia, Czechoslovakia, and South Vietnam before joining the Ohio paper in 1971, Alexander was cited for best investigative reporting by the Associated Press Society of Ohio in 1972 and 1974.

Jack Anderson, author of "Washington Merry-Go-Round," the nationally syndicated column that goes far beyond the base built by the late Drew Pearson. Anderson has become a major guardian of the public interest, defender of the First Amendment, and goad to the clubbier members of the Washington press corps.

Ross Anderson, reporter for the *Seattle Times.*

William E. Anderson, veteran police reporter of the *Indianapolis Star* and key member of the team that won a Pulitzer Prize in 1974 for reporting on police corruption and politics in Indianapolis.

Gene Ayres, reporter for the *Oakland Tribune,* a Professional Journalism Fellow at Stanford University in 1971-1972. He has won several San Francisco Press Club and AP California-Nevada prizes as well as the McQuade Award for work that demonstrates how every reporter can do investigative work.

Charles W. Bailey, editor, the *Minneapolis Tribune.* He spent eighteen years in the *Tribune's* Washington bureau, the last six as its chief, was president of the White House Correspondents Association in 1969 and secretary of the standing committee of correspondents in the United States Congress in 1963. He is coauthor of three books, the best known of which is *Seven Days in May* (with Fletcher Knebel, 1962).

Donald L. Barlett, co-member, with James B. Steele, of the investigative team of the *Philadelphia Inquirer.* He has done investigative work for the *Chicago Daily News* and *Cleveland Plain Dealer* and general reporting for the *Akron Beacon Journal* and the *Reading* (Pa.) *Times.* Since 1970, he and Steele have won thirteen national prizes together, including one Pulitzer, two Sigma Delta Chis, two John Hancocks, and two of the other best-known business-writing awards (University of Missouri-INGAA and Gerald Loeb). For more, see the listing for Steele.

Harley Bierce, member of the *Indianapolis Star* Pulitzer team (see William E. Anderson). The *Star's* police-corruption series also won a Sigma Delta Chi Award, Drew Pearson Award, and other recognition.

George W. Bliss, reporter for the *Chicago Tribune* and one of the most colorful figures in recent Chicago journalism. He won a Pulitzer individually in 1962 for his work on the Chicago Sanitation District, led the *Tribune* Task Force in winning another in 1973, and shared in another *Tribune* Pulitzer in 1976. He has worked also for the Better Government Associ-

The Cast of Characters

ation, a group that assists Chicago media in uncovering and documenting corruption.

Ben Bradlee, executive editor of the *Washington Post*. Although he decries the labeling of reporters as "investigative," he has built the kind of news staff that thinks of and applies investigative techniques to most of its stories.

Jay Branegan, member of the *Chicago Tribune* Task Force. His major projects have included investigations of hospitals (which shared a 1976 Pulitizer) and the Veterans Administration. He is a specialist in organizing such stories.

Howard Bray, executive director of the Fund for Investigative Journalism, Inc., which provides grants for investigative work. In addition to encouraging and supporting my application for a loan from FIJ, he provided innumerable leads and ideas and the moral support a writer needs in tackling a book like this one.

Geoffrey Brown, staff writer for the *Louisville Times*. Geoff worked for me at the *Sun Newspapers of Omaha* where he shared a University of Missouri-INGAA Award for business and financial writing. At the *Times*, his work has included a study of the Louisville power structure.

Warren Buffett, board chairman of the *Sun Newspapers of Omaha*. He built a nest egg running several carrier routes for the *Washington Post* in the 1940s then parlayed it into a fortune. His purchase of the *Sun* in 1968 was the first of several newspaper investments, the most notable of which is in the *Washington Post*, of which he is a director.

David Burnham, reporter for the *New York Times*. He covered criminal justice in the big city for seven years, then moved to Washington to apply similar techniques to coverage of the federal regulatory agencies. His awards include the George Polk Award, 1968; Society of Silurians, 1969; and the Page One Award of the Newspaper Guild of New York in 1973 and 1974.

Richard E. Cady, another member (credited by his colleagues as "the brains") of the *Indianapolis Star* team. Rounding out the team's awards for the police series were the National Headliners, George Polk, and AP Freedom of Information awards.

Lee Canning, executive editor of the *Minneapolis Star,* since promoted to assistant to the publisher of both the *Star* and the *Minneapolis Tribune*. He declined to list his awards and honors, but said, "My proudest achievements have been in working with staff members like Dave Nimmer, Jim Shoop, Maury Hobbs and others on the projects which were truly innovative for a daily newspaper: an in-depth look at the poor, studies of the power structure, consumer investigative projects of sizable scope and an in-depth look at the quality of the news media of the Twin Cities.''

Bob Casey, assistant metropolitan editor of the *Wilmington* (Del.) *Morning News* and *Evening Journal*, formerly assistant managing editor of the Paddock Publications, Arlington Heights, Ill. He was named Suburban Journalist of the Year in 1974 for his investigative work.

Stephen L. Castner, alumnus of the *Milwaukee Journal* and the *Indianapolis Star.* He specialized in financial reporting with the *Journal.* I found him one of the best-organized and most knowledgeable reporters on banking records.

Bo Connor, city editor of the *Indianapolis Star* whose legal name is Lawrence S. He is an articulate and effective city editor whose discussion of staffing for special projects was helpful.

Edward Cony, executive editor of the Dow Jones publications, a Down Easter from Maine who started his newspapering in Oregon after graduating from Stanford, then helped build the *Wall Street Journal* into the best business-oriented newspaper in the nation.

Peter Cowen, reporter on the *Boston Globe* Spotlight Team. He has worked on investigations of private vocational schools, Chappaquiddick, political fund raising in the Boston Fire Department, and corruption in the state liquor-licensing board. His honors include the UPI Public Service Award and the National Press Club Consumer Reporting Award, both in 1974.

William B. Crawford, Jr., member of the *Chicago Tribune* Task Force. A specialist in "inside" work. Crawford was a precinct captain during a *Tribune* investigation of city waste. He received both the Associated Press and UPI investigative awards in Illinois in 1975.

Dick Cunningham, reader's representative of the *Minneapolis Tribune.* His twenty-four years as a reporter and editor have included work in Hartford, Conn., and Durango, Colo.

Gene Cunningham, the investigative specialist of the *Milwaukee Sentinel.*

B. Dale Davis, executive editor of the *Philadelphia Bulletin.* He has been a lecturer at the University of Pennsylvania and the American Press Institute, president of the Society of Professional Journalists, Sigma Delta Chi, and of the Franklin Inn Club in Philadelphia. He spent eighteen years with the Knight Newspapers and was assistant managing editor of the *Detroit Free Press* before joining the *Bulletin.*

Al Delugach, business writer for the *Los Angeles Times* specializing in the Las Vegas gaining industry. He teamed with Denny Walsh in winning a Pulitzer Prize in 1969, and reported for both the *St. Louis Post-Dispatch* and *Globe-Democrat* before moving to Los Angeles in 1970.

Alex P. Dobish, reporter for the *Milwaukee Journal*—and among those with the best sources in that city. He has twice been a winner of regional UPI awards and has been cited by the Milwaukee Press Club and the Inland Daily Press Association.

Thomas J. (Tom) Dolan, reporter for the *Chicago Sun-Times*. A Nieman Fellow in 1974-1975, he has worked on several major investigations for the *Sun-Times*, including corruption in housing, ticket-fixing, and other abuses in traffic courts.

Leonard Downie, Jr., assistant managing editor for metropolitan coverage, the *Washington Post*. He is the author of *The New Muckrakers* (1976), *Mortgage on America* (1974), and *Justice Denied* (1971). His honors include the American Bar Association Gavel Award in 1967 and the John Hancock Award for business and financial reporting, 1968.

John de Groot, reporter for the *Philadelphia Bulletin*. He was city editor of the *Akron Beacon Journal* when it won a Pulitzer for coverage of the 1970 Kent State riots, and was with the *Miami Herald* later.

Robert W. Early, editor of the *Indianapolis Star.*

Rick Friedman, assistant to the publisher, Williams Press (Star-Tribune Publications), Harveyville, Ill. He wrote "The Weekly Editor" for *Editor & Publisher*, then was a reporter and editor with the Paddock Publications before joining Williams Press in 1972. The *Star-Tribune* won general excellence awards from the National Newspaper Association and the Illinois Press Association in 1973.

William Gaines, member of the *Chicago Tribune* Task Force. He worked on a series on waste of city funds that won an Illinois Press Association Award for 1974. Gaines teaches investigative reporting at Columbia College, Chicago.

Tom Gavin, managing editor, the *Rocky Mountain News.*

Richard Gibson, business editor *Des Moines Register*. As business editor of the *Minneapolis Star*, he was repeatedly cited by his colleagues and competitors as innovative, tough, and fair in his coverage of such topics as political contributions by the 3M Company and the business workings of Twin Cities media.

Katharine Graham, board chairman of the Washington Post Company and—on the record of the Watergate case alone—one of the most courageous publishers in American history.

Robert W. Greene, senior editor of *Newsday.* He headed investigative teams that won two Pulitzer Prizes, two Sigma Delta Chi Awards, three National Headliners, two George Polk Awards, five New York State Publishers' Awards, and many others. A lecturer at American Press Institute seminars, he is coauthor of *The Heroin Trail* (1974) and one of twenty-one creators of *Naked Came the Stranger* (1969) the successful spoof of all the sexy novels of the 1960s.

Elmer Hall, city editor of the *Louisville Courier-Journal.* Another editor who doesn't believe in the term "investigative reporter" but turns on one of the nation's better local staffs to show with careful documentation how society's institutions really work.

David E. Halvorsen, managing editor of the San Francisco Examiner, former assistant to the editor of the *Chicago Tribune.*

Howard H. (Tim) Hays, editor and co-publisher of the *Riverside* (Calif.) *Press-Enterprise,* which won a Pulitzer in 1968 for community service. Past president of the American Society of Newspaper Editors and member of the board of the American Press Institute, he works with Norman Cherniss to produce one of the best medium-size dailies in the nation.

Seymour Hersh, reporter of the *New York Times.* Hersh tackles only the toughest kind of stories and is best known for his single-handed exposure of the My Lai massacre, which won a Pulitzer Prize in 1972, and his 1975 revelations about domestic spying by the CIA.

James P. (Jim) Herzog, whom I somehow failed to hire for the *Sun* Newspapers back in 1964. He went on to the *Akron Beacon Journal* where he was a member of de Groot's Kent State team and helped the Knight Newspaper win a George Polk Award, then joined the *Louisville Courier-Journal* where he won a 1971 Meeman Award for environmental writing. He has since moved to the *Courier-Journal's* Washington bureau.

Steve Higgins of the *St. Louis Globe-Democrat.* Between receiving his A. B. from Yale and his law degree from St. Louis University, he sandwiched two years as a district coordinator of the Phoenix program in Vietnam and five productive years at the *Globe-Democrat,* winning or sharing in such awards as the ABA Silver Gravel (1973) and the Scripps Howard Public-Service Award (1973).

Henry Holcomb, city editor of the *Cincinnati Post* and a former investigative reporter for the *Houston Post.* While in Houston, he and Felton

West worked on state government in the early 1970s, culminating their coverage with a widely cited series, "Recipe for Reform."

Janet Horne, consumer reporter for the *Seattle Times* who has won citations from Sigma Delta Chi and from the Washington Press Women. She has worked as a volunteer aide in nursing homes to research stories on the quality of care, and has exposed frauds in a travel agency and in beauty aids sold by mail.

Hugh Hough, reporter-rewriteman for the *Chicago Sun-Times.* He is often Mr. Inside to Art Petacque's Mr. Outside, a combination that won a Pulitzer in 1974 for investigating the investigation of the Valerie Percy murder.

James L. Huston, managing editor of the *Waukesha* (Wis.) *Freeman.* With a staff of fifteen, Huston leads one of the better small daily organizations in the Midwest.

Sherry Keene-Osborn, managing editor of the *Rocky Mountain Journal* of Denver. This weekly specializes in business and real-estate reporting and has grown into an aggressive metropolitan paper examining government and community concerns.

Al Knight, assistant managing editor of the *Rocky Mountain News.* A onetime radio and television reporter who went into newspaper work, he had a distinguished record in investigative reporting in the Denver area before becoming an administrative editor in 1975.

Ron Koziol, investigative reporter for the *Chicago Tribune.* A source specialist, Koziol in 1974–1976 became known as the *Tribune* expert on the Patty Hearst case, beating national competition on many major breaks.

David Kraslow, Washington bureau chief of the Cox Newspapers. A newspaperman since 1947, he distinguished himself with the *Los Angeles Times* Washington bureau, winning the George Polk, Raymond Clapper and Dumont awards in 1969 as a result of the reporting he and Stuart Loory did to produce "The Secret Search for Peace in Vietnam," (1968), first as a series of newspaper articles, then as a book published by Random House. He was a Nieman Fellow in 1961–1962.

Stephen A. Kurkjian, acting editor of the *Boston Globe* Spotlight Team in 1975-1976. A member of the team when it was formed, he shared in its 1972 Pulitzer and Sigma Delta Chi prizes and its 1975 National Press Club consumer-service award. Like many other good reporters, Kurkjian is a law-school graduate.

Jonathan Kwitny, reporter for the *Wall Street Journal.* Author of *The Fountain Pen Conspiracy* (1973) and *The Mullendore Murder Case* (1974). He won the Herbert Bayard Swope Memorial Award in 1974 and first prizes for distinguished public service from the New Jersey Press Association in 1964 and 1967.

William Lambert, investigative reporter for the *Philadelphia Inquirer.* He began covering Teamster scandals for the *Portland Oregonian* and shared a Pulitzer and a Heywood Broun Award with Wally Turner in 1957. Later with the *Life* investigative team, he has also won two Sigma Delta Chis, another Broun, Worth Bingham, George Polk, National Headliners and New York Newspaper Guild Page One prizes.

Timothy Leland, Sunday editor-in-charge, *Boston Globe,* He was the first director of the *Globe's* Spotlight Team and has shared in a Pulitzer, a Sigma Delta Chi for public service, a national Associated Press Managing Editors and a Sevellon Brown Memorial award—all for public service.

Stanford Lipsey, president and publisher of the *Sun Newspapers of Omaha.* His business management helped me build a strong news staff at the *Sun.*

Stuart Loory, the first Kiplinger Professor of Public Affairs Reporting at Ohio State University and now associate editor of the *Chicago Sun-Times.* Besides his work with David Kraslow, Loory has written one book of his own, *Defeated: Inside America's Military Machine* (1974), contributed to others, and reported from Moscow for the *New York Herald-Tribune* and the *New York Times.*

Dan Lynch, editor of the *Rocky Mountain Journal.* A lawyer specializing in real estate, Lynch (with Bruce MacIntosh) bought *Cervi's Journal* in 1973 and helped shape it toward a comprehensive weekly of the kind I believe will become increasingly prevalent in our cities.

Dick Lyneis, investigative reporter for the *Riverside Press-Enterprise.* One of the original Professional Journalism Fellows at Stanford University (1966) and a specialist in labor and labor economics, Lyneis keeps track of the influx of organized-crime figures in southern California.

Kenneth MacDonald, retired editor of the *Des Moines Register* and *Tribune,* and developer of talents such as Clark Mollenhoff, and Nick Kotz.

Stan Macdonald, reporter for the *Louisville Courier-Journal,* specializing in state and local government.

Keith A. McKnight, statehouse (Columbus) correspondent of the *Dayton Journal Herald.* He and Andrew Alexander worked together five years, beginning with a series on corruption in bankruptcy courts in Indiana and concentrating later on abuses in Ohio's mental-health and vocational rehabilitation programs.

Henry MacLeod, retired in 1975 as managing editor of the *Seattle Times*. His staffs won two Pulitzer Prizes—one to Ed Guthman for reporting in 1949 and one to Jerry Gay for photography in 1974.

Marcia McQuern, capitol (Sacramento) correspondent for the *Riverside Press-Enterprise*, formerly assistant city editor of the *Sacramento Bee*.

Alice Marquis, who gave up journalism to work toward her doctorate in history at the University of California at San Diego. As co-publisher of the *Chula Vista Star-News*, she was named Suburban Journalist of the Year in 1972 and won an award from the California Bar Association in 1971. She is also a teacher, artist, and chairman of the San Diego Planning Commission.

Al Messerschmidt, former investigative reporter for the Paddock Publications, now with the *Miami Herald*. He was a co-recipient of Inland Daily Press awards for investigative work in 1974 and 1975 and has also won citations from the Suburban Press Association and the Northern Illinois Press Association.

Philip Meyer, national correspondent for the Knight Newspapers and author of *Precision Journalism* (1973), which won a Sigma Delta Chi Award in 1974. A Nieman Fellow in 1966–1967, he has been an innovator in the collection and analysis of precise data since he put together the *Miami Herald's* 1968 study on blacks in Miami.

Clark R. Mollenhoff, former Washington bureau chief of the *Des Moines Register* and *Tribune*, now teaching at Washington and Lee University. He won the Pulitzer Prize in 1958 and has more than twenty other major awards including three from Sigma Delta Chi, the Raymond Clapper and Heywood Broun prizes, and five honorary doctoral degrees. A lawyer, he is also the author of eight books, the most recent of which are *Game Plan for Disaster* (1976) and *The Man Who Pardoned Nixon* (1977).

Jeff Morgan, staff writer for the *Oakland Tribune* and the only journalist to win both the Nieman and the Stanford Professional Journalism fellowships. He has won more than ten West Coast reporting prizes and has found time to write two books on wines, most recently a second edition of *Guide to California Wines* (1975).

Jeff Nesmith, investigative reporter for the *Philadelphia Bulletin*.

David Nimmer, managing editor of the *Minneapolis Star*. He distinguished himself as a legislative reporter before he joined Jim Shoop and Sue Hovik to form the *Star's* consumer team, which investigated auto repairs, hamburgers, martinis, and a variety of other goods and services.

David B. Offer, reporter for the *Milwaukee Journal*. National ethics chairman of the Society of Professional Journalists, Sigma Delta Chi, he has won prizes in New England and Milwaukee for investigative stories. He received the American Political Science Association Fellowship in 1971 for public-affairs reporting.

Mel Opotowsky, day editor of the *Riverside Press-Enterprise*. A former colleague of Bob Greene at *Newsday*, he directs not only investigative but general reporting for the *Press-Enterprise*.

James O'Shea, Washington Bureau, *Des Moines Register,* former business and financial editor of the *Register*.

Ralph Otwell, managing editor of the *Chicago Sun-Times* and former national president of the Society of Professional Journalists, Sigma Delta Chi. During his term as managing editor, the *Sun-Times* and its staff have won Pulitzer and numerous other major journalistic prizes.

Robert Peirce, reporter for the *St. Louis Globe-Democrat*.

Stanley W. Penn, reporter for the *Wall Street Journal*. Co-recipient of both the Pulitzer and Sigma Delta Chi awards in 1967, Penn wrote a 1966 series for the *Journal* exposing gambling and conflict of interest among government officials in the Bahamas.

Art Petacque, investigative reporter and columnist for the *Chicago Sun-Times*. Among fifteen major awards, he counts the Pulitzer Prize and the Associated Press Managing Editors' Newswriting Award in 1974.

James R. Polk, investigative reporter for NBC News. With the *Washington Star* from 1972 to 1974, he won a Pulitzer, Sigma Delta Chi, and two Raymond Clapper awards, largely for his work on campaign finances, conflicts of interest in Congress.

Edward T. Pound, investigative reporter for the *Chicago Sun-Times*. His work opened up the 1971 Illinois racetrack scandal, which resulted in the conviction of U.S. District Judge Otto Kerner, former governor of Illinois. Pound has won for himself or his newspaper a National Headliner Award, an Associated Press Managing Editors' Award, and two Chicago Newspaper Guild awards.

Myrta Pulliam, reporter for the *Indianapolis Star*. Descendant of a noted newspaper family, she shared in the *Star's* work on police corruption.

James Risser, chief of the Washington Bureau of the *Des Moines Register*. His work on the grain-shipping scandals of 1974–1975 helped the *Register* win the APME Public Service Award and several others, including a Pulitzer for himself. He has written extensively about the environment and consumer issues.

Louis J. Rose, investigative reporter for the *St. Louis Post-Dispatch* whose work has thrice been nominated for Pulitzer Prizes. His specialty is city government, but he has written extensively about bankers and about corporate political slush funds.

Susan Schwartz, "just a reporter," she says, for the *Seattle Times.* Schwartz, however, has a regional reputation for consumer and environmental reporting.

Joseph W. Shoquist, managing editor of the *Milwaukee Journal.* He is a director of the Associated Press Managing Editors Association and was its general chairman for continuing studies for 1975-1976.

Lane Smith, city editor of the *Seattle Times.*

Joan C. Sprout, research secretary of the *Boston Globe* Spotlight Team.

James B. Steele, the other half of the *Philadelphia Inquirer* team. A Kansan who began on the *Kansas City Star*, he has shared with Don Barlett two George Polk Memorial Awards, an Overseas Press Club Award and the Heywood Broun Award, among others. Each of them also won an American Political Science Association Award for public-affairs reporting.

Carol Sutton, assistant to the publisher of the *Louisville Courier-Journal.* She won her share of awards in the field of consumer reporting before she became managing editor and was chosen to share *Time* magazine's "Woman of the Year" honor for 1976.

Robert H. Teuscher, investigative reporter for the *St. Louis Globe-Democrat.* His major work has been in organized crime and its white-collar manifestations.

James F. Vesely, former managing editor of the Paddock Publications, now metropolitan editor of the *Detroit News.* Vesely was named Suburban Journalist of the Year in 1970, for his supervision of staff members in uncovering suburban land hustles and political chicanery.

Denny Walsh, reporter for the *Sacramento Bee*, who has tackled controversial stories wherever he has been: in St. Louis, on the *Life* team, and at the *New York Times*. He has a Sigma Delta Chi Award (1968) and a Pulitzer (1969) among his professional honors.

Henry Weinstein, San Francisco bureau, *New York Times.* A former *Wall Street Journal* reporter, he has worked on such subjects as the Equity funding scandal and the Northrop Aircraft political slush fund.

Peyton Whitely, investigative reporter for the *Seattle Times*. He was a teen-age cub with the *Sun* Newspapers of Omaha before going to Seattle where he has won regional recognition for investigating bank and insurance frauds, among other swindles.

Les Whitten, the indefatigable associate of Jack Anderson who also writes books and translates novels from the French in his spare time. He has shared in the many journalistic awards showered on the Anderson team.

Bill Worth, managing editor of the *Dayton Journal Herald*.

Pamela Zekman, charter member and former director of the *Chicago Tribune* Task Force who moved over to the *Sun-Times* in 1976. With the task force, she shared in two Pulitzers and four Illinois Associated Press newswriting awards.

* * *

I must make special mention of Dr. William E. Hall, director of the School of Journalism at Ohio State University. His gift is the ability to motivate and support people around him to advance journalism scholarship. I met him in the early 1960s when he was building the University of Nebraska School of Journalism into one of the best and was encouraging Neale Copple and Emily Trickey to produce a landmark book entitled *Depth Reporting*, (1964). When, as a beginning academic, I undertook this project, Bill Hall cleared the decks, withstood the heat from my overworked colleagues, and arranged teaching assistance so that I could squeeze time for travel and writing.

I want also to thank especially the directors of the Fund for Investigative Journalism for their decision to grant me a no-interest loan to supplement my own travel budget.

My daughter, Nina Keenan, and a former student, Ann Corcoran, listened to some 60 hours of tape recordings and transcribed them into more than 1,000 typed pages. Ann, whose work extended over more than a year, also maintained my files, typed the manuscript, and helped check many points. And Pat, my wife, was a source of moral support through the conception, outline, research, reading, writing, and final revisions. A journalist who gave up her career to bear and raise our children, she returned to college and the world of work after more than twenty years and has become an editor in her own right.

I
THINKING
AHEAD

1
Winners and Losers

REPORTERS AT WORK

JIM SHOOP orders two cooked hamburgers to go, then asks the waitress: "Can I have a patty of raw meat for my dog? He's out in the car." *Shoop and two Minneapolis teammates are testing.*

In a penitentiary in Fort Madison, Iowa, Art Petacque turns on a tape recorder and starts questioning a convict. *Petacque is solving a murder.*

Pam Zekman sits at the receptionist's desk in a Chicago bill-collection agency, making notes of telephone conversations. *She is doing covert work.*

Jeff Morgan is shaving when the thought hits him: Richard Nixon must not have paid any income taxes in two of the last four years. *Morgan has just had an inspiration.*

Robert Greene sits alone at night in the newsroom, reading memoranda, coding and routing them. *He is building patterns.*

Lou Rose leads a subject through a tedious interview, getting a series of one-syllable responses: "Right." "Right." "Right." *Lou Rose is confirming a single fact.*

Clark Mollenhoff challenges a senior official of the Department of Agriculture: "I don't want any facetious answers. I'm taking notes now, and I don't want any quibbles about my misquoting you." *Mollenhoff is conducting a key interview.*

Months later, Jim Risser, who was with Mollenhoff on that interview, sits in New Orleans, leafing through a sheaf of reports, trying to find out how 18 million bushels of grain disappeared. *He is testing records.*

Don Barlett and Jim Steele sit in their office in Philadelphia, reading from a computer printout. *They are checking numbers nobody has ever seen before.*

Like a Fuller Brush man, Carl Bernstein puts his foot in the door of a suburban Washington home and starts talking fast. *He is interviewing an innocent.*

In New York, David Burnham eats lunch with a friend, talking about police corruption. *Burnham is conceptualizing.*

In the Huntington, W. Va., courthouse, Tom Miller closes one plat book, wearily reaches for another. *He is tracing land ownership.*

Bob Teuscher meets a man in a St. Louis bar, receives a tape cassette, and slips it into his pocket. *Teuscher is using an informant.*

George Condon, Jr., banters with a Cleveland doctor's receptionist, lays down $15, and walks away with an illegal prescription for Quaalude. *Condon is posing.*

In Paris, David Kraslow waits for a telephone call from Stuart Loory in Prague. *They are teaming.*

In New York, Bill Lambert sits with Russ Sackett and a team of *Life* lawyers, discussing a story about conflict of interest by a Supreme Court justice. *They are checking for libel.*

Peyton Whitely settles his 6 feet 4 inches into a deep chair in a Seattle banker's office and unfolds a penciled chart of the ownership of a tottering bank. *Whitely is sourcing.*

Larry Brinton sits in the Nashville office of a telephone company vice president, going over reports of the cerebral palsy association. *Brinton is asking how things work.*

Near Boston, Steve Kurkjian talks to a state patrolman who guards the governor's mansion. *Kurkjian is closing a gap.*

Gene Cunningham threads her car down a narrow road in Northern Wisconsin, suddenly finds herself in a large clearing where thousands of trees have been illegally felled. *Cunningham is checking a tip.*

In Detroit, Mike Graham and Jim Neubacher talk with a man who burns down houses for profit. *Graham and Neubacher are doing a job the legal authorities haven't done.*

All these men and women are investigative reporters. They are using the techniques of investigation to discover new information, to develop news stories that would never have come out through official channels.

Some of them are doing it the old-fashioned way, using private sources to get leads to concealed information. Others are using more modern methods, discovering patterns that once were beyond the ken of the pencil-and-paper reporter. They vary widely in age, experience, and approach, yet each of them is changing the nature of news work. They are breaking away from the conventional beats. They are viewing events as parts of processes. They are challenging and questioning the official version of significant issues.

How great an impact will their published stories have? Will governments tremble and grand juries convene? Will some people go to jail? Will marriages break up and hamburgers improve? Will money, illegally diverted, be returned to public treasuries?

Day after day, year after year, investigative reporters are plagued with the question of whether what they do will change things. For most of them, change is the inner motivation, spoken or not. That it comes slowly, if it comes at all, is the inner frustration. "There are times I have doubts about it," says Ed Pound. "You know, whether or not we've accomplished anything, whether or not people really give a damn. ... Things go on." Pound, of the *Chicago Sun-Times,* is here articulating a feeling that many reporters share.

Kenneth MacDonald, retired editor of the *Des Moines Register* and *Tribune* is inclined to agree. "One of the things that makes so many people feel frustrated these days is that they feel everything is out of control," says MacDonald. "There's nothing they can do about their lives. There are forces here, there and everywhere that have just taken over."

But MacDonald goes on to say: "One of the things a newspaper ought to be doing is telling them how to deal with these forces. Part of this whole news concept is explaining to people how things work and who has the power—how the power is exercised." From a perspective of experience, MacDonald is describing the major impetus behind the kind of reporting that will likely dominate newspapering in the last quarter of the twentieth century: investigative reporting.

In recent years, this is the different approach that many reporters are taking to their work. They still expose specific instances of individual wrongdoing. But more and more of them are pressing beyond, searching for conceptual and structural problems in the American social system. They are doing investigative reporting.

WHAT IS INVESTIGATIVE REPORTING?

The word "reporting" comes from the Latin *reportare*, which implies carrying something back from another place. It is a respectable word to describe the traditional, neutral, official style of reporting that developed during the latter half of the nineteenth century and the first half of the twentieth: the anecdotal reporting of anomalies. Its maxims were simple: be fast, be brief, be accurate. Write about the here and now—what happened in the last twenty-four hours and what is likely to happen tomorrow. Get both sides of any controversy. Carry back to your reader an account of what you or others you trust, like an official source, saw and heard.

The word "investigative," of course, also has a Latin root: *vestigium,* which refers to a footprint or track. The analogy seemed simple enough a few years ago. The reporter went on the trail to find a predator. The quarry did not sit waiting; it tried to escape. But the reporter found and followed its footprints, watched the trees and rocks for claw marks or tufts of fur. He stayed on the hunt day and night, trying to anticipate the quarry's next move. Eventually he bagged it and hung up its hide in public. Much of the thrill was in the chase, and the hunter was honored as a hero for outwitting and capturing a cruel individual beast.

But the game has grown somewhat stale. Americans have learned that it does not keep away all beasts. They want more from their hunters, the reporters, than vicarious sensation. They want to learn about real life and how to live it successfully.

How Things Work

To build a workable definition of investigative reporting for tomorrow, then, start with this injunction: You are here to tell how things really work, not how the civics book says they work.

If you think about and work at reporting with this principle in mind, you begin to find stories where nobody else thought to look. If you start looking at how things work in a business, you try to find out about the relationships between the managers of that business and the agencies of government that are supposed to regulate it. You think about the decision-making process: about the relative priorities given, for example, to profit, to pollution control, to other community or national goals.

Ralph Otwell, managing editor of the *Chicago Sun-Times,* has described just such a prospect: "You can go into the business community and do a major take-out on rate-making by commerce commissions, about the influences brought to bear in that. You might not encounter corruption in the traditional sense, but you do encounter influence peddling and lobbying and all sorts of things that add up to an unfair break for the public."

If you start looking at how a police department operates, you try to determine what internal controls it has, what criteria it uses in deciding which laws to enforce. David Burnham spent eighteen months in 1971-1972 reporting on the problems of the New York Police Department. The resulting stories in the *New York Times*, in his words, describe "system-wide corruption and failure of the top bureaucracy to do anything." The concept he used was to "find and describe the barriers to achieving the stated goals of the criminal justice system in New York City." From the experience, he summarizes as follows:

"Corruption is much more than a moral issue. It really is a failure of the bureaucracy to function. Corruption means the bureaucracy can't recruit the right people. You attract the wrong people and repel the right people. It means the discipline is all shot to hell.... It means, of course, that the laws are not enforced."

Burnham's objective—describing how the New York Police Department works—was a worthy subject for investigative reporting. It was far more worthy than reporting a simple tally of rake-offs taken by patrolmen and sergeants in a single precinct. But telling how things work inevitably leads the reporter on trails far outside the conventional paths of the beat reporter. It leads to another way of defining the challenge: it's a job of pulling things together for your reader.

Pulling Things Together

The investigative reporter is the antithesis of the beat reporter, a fact that accounts for some friction in many newsrooms. The beat reporter is expected to produce several hundred meaty words each day about activities of immediate consequence to thousands of persons; the investigative reporter may work for months without writing a paragraph for print.

The beat man must know and cultivate all of the key people in his building, which sometimes means scratching their backs in exchange for the first break on an official announcement. The investigative reporter, on the other hand, is skeptical if not scornful of the announcement; he devotes little effort to winning friends in the official hierarchy. The beat reporter's world is bounded by the walls of his courthouse or police station; the investigator views these buildings as way stations along a torturous trail of observation, documentation, and interview. The beat reporter's job is to report that something happened. The investigator's challenge is to find out why, and to tell why it may happen again. His job is to pull things together. Not surprisingly, this challenge leads the reporter, after training on the beat, to abandon the beat.

Penetrating Secrecy

In addition to telling how things work and pulling things together, there are two other aspects of investigative journalism: penetrating secrecy and preserving the system. "Investigative reporting," says Robert W. Greene, "usually involves the gathering of important information which some person or agency is trying to keep secret. This definition...presupposes that the information gathered is the original work of the reporter, not the investigative product of another person or agency." Greene's definition emphasizes "the original work of the reporter" and stresses the penetration of secrecy. Unless these elements are present, Greene believes, reporting may be called good, but it cannot be called investigative.

These are tough standards—but valid ones. The important point is that the reporter goes beyond the official version of an event or circumstance. He looks at things not from the self-interested viewpoint of the prosecuting attorney, for example, but from the viewpoint of the reader. Experience tells the reporter to examine critically every record, every leak, every opinion offered by an official source. Carl Bernstein and Bob Woodward proved the wisdom of such a policy early in the Watergate experience. Art Petacque and Hugh Hough practiced it when they forged a new chain of evidence in the Percy murder. Don Barlett and Jim Steele challenged the official version when they applied factor analysis to the court histories of a thousand defendants in Philadelphia. Jeff Morgan had the idea when he parsed every sentence of the White House release and punctured the official version of Richard Nixon's financial status.

By far the toughest aspect of investigative reporting is the penetration of secrecy. It requires ingenuity, resourcefulness, planning, guts, guile, salesmanship, and obstinacy in the face of hostility. If you are afraid to argue, if you dread being shoved around, if you hate to go back after your polite requests for information have been refused—then you probably will not be a successful investigative reporter. If you believe something is true simply because a person in authority says it is true, you are in trouble. "The lies," Ben Bradlee points out. "Layers upon layers of them. Day after goddam day. As a reporter today, you have to move up the list the possibility that somebody is lying to you."

Preserving the System

But why challenge the system? Can't we report some good news for a change? Aren't the people in charge aware of the problems, and aren't they working on them? Despite its shortcomings, isn't ours still the best political and economic system in the world?

You can answer "yes" to all these questions and still argue the need for investigative journalism. Yes, the people in charge are aware of problems, but time and again we have seen them make serious errors of policy and tactics because they misread the public's perceptions of important problems and their causes. Yes, we can and do report good news, tons of it.

Investigative journalism does not and should not preclude the reporting of good news. We should continue both kinds of reporting in order to keep our sanity and our perspective. And yes, we have probably the best constitutional system in the world, but to preserve it we must report on people and institutions that seek to subvert it.

"A free press," Walter Lippmann said, "is not a privilege but an organic necessity in a great society."[1]

The press is not free solely for its commercial good, nor because publishers and editors should have special license to vent their spleen. Its freedom is based on the common right to know not only what is going on, but what ideas to do things differently are abroad in the land. The latter right is every bit as important as the former. It makes change possible.

Political scientists and lawyers will continue to argue about precisely how our journalistic right to free inquiry and debate fits into the system, but the evidence over 200 years of American history seems clear: its main purpose is to help citizens participate in the decisions that affect their lives. The system has never worked precisely that way. Perhaps it never will—but the ideal is there and is worth striving for.

THE DEMANDS ON THE JOURNALIST

Given the complexities of life today, finding out how things work is a full-time job. The individual citizen cannot do it without skilled help. Preoccupied with his work, his special interests, his own biases, the citizen may be a victim or even a supporter of some questionable practice or institutional policy whose implications he is not aware of. The investigative reporter can help him find out about these implications and regain some degree of control over his own life.

Such work makes special demands on the journalist. It calls for personal integrity and a strong sense of right and wrong. "You must have a low threshold of indignation," is the phrase Bill Lambert used in describing it to reporter Robert Daley of *New York* magazine.[2] In discussing the phrase with me, Lambert added: "I get indignant where I see people trying to pervert the processes of the system, whether it be corporate or public." Note Lambert's stress on "the processes of the system." Uncontrolled, mindless indignation, he was careful to point out, leads to irresponsibility:

"I'm disturbed about this tendency to do one-source stories. I'm disturbed that this kind of reporting, which is cheap reporting, becomes a kind of standard for investigative journalism.... From a standpoint of ethics and from the reputation of the press in general, every mistake that comes up is going to be turned right around and stabbed at all the rest of us. It just simply is not good journalism and certainly is anything but investigative."

Stories based on a single source are, by definition, not descriptive of how investigative reporting is conducted. They do not pull things together.

They perpetuate and give stature to the biases and special interests of the single source. They contribute to misunderstanding. The reporter who lives on them is denying the very basis of investigation, which is to compare and contrast, to strip away irrelevancy and obfuscation, to provide solid information.

Even the most careful investigative journalism carries the seeds of harm to others. Dick Lyneis had been working for months to trace the background of a man who was trying to start a new business in Riverside County, California. "The general knowledge that I've been working on this guy for a long time has almost rendered him inoperable," Lyneis recounts. "His permit, his chances of putting up his building have been lost. And I haven't written the story yet. The pressure of the newspaper looking upon him can have more effects than people would recognize." In this instance, Lyneis didn't feel too bad; the man in question had a lengthy criminal background and was fronting for a Mafia-financed business.

For years, Matt Danaher climbed up the political ladder in Chicago. Then Ed Pound and Tom Moore produced documented proof that Danaher and a brother-in-law were operating a scheme to squeeze home-building contractors for phony real-estate commissions in exchange for zoning approvals and other favors from the city. The *Sun-Times* broke the story December 15, 1973. Danaher was indicted by a federal grand jury on charges of income-tax evasion and conspiracy. His wife filed for divorce. Within a year, Danaher was found dead in a hotel room. The official verdict was heart failure. "That was a sad case," Pound says. "I don't know how much effect [the *Sun-Times* stories] had on him, because he was already drinking heavily, probably taking pills or whatever...."

The investigative reporter must be able to live with such results of his work.

Bad reporting, of course, can have different results. For one thing, it can do great harm to a newspaper. The *Detroit Free Press* basked briefly in glory in 1973 when a by-lined series by Howard Kohn brought the indictment of twelve policemen and sixteen alleged drug dealers. Soon afterward, Kohn reported he had been kidnapped and shot at by an unidentified gunman. Five days later, investigation by other *Free Press* reporters found discrepancies in Kohn's story; he then admitted that he had made it up. The *Free Press* fired him. Within a month, one of the men named in Kohn's series filed a $60 million libel suit against the paper.[3]

The pressure of investigative work cannot only place severe strains on a reporter, it can sometimes sour his outlook. Denny Walsh shared a Pulitzer Prize with Al Delugach at the *St. Louis Globe-Democrat*, then went on to become a member of *Life's* investigative team with Bill Lambert, Sandy Smith, and Russ Sackett. He became involved in the investigation of San Francisco Mayor Joseph Alioto. He pursued the project for the *New York Times* after *Life* went out of business. When the *Times* refused to publish his story on Alioto, Walsh was fired after a public argument with the *Times* management that became the talk of the newspaper industry for a few months in 1974.[4]

When I interviewed Walsh in 1975, he was working for the *Sacramento Bee-News*. He said he had come to California because he "just wanted to work again as a general assignment reporter, and to get to know my family better." But he had some rather acerbic things to say about the newspaper business:

"What it comes down to is that this is a business, just like any other business. The people who run this business are interested in only one thing, and that is the color of the ink at the bottom line. There's nobody who has any control over this business who has any altruistic motives. The people who go into this business with altruistic motives are sooner or later going to be brought up very short and very sad. I'm not bitching about it. I'm just saying that that's a fact, and to pontificate about methodology or process, thought or otherwise, or hard editorial decisions is nothing but public masturbation."

Walsh was still doing investigative stories for the *Bee,* however. He simply maintained that he had learned better how the journalistic system works—and hence had lost many of his illusions. "I just feel uncomfortable talking in theoretical terms about reporting," he said, "because as far as I'm concerned a reporter is nothing more than a chattel, and to pretend otherwise is to kid yourself."

Obviously, the everyday challenges and problems of investigative reporting are not for everybody. It is a much more demanding form of journalism than reporting the visible, daily activities of life—the wins and losses that a professional football game symbolizes or the personal struggles of men and women trying to cope with a system they cannot control.

But the rewards can be enormous. The investigative reporter can shed light on the future. By describing the systematic weaknesses in his local court system, for instance, he can help preserve the system of justice for all. He can help explain the problems of the computerized society. He can discover and report the impact of commercially oriented energy policy on American foreign policy. By reporting the diversion of charitable dollars to private purposes, he can help the public develop new policies. In short, by telling how the system works, by pulling together the various aspects of the system, the good as well as the bad, the investigative reporter can offer the public an accurate image of its society. Only seen clearly, can the system be improved.

The reporter who decides to follow the investigative route will be exploring the frontiers of journalism. But before he embarks on it, he will need to reexamine his standards, his thought processes, and his reporting techniques.

2
Thinking About It

THE INTELLECTUAL PROCESS

INVESTIGATIVE REPORTING is an intellectual process. It is a business of gathering and sorting ideas and facts, building patterns, analyzing options, and making decisions based on logic rather than emotion—including the decision to say no at any of several stages.

The fundamentally intellectual nature of the discipline eludes many would-be Bernsteins, Steffenses, Hershes, and Tarbells. Because some reporters have a tip, can surround it with circumstantial evidence and can dash off a sensational story, they think they will blow the lid off the town. Instead, they come up with a one-day, one-source story that falls flat. They then complain about public apathy because nobody reacts. They have failed the test of finding out everything their readers need to know. They have failed to prove anything because they have failed to pull everything together.

"The hardest thing to do in any reporting," Seymour Hersh says, "is not write when you don't have a story."[1] His statement crystallizes the greatest daily pressure on the investigative journalist. His colleagues, his boss, his sources—even he himself—all expect to see some results from all that sitting around and reading, that clipping and indexing, that traveling and telephoning. Too often under such pressure, the reporter hypnotizes himself. He begins to believe that the story is there. He ignores or fails to look for evidence that it isn't. He refuses to accept the idea that he has found only pieces that fit. He tiptoes around the big holes in his jigsaw puzzle. "Investigative reporting carries a sterner responsibility [than daily news]," says James R. Polk. "The reporter is responsible for the truth of every word in that article, that an allegation, a second-hand bit of knowledge is not a fact.... You have to satisfy yourself that the content of what [your source] said is true. It is no excuse to come back later and say, 'My source was mistaken.'"[2]

To guard against these pitfalls, as well as to select and pursue valid stories to their conclusions, requires a disciplined mind. In casual conversation, relatively few experienced professionals describe it that way. They talk about the tedious digging, the loneliness, the blind alleys, the hostility of key interview subjects. Often, when asked how they got to the core of a story, they say something vague about "feeling things just didn't look right." But when the specific steps they undertook on a given story are analyzed, a pattern begins to emerge. What is found is a definite order of activities arranged in such a way that no lead was passed up, no bit of information unevaluated.

The veteran has ingrained within himself a special style of reasoning. He knows how things normally work. If he observes a phenomenon, an effect, he wonders what caused it. He develops a hypothesis and begins checking it against observable facts. He works to back up the chain of facts, searching for information that will either support or negate his hypothesis. He tries different combinations of conflicting versions of a story until he finds the one in which salient points overlap.

Many established investigative reporters have been trained in the law, and some have worked as investigators for congressional committees. Clark Mollenhoff says his legal training causes him to think in terms of evidence and proof. David Burnham was on the staff of the National Commission on Crime and Justice before he joined the *New York Times*. Bob Greene, a former congressional investigator, refers as follows to his Jesuit training: "The Jesuits go in very heavily for Aristotelian and Aquilian logic: syllogistic, deductive, inductive logic, and I find that an ideal way to build an investigation."

How It Works

What is this intellectual process? How does it work?

There is no magic formula, but the methods used by the experts do form a pattern, a workable plan, a roadmap along which there are certain

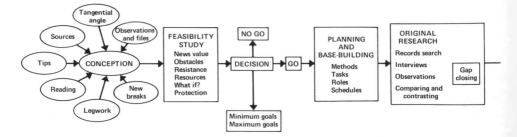

mileposts. The mileposts represent steps along the way against which you can measure you own progress in the intellectual process. These major steps, as shown in the figure on pages 14 and 15 are as follows:

- Conception
- Feasibility study
- Go/no-go decision
- Planning and base-building
- Original research
- Reevaluation
- Go/no-go decision
- Key interviews
- Final evaluation
- Final go/no-go decision
- Writing and publication

Consciously or unconsciously, formally or informally, each of these steps must be taken. At each of several points, options must be evaluated and decisions made about whether—and in what direction—to proceed. Or not proceed.

The crucial area is original research. Think of it as a loop, a circuit that may have to be traveled two, three, four—many—times before you move on to key interviews. It is in this loop that the wise reporter spends most of his productive time. It is here that he carries out Jim Polk's injunction to be "responsible for the truth of every word."

CONCEPTION

Let's examine each of the steps in this intellectual process beginning with the conception—the germination time—part chance, part calculation. We'll look into tips, sources, reading, news breaks, legwork, tangential angles, and observations and files.

Tips

If you are an established reporter, you get lots of tips. Some are single sentences spoken in a half whisper: "You ought to check the bidding on that furniture contract, friend." Many are telephoned, with little or no identification. Some come in letters, signed or unsigned.

Never throw away a tip without giving it some screening. It can be the basis for a story. Look for proof of two or three essential facts that might support the tipster's claim. Usually this means a few quick calls to sources to see if the thesis is plausible. Says Al Delugach: "I just look for somebody in the community who would be in a position to know if the tip is reasonable." Often the screening of a tip involves a trip to the courthouse, the library, or some other repository of records.

Equally important is evaluation of the tipster, if she or he is known. Is it reasonable to assume that this person knows the facts? Is there any information about the tipster in the morgue? Is the tipster known by other members of the news staff? What ax does this person have to grind? If a story develops as a result of this tip, will the informant personally benefit through job promotion, financial gain, advancement of political interest? Is he or she trying to "get" somebody? An ex-boss? An ex-lover?

Joe Shoquist recalls waiting too long to screen a tip. The lady claimed to have been the girlfriend of a county official and said he was living a double life. The tip came about a week before a *Milwaukee Journal* staffer came back with a report on her that caused Shoquist to say, "We'd better get her in here and talk more to her." By that time it was too late. She had taken her story to the opposition *Sentinel*, and Shoquist's staff had the embarrassment of trying to catch up on a fairly sensational story. They eventually did: David Offer followed a trail to Antigua and found that the county official had been there—complete with false mustache and alias—living a Dionysian life.[3]

One can forgive Shoquist's caution. The investigator must always be skeptical. When it comes to tipsters, that skepticism must include the operating principle that hardly anybody, ever, provides a tip without an ulterior motive. The motive will likely bias the tipster's version of whatever is going

15

on. You do not want to rush into print with a story that can damage a person's reputation. Still, tips, handled carefully, can provide the conception for a story.

Some tipsters are true con artists. A smart one can disarm you completely. If you challenge his shady background, he admits it, enriches it, and then points out it's all the more reason why his story is plausible: "So what if the straight guy claims he never saw me, buddy? You don't expect him to admit it, do you? Of course there's no record of our deal. He didn't want it traced back to him."

Although months had passed, Dave Nimmer was still smarting at the knowledge that he might have been thus conned. Both the *Minneapolis Star* (Nimmer's paper) and the opposition *Tribune* had the same tip. It was from a convict in the state penitentiary. The man claimed he had been part of a burglary ring with several policemen. He seemed to know a lot, and general circumstantial evidence fit what he claimed. Sources said his claim was possible, but there were no records, no physical evidence. Nimmer talked to top police officials, who said they were investigating the same tip. Nimmer waited. Finally convinced the officials were covering up, he published the story. A grand jury was convened—and failed to come up with a single indictment. To this day, Nimmer doesn't know if he had a case or not. He does know that he didn't have proof, and that publishing the story blew away all chances of getting further evidence.

I have had similar frustrations. Early in my career, I got a tip from a worker in a government tool-storage program. Scandalous waste of money, perhaps even illegal diversion of government funds, he claimed. I talked to two of his cronies who supported his story. I went to the people in charge, and they knocked me over with records, unbelievably detailed, proving the impossibility of my tipster's claim. And (though I thought I was protecting my source) they also showed me files on him and his cronies, indicating he was indeed trying to "get" his supervisor. The upshot was mostly personal embarrassment, but it also cost the *Omaha World-Herald* several hundred dollars worth of my time.

Sometimes the tipster has no motive but good citizenship. Al Knight remembers a woman who brought the *Rocky Mountain News* a list of license numbers on cars that showed up at odd hours outside the home of a neighbor. She didn't like the man because he had shot an injured dog. Knight and Richard O'Reilly checked the license numbers. They were from several states and their owners had a variety of backgrounds. Eventually, however, the reporters found a pattern and published a story about corruption of a Small Business Administration official by a shady business promoter.

Your final evaluation of a tip should be based on the provability of the allegations it involves, not on the character or motives of the tipster. Even if your tip doesn't pass your first screening, it is a good idea to file and cross-index it two or three ways: activity, names of persons involved, general subject. Some day, another bit of information may come your way that fills a gap in your fragmentary knowledge—and suddenly a story begins to take shape.

Sources

Sources are not tipsters. Sources are people who are in a position to tell you what is going on. They do not just show up on your doorstep or call you from a phone booth. Sources are acquired, developed, checked, and protected over a period of time.

Every time you make a new contact on a story, you have found a potential source. As you go along, you acquire sources in law-enforcement agencies, in banks, in key government agencies, in the criminal community, in the professional fields (law, medicine, engineering), in public relations, in labor, in politics, in the courts, in education, in science—ideally in every field of human endeavor.

If you do your job professionally, you can even make good sources out of former targets. "We have sent these guys to jail," recounts Bob Greene of *Newsday*. "They come out of jail and we'll go out drinking together." Such people, for instance, may carry grudges against former associates. "They want whoever they're dumping on to do a professional job," Greene explains. "And they know we go after Republicans and Democrats alike. When the Republicans want to dump, they dump to us. When the Democrats want to dump, they dump to us."

An intelligent, discreet, and well-placed source is a help in story conception, an adviser in appraising tips, a guide to valuable research records, and a knowledgeable interpreter of your research. There are cautions, however, about dealing with sources; these are covered in Chapter 4.

Reading

A great deal of information floats by you every day. If you scan it intelligently and analyze it properly, you can do several things:

- Define broad issues
- Learn better techniques
- Get specific story ideas

Most good investigative reporters find time to scan one national newspaper and one other state or regional newspaper every day. Most of them see at least one radical, alternative, or street newspaper regularly (indeed, they often free-lance pieces for such papers). The thoughtful reporter also reads one or more journalism reviews a month, governmental and trade publications (especially if he or she specializes in a particular field), and *local* newsletters, bulletins, and trend reports. He reads, at a minimum, several books a year, not only while killing time on or between planes, but while working on stories. The search for issues is general. It becomes a subconscious process of spotting trends and changes in society and of testing ideas for local application.

The search for technique is more specific. If, for instance, you were reading a paper that used the Knight News Wire in July, 1974, you might have encountered a fascinating story about how reporters Mike Baxter and James Savage of the *Miami Herald* traced a scandal in local administration of the Federal Housing Administration to the doorstep of a United States senator.[4] If you read (*More*) in 1973, you would have seen a number of stories about reporters uncovering the growing scandal in nursing-home ownership, management, and political influence. If you lived in the Upper Midwest in 1974, you might have seen the *Des Moines Register* and deduced how Don Muhm uncovered misallocation of federal disaster-relief funds.[5]

The search for story ideas is unending. Story ideas can come from any-where—legal advertisements, estate sales, bankruptcy notices, transfers of business executives, company and professional newsletters. The bulletin of the local dental society, for example, once provided one of my reporters, Mick Rood, with a story. He read a one-paragraph item about disciplinary action being proposed against two dentists. Why? He asked questions, found some public records, and established that the two had been milking Medicaid with false billing—and that the local prosecutors were waffling about whether to file charges. We published the piece, and shortly afterward criminal charges were filed and the men pleaded nolo contendere.[6]

News Breaks

This form of story conception derives directly from daily spot journalism. It is simply a matter of reading your own newspaper every day and asking that why question about major news breaks. If the beat reporter who covered the story is too busy to carry on the inquiry—or if he or she does not grasp the possibilities of a really big story—you may do some quick "sourcing" (in your new jargon, "source" is also a verb) and recommend a sort of blitz approach to shake loose the answer.

There are times when you scrap the whole formal process and just start pressing for day-to-day stories that will shake informants and information out of the trees. The *Washington Post* coverage of the Watergate affair is a classic example. Carl Bernstein has reported: "We made sources as we went along. ... You can see how the stories progressed. ... Most of the early stories referred to 'sources close to the investigation'. ... Later, you would have seen some stories attributed to personnel of the Committee to Re-elect the President. ... As we learned more and more, we found more and more people we could go to.'"[7]

In a story that put as many pressures on as many people as Watergate did, potentially valuable sources want to be sure you and your paper will believe them, protect them and follow their leads all the way. Publishing hard stories is sometimes the best way to convince them. The news break itself, in other words, can serve as a basis for the conceptualization of a story.

Legwork

It is easy to lock yourself in an office and rely on internal information. The smart reporter, however, makes a point, even while carrying on a major investigation, of moving around, of seeing people outside of the news business. Don Muhm, who is among the most-honored farm editors in the nation, still goes to local hog shows in Iowa. "I'm not so much interested in the damn grand champion hog as I am in the guys who are at the show and what they've got to say, what their concerns are," Muhm explains. "You've got to get out."

Tangential Angle

There are times when, in the middle of one investigation, another story possibility is conceived, something that might be called the tangential angle. It's a new angle, but one you can't chase down right away. So you write a memo on it to review at the end of your project.

In 1972, for instance, Ed Pound was investigating a minor political kickback scheme in Chicago's 43rd Ward. A friend told him about a young man who was being intimidated by John J. (Jack) Clarke, a probation officer. Pound made a note, went back several months later with colleague Tom Dolan to find out who Jack Clarke was. They found that Clarke was more than a probation officer. For special missions, he reported directly to Mayor Richard Daley and to Judge Joseph Power, former law partner of Daley's. The reporters found Clarke also drew $1,500 a month as a consultant to the police department, and that he further drew questionable fees as a security consultant to the Port of Chicago. In a series of stories in April of 1973, the *Sun-Times* exposed Clarke's multiple and mysterious roles. Within eight months Clarke was indicted for income-tax evasion and obstruction of justice, pleaded guilty, and was sent to jail. It was a dramatic payoff to systematic pursuit of a tangential angle.[8]

James B. Steele says that when he and Donald L. Barlett finish a subject, they always have about a half-dozen more ideas they'd like to pursue. When they were working on their series "Oil: the Created Crisis," they came across an IRS audit of major multi-national oil companies in the Middle East. The IRS had apparently assessed the oil companies for half a billion dollars in unpaid taxes.

"We'd read about tax loopholes for years, but the thought occurred to us based on this IRS thing. This isn't a loophole," Steele says.

The results of their investigation into how the IRS annually fails to collect billions, accepts fraudulent returns, and concentrates its efforts in the wrong areas was a seven-part series, "Auditing the IRS."[9]

And Clark Mollenhoff agrees that dozens of tangential leads accompany stories he's working on. "You make a file and observe; otherwise, you forget," he said. "But you remember even those you forget when something comes up at a later stage."

Observations and Files

Sit and stare at the wall and ask: "What things happen in this town that affect a lot of people but are never written about? What institution—public, educational, nonprofit, corporate—manages to stay out of the news?"

Sometimes a subject emerges clearly. More often, you will decide to start building a file on the basis of conversations with people around the institution. Then, if the initial results confirm your suspicions, you go into the next phase of story development. The Boys Town story (Chapter 9) is an example.

On a different level and in a different metier, but still using observation and files, David Kraslow and Stuart Loory put together a story of misdirected American diplomacy. Their work originally appeared as a series of articles in the *Los Angeles Times* in 1968, then was published as a book, *The Secret Search for Peace in Vietnam.* The problem, as Kraslow recounts it, was that the public was getting only the government's version of the efforts to end the war, and there was "reason to believe the public was not being given the whole truth." Their information was that at least one peace initiative "had been sabotaged either deliberately or accidentally," Kraslow recalls, perhaps due to faulty or purposefully blocked communication between military and diplomatic leaders. The reporters' problem was complex: the war was still going on; their prospective sources were scattered around the globe; most of them were contemptuous of every newspaper reporting of international diplomacy. "They think [of daily journalism] as an ephemeral sort of thing, that [the reporter is] not really serious enough to bother with," Kraslow says.

The sources also had problems of conscience. "We argued—and we meant it when we argued—that in light of all that was at stake in the war, of the apparent evidence that the American people were not being told what their government was up to, that a public servant would be serving the higher public interest by cooperating in a responsible examination of the policy," Kraslow adds. "It was really kind of an appeal to patriotism."

Before they started interviewing, however, Loory and Kraslow went through a meticulous base-building effort. They hired a full-time researcher to compile a careful chronology of public records on Vietnam diplomacy beginning in 1964: *New York Times* files, clippings from the foreign press, white papers, testimony at congressional hearings. They also pieced together the federal "information grid," the routings of various categories and classifications of information to high-level government officials.

"There were a lot of sources who knew only bits and pieces and didn't have access to other bits and pieces," Kraslow explains. To put together the history of a given incident or peace initiative, the reporters had to know who was on the information grid. They then interviewed people at different levels in order to compare and contrast different versions. As they did so, they began to build credibility with sources who had previously been diffident. "They began to appreciate that they might even learn something from us," Kraslow said, "because we were picking up information that they were not privy to."[10]

FEASIBILITY STUDY

Bob Greene calls this stage in the intellectual process "the sniff"— the stage in which a reporter is assigned to sniff out the possibilities and problems surrounding a story idea. Whatever it is called, you should ask yourself: Is it possible to do the story? Is it feasible? Are people, time, money, and technical skill available to pull it together? Will the story literally sit still long enough for our examination? What stands in its way from being fully and accurately told? And the most basic question of all: Does the story mean anything to my reader? At the *Dayton Journal Herald*, Andy Alexander and Keith McKnight call it the WGAD Rule: Who Gives a Damn?

For major projects, your feasibility study should result in a memo written to your editor. This memo should describe the story's potential, your investigative assumptions and problems, the kind of active and possible sources of information you can identify, the leverage and resources you have to get at nonpublic records, and an assessment, if the story pertains to an individual, of your target's ability to resist investigation. Phil

Meyer thinks of feasibility in the terms of a social scientist. How can I measure this phenomenon? Where will evidence of it be visible? What forms of measurement can I use, both direct and indirect?

The feasibility study may consist of a twenty-minute talk with your editor, or it may involve a couple of weeks of intermittent conversations. However it is done, on paper or in conversation, it should cover these points:

News Value

How many readers does it affect? Is the effect clear and direct, or is it abstract and theoretical? Is it something a significant segment of the audience needs to know but can't find out?

Obstacles

Are records available? Will sources talk about the subject? Is there time to do the job properly before, say, the next election or the next session of the legislature or the next meeting of the city planning board? Do you (or your colleagues) know how to interpret the technical material related to the story?

Resistance

Has the county attorney asked (or will he ask) the judge to seal the records? Will the target of the investigative story apply pressure on people not to talk to us? Will he sue?

Resources

How many people are needed to do the investigative-reporting job? What kinds of skills must they have? Can temporary help be hired to screen 10,000 documents in the court clerk's office? Can the university computer genius help us sample land ownership in the slum area? Can the business editor help with the project for a week? Can you carry the job alone, with only one veteran to help double-team the key interviews?

What If?

The "what if?" phrase, along with its implications, comes from Mel Opotowsky of the *Riverside* (Calif.) *Press-Enterprise,* and it should not be forgotten. If you get the story and your paper runs it, what will happen to the paper? Can it afford to defend the expected lawsuit? Will advertisers pull out? Will readers boycott it? Is this a subject your publisher does not want to go into? You don't like to think of some of these questions, but you are making a mistake if you don't. The publisher may not order you off the story, but he can give you a hard time. You are wise to lay out all these questions at the start, rather than run into them near the end and see months of investigative work go down the drain.

Protection

There are two aspects to protecting your story. The first is to preserve security within your own organization in order to prevent knowledge of the investigation from leaking back to the target. Although the general idea will get back to the target soon enough after interviews begin, it is wise to keep details of your findings protected as long as possible. Keep your files or memoranda and documents locked up and discuss the project with others only on a "need to know" basis.

The second aspect of protection is to prepare for the backlash or counterattack from the target. As part of the "what if?" discussion, the editor and reporter should consider ways in which to protect the reporter and the newspaper from public attack. These may include alerting trusted public officials to the nature of the investigation, working with appropriate congressional or legislative oversight committees, or filing a registered letter in a safe-deposit box. If, for example, the reporter needs to adopt a covert role to gather information, such a letter may be sealed before he begins work and opened later in the presence of a public official—such as a trusted judicial officer—if the reporter is unmasked and his motives questioned.

GO/NO-GO DECISION

The upshot of the feasibility study is a decision on whether to proceed with the investigative story. This go/no-go decision is the first of at least three to be made before publication of the story. If you have asked and answered the right questions, the editor will now be able to tell himself either that at least a minimum story can be delivered that the reader gives a damn about—or it can't.

Goals

Encompassed within that decision, of course, is the matter of goals: what the paper hopes to accomplish by publishing the story. Note that I said "goals," plural. The best reporters and editors think in "minimax" terms. Bob Greene gives a vivid illustration of the necessity to determine goals:

"We received information that the Metropolitan Transit Authority had bought an airport here on Long Island, then leased it out to a fixed-base operator at incredibly advantageous terms to the operator. We got a copy of the contract. On the face of it, it was unbelievable, because there was literally no accounting from the fixed-base operator. You just had to take his word for it. What had been run as a private business at a $250,000 annual profit, one year after MTA took over, was running $600,000 in the red. So we said all right, we have a minimum and a maximum here: the minimum is that we can show there's been a huge waste of taxpayers' dollars—and that's a hell of a good story—and the maximum is that we can show that somebody's been paid off."

This approach toward determining goals makes life easier at both the start and the finish of an investigative project. If the goal is defined only in terms of finding a payoff scheme, the editor may say no go because the odds against identifying the participants in the scheme are too steep. Or if he says go, he will be disappointed when you come back with proof only of a waste of tax money.

If the goals are clear, the go/no-go decision is far easier to make. If the editor has a good idea what story is there, how it will be gotten, and how much it will cost to get it, and if he believes the newspaper can survive the pressure incurred in putting it together and publishing it, he is most likely to say: "Go."

If, on the other hand, there are too many unanswered questions about the feasibility of the story, or it is one that the editor feels the reader won't give a damn about, or is too expensive to get and too uncertain in the getting, the editor is likely to say: "No go." Even if the answer comes out no, you should be able to satisfy yourself that you've given your best. You can close the file—or put it in the "observation" category—and move on to your next idea.

But if the decision is go, you can start planning how to do the job.

PLANNING AND BASE-BUILDING

Any investigative story involves planning. It also involves learning and understanding the norms of the subject area under study, what might be termed base-building. Planning pertains to methods, tasks, roles, and schedules.

Methods

Information obtained along the way in pulling together an investigative story must be compiled and organized. Don Barlett and Jim Steele design forms for each project. For their study of criminal justice, for example, they worked out a form designed for the transfer of information to computer-data cards. They usually do a preliminary exercise. They sample a few public records, then design a form of their own and field-test it on a bigger sample before settling on a final form organized in the way they need it.

Maintaining files is also an important method. "Let your files do your investigating for you," Bob Greene says. Files should be organized so that related information falls naturally into patterns. Editor Greene insists on daily memoranda from each member of his teams. He himself goes through the memos nightly, "breaking" and annotating them. The next morning, the team's researcher-clerk makes copies and files them. Greene explains the process this way: "Say we're working on one guy, but this guy Joe Jones—a subordinate or close operator with him—seems to be developing as a major character. Then I will mark on the top of the memo: 'Start new file on Joe Jones.' The researcher will start a new file and will also go through every previous memorandum for any mention of Joe Jones. Those memos will be duplicated and copies will go into the Joe Jones file."

If you don't have a file clerk, of course, you develop your own method. On all but the simplest projects, you will need some form of cross-index. The standard three-by-five-inch card index can be helpful. The simplest way of all is to tab a file folder on each major character and event, then write cross-references on the outside of each folder.

A chronology is another basic method. It is essential for an understanding of any long or complicated sequence of events. A loose-leaf notebook is a good way in which to organize it. If you are studying a year's activities, put in 365 blank pages, writing only a date at the top of each one. As you reconstruct activities, write short notes on the pertinent pages.

Tasks

Tasks are specific activities you will have to perform in connection with any investigative story: records to be checked, persons to be interviewed, data to be put on punch cards and processed, files to be maintained, references to be read. Given some thought, tasks can be tagged with fairly concrete time spans: two days for checking courthouse records, three weeks for getting a job inside a target organization, one day for a trip to the state-house, one day a week for reviewing files. As best you can, try to estimate the time your tasks will take and pencil them in on a calendar in the order in which they are to be done.

Roles

Assuming that you have help on your story, it is important to fix responsibilities. Who will do what jobs? If one person is particularly familiar with the public records in your target area, he may become responsible for all records search and perhaps for weekly file maintenance. If another has a talent for getting people to talk, he or she may carry the bulk of interviewing. You may organize roles in any of several ways; simply be sure that every task you have identified is covered by someone who knows that is his job.

Schedules

What is the best order in which to do the assigned tasks? If your project involves a public-attitude survey, for instance, there will be at least five steps to it: design, field-testing, data collection, tabulation, and evaluation. Schedule these tests early and delay most of your interviewing until the survey results are in hand. Normally you stay away from the key interview-subject as long as possible, but there are times when you may want to visit that person early for a soft interview in order to get information that won't be available later. In that case, scheduling is important.

Base-building usually begins during the feasibility study and becomes more formal during the planning stage. Its purpose is to define the historic, legal, statistical, and ethical boundaries of the subject area. The law and history are fairly easy to find in public or academic libraries. Statistics can be compiled from trade literature, government reports, and institutional files. The ethics and accepted practices of a field of endeavor are learned from conversation with experts, from the files of professional and public regulatory agencies, and by inference from reading the trade press.

Peyton Whitely of the *Seattle Times* recalls investigating a questionable insurance agency and finding that it had advanced $163,000 to finance one of its directors to begin business as a general agent for the company. The transaction was listed in a state-required report and meant little to Whitely until he discussed it with an expert source. "An advance of $163,000? Unheard of," declared the source. This discovery of self-dealing became a basic reference point for Whitely's subsequent stories about an ingen-ious circular hustle involving the insurance company and a small bank in

Washington acquired by California promoters. Both firms subsequently collapsed.

The goal of base-building may be defined simply as understanding the norms of the area under journalistic investigation. If you don't understand these norms, you won't have a story. You may write one and somehow get it published, but you will not have asked the right questions and your reader will not understand what you are trying to say. Moreover, your target will be able to shoot holes in your story. Indeed, he may be able to get other reputable experts to do the shooting while he stands aside, looking righteously aggrieved.

ORIGINAL RESEARCH

There are three major kinds to research activity, each of which will be discussed later in detail: records search, interviews, and observation. If you are not working solo, the comparing and contrasting of information gathered by others is also an essential activity. As a practical matter, you do not want to fragment these activities. Sources lead to records; records suggest interviews; interviews suggest other interviews, and so on. Comparing and contrasting becomes part of the daily routine. Every day, you (and your teammates if you have them) must sit down and record what you did that day.

Research Records

Written evidence of what the reporter sees, to whom he talks and what the person said, observations, and speculations are the seeds of investigative stories. They build a consolidated record that fertilizes the investigative imagination. As James B. Steele says: "The record provides an incredible amount of information." The records suggest, as no other method can, a pattern the investigator can follow. Write a separate memo about people you see, records you look at, observations you make. Every day. Unfailingly. Slavishly. And be sure that this information is properly filed and cross-indexed.

Interviews

Transcribe your interview notes in clear English. Keep direct, usable quotes completely separate from off-the-record material. At the beginning of the interview notes, write a brief statement of your own about the color and circumstances surrounding the interview: where it was, who else was present, how the interviewee acted, one-sided telephone conversations you may have heard, questions that may not have been resolved in the interview. It may be two or three months before you write a story. Therefore, make your interview notes as lucid and as solid as possible so that when it's time to write them into a story, you and your teammates will be able to understand them.

Observations

Direct observation places the reporter at the action scene. He may watch from a distance, he may be an anonymous participant, he may play roles. All of these activities force the reporter to weigh and examine his ethical values.

Comparing and Contrasting

Finding the piece in the puzzle that doesn't fit, the extraneous fact in all of the collection of data, is what starts the investigator on the trail. Comparing and contrasting as the reporter sifts through the accumulation of records, he develops nerves closer to the surface than most people, an instinct for the telltale clue—the fact unlike in all the facts alike.

Gap-closing

If you are working alone, sit down at least once a week with the material and review it, bringing your chronology book up to date and deciding whether the new information points in a new direction or requires further checking. This procedure is gap-closing. Bill Lambert calls it "triangulating." It is the business of resolving conflicts among your different records, observations, and interview notes. Do the files from the building inspector's office agree with the architect's plans in the building-permit office? Is there a requisition in the purchasing office that agrees in every detail with the city council resolution? Do Joe Smith and Richard Roe have the same version of what Councilman Doe said when they had lunch? No? Then in each case, you have a gap.

Why does the gap exist? Could the building inspectors simply be slipshod in their work? Are dated or serially numbered records incomplete or out of order? If so, you had better look up the supporting documents on this case in the city clerk's office. Or you had better talk to Councilman Jones, who knows both Joe Smith and Richard Roe and can help you evaluate the conflicts in their stories.

In these situations and in countless others, you may decide to recycle—to reinterview and recheck records until you have resolved any conflicts. In any event, no matter how many record searches, interviews, and observations you have to make and no matter how often you and your co-workers compare and contrast the information gathered, the gap must be closed.

REEVALUATION

The boss—your line editor—should be in on any reevaluation of the story's progress. The purpose of this step is to find out where you are with respect to minimum and maximum goals. You can expect one of several outcomes from a reevaluation of your story progress thus far:

- You are told to drop it. You are not getting anywhere.
- You are told to file it but keep watching for leaks, tips, or leads that may reactivate it.
- You are ready for key interviews to complete the minimum story.
- You have the minimum story in hand, and the maximum looks possible.
- You are ready for key interviews on the maximum story.

The last possible outcome is, of course, the most palatable. And if the green light to proceed further is given, you are ready for your most important interviews.

KEY INTERVIEWS

Key interviews are to be saved for the last. There may be only one, or there may be as many as half a dozen. However many, the reporter sets them up only after he is satisfied that he has isolated the central figures behind his central thesis.

Much of Chapter 4 is devoted to the complexities of the key interview. Here, however, let it be said that there are three important points to remember about it: you should prepare for it carefully; you should keep control of it, and you should use it to gain new information.

Preparation

Reread all of the files. Bring the chronology up to date. Check and recheck crucial documents. Study all of this material until you can talk about any aspect of it without fumbling. Write down the questions. Study them and arrange them in a logical order, going from the most general and least difficult ones at the start to the toughest and most specific ones at the end. With the person who will accompany you on the key interview, go over the questions carefully and agree who will carry which lines of questioning.

Control

In most cases, the interview becomes an intense contest of wills and wits. Proper planning and execution enables you to keep control of it.

New Information

Too many people think of the key interview only as the formality of letting the target person comment on or give excuses for the illegal or immoral activities that you have documented. But another, admittedly difficult, objective in conducting the interview is to get new information. If you have not planned the interview well, you will run into a stone wall of "no comments"—or suggestions like "get out of here," among others. These reactions may make the target person look bad, but they do little to enlighten your reader.

Don't shirk the key interview. The target person may not want to see you, but don't use this as an excuse to avoid the interview. If he won't answer the phone, go to his house. If he won't answer the door, send him a registered letter. If he won't accept the letter, get to him through his attorney, his employer, his business partner, his family, his party chairman. Not until you have tried all approaches can you conscientiously write, "Mr. Doe refused to comment."

FINAL EVALUATION AND FINAL DECISION

Even if you left the key interview with the happy feeling of having gotten all you needed, sit down in a quiet place with your interview partner and recheck the information gathered. Test each point against documents and files. One of you should be the devil's advocate and argue for other interpretations or further documentation. If the interview was taped, play it over, stopping and backing up at important points to be sure that the context is clear. Was your question clearly phrased? Was the answer directly to the point, or did the respondent leave himself an opening? If he gave an alibi, can it be checked?

At the end of this last evaluation comes a final go/no-go decision. If it's no-go, so be it. Discuss the negative decision with your editor, but do not talk yourself into a go decision just "because of all the work we have put into it."

"I spent weeks reading transcripts of court material and several thousand pages of transcripts and depositions," says Al Delugach, *The Los Angeles Times.* (The original tip was to have led to some hanky-panky in a national political campaign.)

"After talking to a number of people," he says. "I decided it was not the story that it was cracked up to be.... It didn't have the potential."

"Relatively few professionals describe investigative work in intellectual terms," says Dick Lyneis, *Riverside Press-Enterprise.* "They talk about digging, frustrations, finding blind alleys, obstinacy of sources. I say it in a little different way.... You have to develop such a tremendous self-discipline to deal with this frustration of finding blind alleys. You can go off and work your ass to the core pursuing this thing, and then you have to go back and tell an editor, "I spent ten days, and I haven't got a goddamn thing for it."

WRITING AND PUBLICATION

If the decision is go, then the writing and the production of the story, which are discussed in detail in Chapter 7, are the last steps to be taken in the process of telling it to the reader. Most likely, the story is quite complex. Identify a main story theme so that the reader can understand it the first time through. Everything else—tables of numbers, technical explanations, question-and-answer transcriptions, comments of peripheral sources—should be put in sidebars or illustrated with photos and graphics—all brightly packaged and arranged for easy reference.

Write only what you know. Write with conservative accuracy. Editors want bright, strong, snappy leads. The editor who was so conservative at all the evaluation points may now want a strong, unequivocal lead to support a sweeping, accusatory headline. But firmly, as reasonably as possible, hold your ground and write only what the facts support.

You can write from the facts and still have a readable piece. Do not think automatically of a summary news lead. Think instead of introducing your subject with a sound, color-laden few paragraphs that speak to the reader in familiar language of problems he is concerned about. And promise to inform him. Not incidentally, it is often best to write the central part of the main story before you decide on the lead and the ending. If you can put together a clear narrative, organized chronologically or in some other easily understandable manner the lead may suggest itself.

Checking and Production

Every good investigative story should have the best possible exposure. To accomplish that result requires cooperation and coordination among editors, lawyers, photographers, proofreaders, artists, the back shop, and anyone else involved in presenting the story. Once the key interviews are finished, you have effectively created a deadline: get the story published before the subject can tamper with records or witnesses or mount a counter-offensive. Nothing can be more frustrating than having publication delayed because others in your organization don't know what's coming or what they are supposed to do.

Publication of the story also involves the checking and rechecking of all story elements one more time. Your name and reputation, as well as the credibility of the paper, are at stake. Check the headlines to see that they reflect the sense of the story. Look at the photos to see that no one has cropped out an important element or emphasized the wrong element. Check the graphs to see that the artists have the correct numbers on the appropriate bars, that the wording of the legend is properly spelled. Read the cutlines. Read the galley proof and the page proof. Read the very first copy of the paper as it comes off the press.

Follow-up Plan

People go about following up on their published story in different ways, but all agree that the follow-up is necessary. If you are working alone, plan to get daily reactions from official agencies, from institutional leaders, from public spokesmen of all kinds, during the week after your story breaks. Keep asking the target spokesman for comments as follow-ups themselves develop into stories.

If your paper is like too many others, your follow-up will fade out in a week or two. And this may suit you. You may decide that you shouldn't do any more, that you have provided the best information you can, and that it has been absorbed into the public consciousness. If it takes months or years before the public decides to react, that is an acceptable circumstance so far as you are concerned.

You may, however, want to do something to prevent your story from fading out of the public consciousness. In that case, you might want to set up a program for six-month, one-year, and two-year follow-ups. These amount to mini-investigations and should be scheduled to start a couple of weeks to a month before the actual anniversary. Or you might choose to work with appropriate legislative or congressional committee chairmen or staff members to get hearings scheduled. Clark Mollenhoff and Bill Lambert are among many strong believers in this approach. Others avoid it, saying that they do not want to be identified as advocates of a particular cause.

Still another way in which to keep your story alive is to proceed from investigation of a particular event or "deal" into investigation of the institutional machinery that is supposed to govern such things. If your paper is given to continuing series, this approach may become part of your operating plan. Or you might prefer to arrange to have someone else carry out the follow-up while you move on to fresh ground. Some say that this method should be standard practice in order to prevent the investigator from being labeled a hatchetman. *Newsday* introduces a follow-up reporter (quaintly called "the vulture") into the process as final writing of the series begins. He reads the whole file and develops a plan for a series of follow-ups. *Newsday's* promotion department also gets into the act, arranging special delivery of the investigative series to appropriate legislators, congressmen, the governor's mansion, the White House, or to any other official who has the power to correct the wrongs described.

There is an element of self-protection in planning the follow-up to any controversial story. "If you're doing a story about a prominent politician," says Bill Lambert, "you're going to get an enormous amount of backlash. He's going to try to figure out some way to destroy your story. I try to consider the possible lines of counterattack and figure out some way to counter them. That's one of the reasons that I don't believe in the idea of the purity and the total disassociation of the reporter from government.... There are instances where agencies of government can step in afterward and help bolster a story."

Lambert recalls a 1967 story he did about the ethical conflicts of a United States senator who headed a major committee. The senator counterattacked, and the ethics committee supported him. After Lambert did a follow-up story citing failure of the ethics committee to pursue the evidence, the committee chairman invited him to outline steps the committee should take. Lambert did so, and the committee staff went to work. The question became moot shortly thereafter: the senator was defeated in a primary election.

There is no single way in which to do the investigative story. There is—or should be—no "typical" investigative story. Circumstances alter cases. The essence of investigative work is imagination and motivation. You can read the chart until you're cross-eyed, but nothing will happen until you apply creative thought to unexplained facts. Particularly if you are not experienced, signs and patterns of irregularity may not leap out at you as they would at a veteran.

As an advanced college student or a young practicing journalist, you should not feel that your experience is too limited to attempt investigative reporting. It may well be a challenge to find a subject on which to begin investigative reporting, and initially you might feel overwhelmed by the prospect. But put your intellectual processes to work in asking how or where you should start. Perhaps you'll find that the way in which to start is by first caring about something around you that seems wrong and then developing a commitment to do something about it.

And a way in which to begin developing ideas is to start on significant but not sensational "depth" stories about local issues. "At least do the motherhood issues," says Bob Greene. "Crime on the streets, drug addiction among the young, this is the sort of stuff that you want to work on first. These are motherhood issues. You know that your advertisers will applaud...but at least you're starting to accomplish some good.... If you can get people used to that profile, then put your foot in. Put another step into the water and keep going. Go as far as you can."

II

DOING THE
WORK

3

Needles
and Haystacks

THE MATTER OF RECORDS

THE FIRST and great commandment of investigative reporting is this: get the record.

All reporters and editors know there are public records in the city hall, the courthouse, the statehouse. They publish some of these records—real-estate transfers, births, marriages, divorces—as routine news matter, some as legal advertising. They get a lot of stories out of records of police activity, fire calls, zoning applications. Unfortunately, that's about as far as most reporters ever go.

The investigative reporter looks at records in different ways. First, he recognizes that there is an institutional record of almost everything. Second, he does not limit his search to standard public sources. He reasons that all sorts of records, including many that are customarily thought of as private, are worth digging for. He knows that records are often the best evidence— far better than prejudiced recollections or oral accounts — of what happened.

He also realizes that no single record—public or private—is certain to be complete or accurate for his purposes. He constantly thinks "compare and contrast.'' He knows that a record may reflect clerical lapses, typographical errors, biases, or outright deception. At the very best, a document is a record of a situation at a single point in time, usually from a single viewpoint, and for a single reason.

So the investigative reporter explores all records pertaining to his story. As he does so, he develops additional dimensions to his research. Records lead to other records. Masses of records lead to patterns and links. In the past, reporters have often been stymied by the sheer bulk of the records-search job. But gradually, as computer technology arrives in newsrooms, new methods of screening records are being discovered, some of which are discussed in Chapter 6.

The investigative journalist knows that before he begins interviewing, he must build a firm documentary base. He knows that he must develop points of reference from which he can check the accuracy of the paths (often primrose-bordered) suggested by people he talks to. And he knows a secret that other reporters sometimes never learn: record-keepers can be great sources. During his cub and journeyman days, he learned to get acquainted with clerks, librarians, bookkeepers, auditors, purchasing agents —all sorts of people who maintain records. He also learned that many of them know more than what may be found on the pieces of paper in their files—and that many of them will let their friend from the newspaper know when a special record passes over their desk. Nick Gage has told of a friend in the federal customs service who spent days sorting through 16,000 documents to find the key link for Gage's story about the illegal shipment of a stolen antiquity to the Metropolitan Museum of Art.[1]

In short, the investigative journalist develops a sense, a feel for records. Even while exploring the feasibility of a story, he considers what kind of records may exist. When it appears that traditional public records will not produce all the evidence he needs, he thinks of ways in which to review private documents. His need to get the record does not stem from mindless malice. It is based on the premise that every hypothesis, every biased allegation a tipster may have made must be checked but in the best possible way. He wants to see if a given record can be confirmed and fleshed out by other records. He is also learning as much as he can about his subjects so that his key interviews will be productive.

FILES AND PROFILES

From his experience with records, the reporter learns to do two things:

- To keep his own file of records
- To build profiles of people

In working with public and private records, the investigative reporter soon realizes the advisability of keeping his own. In Chapter 2, I mentioned the special forms that Barlett and Steele design for each project. Clark Mollenhoff uses "bank boxes" (cartons designed for nine-by-twelve-inch file folders) for each case he works on. Jack Tobin stresses the importance of getting certified copies of many types of records filed in California, for instance, because many of them are legally destroyed after three years. "If you don't write for five years [and then] if you've got to go to court to prove your point, you've got to have something that is in the public record [now] . . . not one that was there five years ago and has been destroyed,"[2] says Tobin.

Dan Paul, a Miami attorney who has represented many a defendant in libel cases, agrees on the need for reporters to keep accurate records. In light of the *Gertz* decision (*Gertz* v. *Welch,* 1974, in which the court held that a "private person" regardless of involvement in a public event, might recover damages from publication of a defamatory falsehood without proof of actual malice by the libeler but with proof of negligence as determined by a state standard), he says, "You've got to be a little more careful [in] keeping records of how you produce a story because . . . the burden may now be on you to prove you used due care. . . . You've got to ask . . . whether the person being written about is a private individual, and if he is, you've got to document the steps you've taken to verify accuracy."[3]

The digging reporter, of course, does not restrict himself to records of transactions and events. At the very start of his project he begins to build profiles of people. He thinks of all the human activity—birth, death, marriage, divorce, travel, major purchases, licenses, education, military service, credit applications, voting, organizational membership—that is preserved in records, and he then sets out to draw documentary pictures of the people he is dealing with.

Lou Rose is a records specialist. "There are people I've constructed whom I've never met," Rose says. "But I can tell them, totally from the public record, when and where they were born, the color of their eyes, how many cars they own, what they paid for them, where they borrowed the money for them, how often they trade cars, whether they have been divorced, whether they've gotten traffic tickets, how long they've owned their home, the whole history of their real property, what their credit reports are."

THE LAW

To get public records, you must know the laws governing them. There are three major sets of laws pertaining to public records:

- Open-meetings laws
- Open-records laws
- Freedom of Information Act

You also should take an active interest in seeing that public access to records is not unduly restricted. Such efforts occur periodically; major First Amendment threats followed the Watergate affair, particularly between the courts and the press. The Society of Professional Journalists, Sigma Delta Chi, American Society of Newspaper Editors, American Newspaper Publishers Association, state press associations, the Reporters' Committee for Freedom of the Press, and others monitor new legislative proposals and court decisions pertaining to public access to records, prior restraint, and censorship. It is worth the reporter's while to join and support more than one of these organizations.

Most states have "open meetings" and "open records" laws, though their content varies widely. Usually, they have been drawn by legislative compromise and give bureaucrats numerous loopholes. Since most reporters don't have the personal resources to carry appeals to courts, they must have either (1) a publisher who cares about the public right of access, or (2) the personal persistence, mental toughness, and ingenuity to induce or embarrass a recalcitrant record keeper into opening his publicly funded file cabinet.

If you haven't read your state's "open meetings" and "open records" laws, do so today. You will find that they are not "free press" laws. Generally, they define the right of every citizen to know what his official hierarchy is doing and especially how public money is being spent. Common features of most of these laws are as follows:

Open-meetings laws: Also called "sunshine" laws, these statutes prohibit public boards, councils, school boards, and similar public boards from taking official action behind closed doors. Usually, they set minimum requirements for public notice of meetings. But more than a few such laws, explicitly or implicitly, also allow "executive sessions" which exclude the public and at least partly nullify the effectiveness of the laws.

Open-records laws: Usually these laws require that formal records of any instrumentality of the state must be available for any citizen to inspect and copy if he wishes. There are, however, catches in many such laws. Certain types of records—especially having to do with medical matters, criminal investigations, official negotiations, and, sometimes, with personnel actions—are exempted. In many cases, the only "open" records are legislative and fiscal ones, while the real story of what happened may be hidden in memoranda, working papers, or "investigative" records.

The federal law: On the national level, the Freedom of Information Act is the major legal tool of the reporter. It permits access by any citizen to federal documents except medical reports, internal-agency rules and regulations, confidential trade secrets, and foreign-policy and national-defense information that has been classified as secret by Presidential order. It sets time limits for compliance by a federal agency with a proper request for information from a citizen, and it provides punishment for bureaucrats who withhold information improperly. If you have to go to court to force compliance, and if you win your case, Uncle Sam will pay your court costs. Because of the time lags built into the procedure, however, many newsmen have failed to use it. Difficulty in getting information from one agency should not be a problem for an investigative reporter on a major project. He knows other ways to dig out the facts.

BEATING THE BUREAUCRATS

What happens when information is withheld? Suppose, for example, a state or local government record you want is being restrained, and suppose your publisher and his lawyer tell you it will be a long and expensive job to get it by going to court. What are your alternatives?

The first principle to remember is to go only as high as necessary to get access to public records—no higher. Jack Tobin, now a freelance writer and a former investigative reporter, in checking on the use of National Park Service employees at Richard Nixon's Western White House at San Clemente, called his headquarters in New York and suggested checking with the NPS. A reporter in Washington went to a senior NPS official who denied the people in question were park service employees. Tobin finally got "another man to go in the back door, not to the head of the department but to the man administering the payroll—there, big as life, were the names [that Tobin wanted]."[4]

Only when denied at the lower level do you go higher, first through the civil-service hierarchy, and finally to the political-appointee level. At each level, be prepared to quote the law by section and paragraph number. It is good also to quote case law, if it happens to be recent and on your side, and to demand the legal citation under which access to the records is being denied to you.

But your main tool is your own controlled indignation: "Are you, John Doe, acting against the will of the legislature and the people of this state as expressed in Sec. 21-104(b) of the Revised Statutes? Are you denying me information that is legally open? Do you really want me to tell my readers, the voters and citizens, that you personally refused to let them know what you are doing with their money? Are you protecting malfeasance of office? Do you want me to go to the governor [or the secretary of state or the attorney general—whoever happens to be of the opposite political party] and tell him you refused to reveal those vouchers to the public?''

There are times, of course, when you don't want to make this kind of scene. To keep your investigative target (and other reporters) from knowing what you're interested in, you want to get the records with a minimum of fuss. In such instances, look for a way around the obstruction. Try going to a friendlier person in another section of the same department. Or go to a source in a different department who has access to the records in the course of his official duties. He can ask for the files, then make photocopies for you.

Another tack is to look for similar or partial records in another office. The secretary of state may have summaries of more detailed records that you could not get from the department of commerce; the environmental-protection division may have a form that asks some of the same questions that appear on the form you were denied in the department of mine safety. Get all such documents, interpret the gaps with common sense, then go back to the mine-safety department and ask for information to fill the gaps. The approach can be quite effective, especially if it causes a senior function-ary to think he will look silly because he can't answer reasonable questions or clear up reasonable inferences.

Get It All

Whatever you do, when you get the record, get all of it. Photocopies are best, but if you have to copy the information by hand, copy *all* of it, including the initials of persons who approved it, the routing, the dates of various actions, the serial or file number, marginal notes scribbled by file clerks or previous recipients.

Early in a story, you may not know what clues, what patterns and links you are looking for. Mike Baxter of the *Miami Herald* has told how he looked futilely at papers of scores of real-estate corporations before finally discovering the connections: they were all notarized by the same person, the one who also notarized papers for the target person in an FHA scandal he and James Savage were investigating.[5] Another reason for copying every-thing is the possibility that before you can get back to the records again, they may be shipped to a remote warehouse or destroyed. Such experiences make paranoiacs of experienced investigators.

I cannot give you a complete guide to public records. There isn't room. A colleague, Stephen Hartgen, set out in 1975 to write a compact journalist's guide to public records in Minnesota. He and a researcher spent two months and managed to keep the guide to 385 pages—by not going into federal records. A good, if slightly dated, book to help you explore public records is *What's Where*; it was compiled in 1965 by Harry J. Murphy of the Central Intelligence Agency to assist federal investigators, particularly those doing personnel checks. It has since been declassified and published by Quadrangle.

What follows is a brief and general outline of public offices that maintain public records. Its purpose is to help you think about the jurisdictions within which you operate and the records they offer. Titles, functions, and organizations, of course, vary from city to city and state to state. And some offices are more important than others. The city council, for example, is a highly valuable checking point for any activity requiring council approval. The official version of any local legislation or appropriation is usually the one in the city council files.

LOCAL RECORDS

I. Administrative Offices
  A. Mayor's Office
    1. Staff reports
    2. Information copies of major departmental correspondence (for comparison purposes)
    3. Citizen complaints and action thereon
    4. Reports on special programs, especially federal ones
  B. Police Department
    1. Blotter (booking record)
    2. Incident or offense reports
    3. "Special" (usually means secret) reports
    4. Crime statistics (should conform to FBI Uniform Crime Reports)
    5. Radio logs or tapes
    6. Duty rosters
    7. Traffic-accident records
    8. Traffic-ticket records
    9. Investigative reports
    10. Individual criminal records or "rap sheets"
    11. TV tapes or stop-action films
    12. Gun-permit applications
    13. License applications for taxi drivers, bartenders, nightclub performers
    14. Squad, precinct, and subordinate-unit reports (for comparison with central records)

C. Fire Department
  1. Fire-alarm logs, rescue-squad logs
  2. Arson investigations
  3. General fire statistics
  4. Duty rosters
  5. Inspection reports, both businesses and homes
  6. Records of individual stations and companies (for comparison with central records)
  7. Permits for special hazards—fireworks, explosives, flammable materials
D. Permits and Inspection Division
  1. Weights and measures of goods sold
  2. Pollution (air, water, sewage) permits
  3. Building plans, permits, and compliance inspections
  4. Air and subway rights
  5. Occupational licenses
  6. Records of housing-code compliance
E. Finance, Treasurer, Auditor
  1. Citywide consolidated budget
  2. Departmental and special-program budgets
  3. Payroll records (compare with personnel records)
  4. Bank deposits, check registers
  5. Bond-issuance and amortization files
  6. Expense accounts, travel vouchers, etc.
  7. Purchase orders, requisitions, and payment records (compare with departmental records)
F. Planning and Zoning
  1. Plat and land-development records with supporting documents, covenants, and correspondence
  2. Requests for zoning variances
  3. Detailed maps, current and historical
  4. Special local censuses and other demographic studies
  5. Reports from consultants on various problems such as traffic flow, parking, parks
  6. Minutes and correspondence of planning and zoning boards
  7. Proposals for rezoning, housing projects, private-business promotions
G. Public Works
  1. Capital-improvement plans and budgets
  2. Invitations to bid or requests for proposals
  3. Plans and specifications—historical, current, and proposed—for public buildings, sewers, roads, water systems, street lights, underground service systems, and utilities

      4. Work-progress reports and partial-payment claims from contractors
      5. Field-inspector and lab-test reports
      6. Background files on architects and engineers doing business with the city
   H. Purchasing Department
      1. Requisitions, purchase orders, invoices for purchases made with general funds (not always for federal programs)
      2. Catalogs, specification sheets, price lists, standards for city purchases
   I. Public Health
      1. Reports on communicable diseases and epidemics
      2. Birth and death certificates
      3. Inspection of hospitals, nursing homes, clinics, child-care homes, etc.
      4. Reports of food poisoning, sometimes industrial-poison cases
      5. Laws (local, state, and federal) covering public health
      6. Restaurant inspections
      7. School health statistics (compare with school records)
   J. Offices having special fields of interest (parks, city property, personnel, civil service, housing, stadium, auditorium, etc.)
      1. Contracts, franchises, concessions
      2. Original files, requisitions, correspondence
II. Legislative Offices
   A. City Council
      1. Ordinances and resolutions, historical and current
      2. Meeting agendas, usually in detail with supporting exhibits, approvals, authorizations
      3. City budgets and supporting data
      4. Correspondence from executive departments concerning budgets, programs, citizen requests, etc.
      5. Contracts and franchises
III. Judicial Offices
   A. Municipal courts
      1. Arraignments or preliminary hearings
      2. Appeals to higher courts
   B. City Attorney's Office
      1. Ordinance books, historical and current, plus good state-law library
      2. Legislative history of ordinances, resolutions, etc.
      3. Records of legal service to municipal or quasi-municipal agencies
      4. Legal opinions and supporting briefs for city departments
      5. Copies of many leases, contracts
      6. Criminal-prosecution records for inferior (misdemeanor) courts
      7. Records of mayor's pardons, special paroles, etc.

SCHOOL RECORDS

I. Academic (recent trends have made many of these records secret, but it never hurts to try to see them)
  A. Attendance
  B. Achievement (grade averages, honors, scholarships)
  C. Discipline
  D. Progress (grades completed)
II. Curriculum
  A. Standard course content
  B. Book lists
  C. Special studies and proposals
III. Professional
  A. Teacher certification
  B. Teacher employment
  C. Teacher evaluation
IV. General Administrative
  A. Budget and finance
  B. Purchasing
  C. Food service
  D. Building operations
  E. Insurance and other contracts
  F. Planning office
    1. Censuses
    2. Capital improvements
    3. Historical records
  G. Transportation
    1. Contracts with bus firms
    2. Bus inspections, maintenance and safety

COUNTY RECORDS

I. Administrative Offices
  A. Recorder (register of deeds)
    1. Land ownership and history
      a. Deeds
      b. Liens (tax, mechanic's, etc.)
      c. Mortgages
      d. Chattel mortgages
    2. Personnel
      a. Military discharges
      b. Other valuable documents as authorized by law

3. Commercial records (recorder's office, county clerk's office)
   a. Corporate charters
   b. Articles of incorporation, lists of incorporators, officers, directors, resident agents
   c. Minimal annual activity reports (sometimes)
   d. Occupation-tax payment
   e. Notices of business dissolution (may be in state records), including disposition of assets
   f. Major corporate financial obligations (see state records, I, A, 2)
   g. Utility-company franchises, special permits, easements, etc.
   h. DBA, business name, "fictitious name" files
B. Clerk of Court (often in divisions such as juvenile, domestic relations, civil, criminal, labor relations)
   1. Dockets
   2. Trial transcripts (not always)
   3. Depositions, pleadings
   4. Final orders
   5. Briefs
   6. Convictions and sentences
   7. Pre-sentence investigations
   8. Alimony and other kinds of payments ordered by courts
   9. Divorce settlements
   10. Wills, estate inventories, executors' reports
   11. Grand jury reports
C. Tax Assessor (treasurer's office, auditor's office, various combinations)
   1. Levies
   2. Valuations
   3. Assessments and collections
   4. Exemptions, waivers, refunds
   5. Equalizations and adjustments
D. Sheriff
   1. Police functions in unincorporated areas (see local records, I, B)
   2. Tax collections (distress warrants)
   3. Annual or semi-annual tax sales, unclaimed property
   4. Operation of county jail (see also county boards, II, A)
E. Welfare Department
   1. General records (varying levels of secrecy surround personal records)
      a. Aid for Disabled-Dependent Children
      b. Blind
      c. Aged
      d. Job relief
      e. Emergency welfare

    2. Joint records
        a. County-federal programs
        b. County-private charity programs
  F. Auditor, Treasurer (usually two different offices, with different or duplicate combinations of accounting)
    1. Countywide budget, broken down by accounts
    2. Departmental budgets, likewise
    3. Tax collections for subdivisions that don't have treasurer/auditor functions
    4. Payroll records
    5. Information copies of audit reports on federal revenue-sharing programs
  G. Other
    1. Personal records
        a. Election registration and voting history
        b. Driver's license
        c. Auto registration and title (including liens)
        d. Jury duty questionnaires
        e. Applications for professional and occupational licenses (see state records I, D)
    2. General (different offices)
        a. Summary reports of subordinate governments
            (1) Municipalities
            (2) School districts
            (3) Special districts
        b. Personnel records of county employees
II. Legislative Offices
  A. County Boards (Supervisors, Commissioners, Trustees)
    1. Zoning matters
    2. Tax levies and equalization
    3. Budget and payroll records (compare with auditor, treasurer, other departments)
    4. Public works, especially highways
    5. Institutions
        a. Jail
        b. Hospital, poor farm, etc.
        c. Branch buildings, garage, maintenance sheds
    6. Official administrative records, historical and current
III. Judicial Offices
  A. County (or District) Attorney
    1. Criminal-prosecution files
    2. Bad-check collections (in some states)
    3. Complete state-law library

4. Files on litigation to which county or its subdivisions and agents are a party
5. Legal opinions and briefs for public officials
6. Correspondence with probation authority, parole board, and penal officials
7. Involuntary commitments to mental institutions (may be function of court or a special board)

STATE RECORDS

I. Administrative Offices
  A. Secretary of State's Office
    1. Corporation files (often more complete than in county records, I, A, 3, a-e above)
    2. Uniform commercial code
      a. Records of major financial obligations
      b. Bank loans
      c. Equipment and land trusts
    3. Reports on public functions established by state law
    4. Political-contribution records
    5. Financial and conflict-of-interest (ethics) statements from public officials
    6. State election records, abstracts, recounts, audits, certifications
    7. Compilation of laws and legal history of state
    8. Reference indexes for records of state-agency meetings, hearings, etc.
  B. Governor's Office
    1. Correspondence, official messages, proclamations, etc.
    2. Summary reports from state agencies
    3. Petitions and documents relating to pardons
    4. Political activities (seldom labeled as such), including travels, meetings, appointments, contacts with political personages. (Information may be obtained from appointments secretary, legislative-liaison official, public-affairs officer, or similar functionary)
  C. Public Works Office
    1. Planning studies
    2. Working drawings, specifications, and other documentation for highways, buildings, parks, bridges, airports, piers, dams, monuments
    3. Lists of architects, engineers, contractors (including financial conditions, experience, management) qualified to do work for the state

        4. Lists of field-office personnel (sometimes havens for star football players, relatives of politicians, and other privileged classes)

D. License Bureaus
   1. Hospitals, nursing homes, rest homes, foster homes
   2. Private schools
   3. Doctors, nurses, dentists, allied health-field workers
   4. Engineers and architects
   5. Educators
   6. Barbers, cosmetologists, funeral directors
   7. Mechanical tradesmen—plumbers, heating contractors

E. Other State Executive Departments
   1. Labor
   2. Welfare
   3. Commerce
   4. Industrial development
   5. Conservation (natural resources)
   6. Environmental protection
   7. Institutions
      a. Vocational schools
      b. Schools for the handicapped
      c. Prisons
      d. Hospitals
   8. Education
   9. Regents (state colleges)

F. State Treasurer, State Auditor
   1. Scaled-up records as noted under IV, K above (If no state treasurer/auditor, there will be a department or division of revenue or taxation.)

G. Regulatory Agencies
   1. Telephone and telegraph
   2. Cable television
   3. Intrastate truckers
   4. Railroads, buses, local air services
   5. Pipelines

H. Judicial Offices
   1. Supreme (or highest appellate) court
      a. Records and transcripts of cases heard on appeal
      b. Administrative records of lower courts
      c. Indexes of litigation in other states and the federal courts
   2. Attorney general
      a. Criminal records
      b. Civil records
      c. Corporation records

       d. Consumer-affairs records
       e. Utility-company records
       f. Records of paroles and pardons
       g. Files on state lawsuits
       h. Opinions submitted to state agencies
       i. Exhibits, briefs, appeals
       j. Law library usually, the best in the state)

II. Legislative Offices
  A. Clerk
    1. Legislative history of bills
    2. Legislators' payrolls, expense accounts, ethics statements, etc.
    3. Official correspondence between the legislative houses, and with state executive and judicial offices
    4. Minutes, voting records, daily chronicle and calendar
    5. Certified lists of lobbyists, their activity and expenditure reports
  B. Legislative staffs
    1. Committee reports
    2. Hearing records, testimony, and exhibits
    3. Indexes and research files on subjects and issues before the legislature
  C. Party caucus clerk
    1. Minutes of meetings
    2. Correspondence

Special Districts: Before discussing federal records, there is one other state jurisdiction that has its own records: the special district. Special districts vary widely in title and powers. In addition to flood control, pest control, and rural fire protection, the most common special district is the development district. The development district has extensive power to levy taxes, issue bonds, let contracts, and perform such functions as building and maintaining streets, parks, water systems, sewage systems, and lighting systems in unincorporated areas. There are also special proprietary districts, authorities, and agencies of municipal government that perform functions authorized by the city council. Often, these bodies are not bound by open-meeting or open-records laws—a fact that should attract your attention.

FEDERAL RECORDS

Washington is big, complex, and frustrating. A list of federal record keepers and records would be monumental. Therefore, before you make a research trip to Washington, know what you are looking for and where to look for it. Operating records of matching programs and information on categorical grants, revenue sharing, and most established departments of government are often in their most complete original form (with supporting documents and working papers) in regional offices—not in Washington. Unfortunately, federal agencies cannot agree on a short list of regional cities, and each new administration shuffles some regional offices to reward its best vote-getting cities. Even so, regional offices are easy to find.

If you do decide to go to Washington, allow plenty of time. Phone ahead for appointments and be as specific as you can about what you are looking for. If you don't know exactly where to go, find someone who does —someone familiar with the hierarchy and handy with the scissors that cuts red tape. That person could be on your congressman's staff, or be a staff member or investigator for a congressional committee, or your paper's Washington correspondent. Regional specialists for your paper's wire services can also be helpful. The syndicated columnists that your paper publishes are busy, but they can often give you quick, precise advice. So can the Library of Congress; the General Accounting Office, which compiles data for Congress; the Office of Management and Budget, which has indexes of virtually every kind of form required by federal agencies, and lobbyists for trade associations or public-service organizations.

If you start at the public front desk of any agency, you face frustration and delay. Your goal is to find the most direct route, not only to the office but to the responsible bureaucrat (by name) in the office that has the records you want. The Congressional Directory is reasonably helpful. So is the Hill and Knowlton Directory of Government Employees. The public telephone directory is virtually useless. People, functions, addresses and telephone numbers change often.

Washington, of course, is a source town. But it takes months just to get the feel of it. Professional journalists covering Washington concentrate on developing sources in key agencies who can refer them to exact locations and custodians of records. So, again, if you're coming from out of town to pursue your investigation, allow yourself plenty of time to thrash through the federal record maze.

Not only in Washington, but everywhere you go, the paper network can overwhelm you. Develop strategies and tactics for finding records. In the best of times, you can get help from sources. But lacking sources, you need to think of indexes and of places where records gather.

DIRECTORIES AND REPOSITORIES

A directory is a kind of index. Start with the telephone book, crisscross directory and city directory, all standard equipment for any newsroom. From them develop a beginning profile on your subject's home address, family, business address, home ownership, neighbors, business connections.

There are many other kinds of directories besides those in the newsroom. Internal institutional directories, for example, were used by Bob Woodward and Carl Bernstein to chart the organization of the Committee to Re-elect the President.[6] There are trade-association directories, professional directories, national and regional Who's Who, official state blue (or red or green) books, institutional brochures, social and fraternal club directories. *What's Where* has a good section on such publications, and more than 3,000 are listed in the *Guide to American Directories*.

Checking institutional brochures helped Marcia McQuern find a chink in the phony exterior of Riverside (Calif.) University. She noted that key points in biographies of some faculty members kept changing, getting more and more impressive. She checked their out of state "alma maters" and found that several faculty members had fake degrees.

Besides your own paper's morgue and library, check the files of other newspapers. Sources of major newspapers now have their files computer-indexed, and these can be viewed on video screens in a few large libraries. But remember, errors in such files can be preserved and repeated until they become a part of modern mythology. Check—and recheck—wherever you can.

There are several places where records tend to gather, and you should think of them as repositories for information. Listed below are five such general repositories that contain useful records.

Audit Agencies. Any public activity that spends money (and some that don't) eventually passes through an auditor's office with supporting documents. Public-audit agencies are generally cooperative, particularly if you are willing to do the detail work. As a rule, ask for a batch of documents rather than a single one. If you ask only for voucher C-34533, you can get it—but you will tip everyone in the office as to the exact nature of what you are looking for, and you will fail to find out that vouchers C-33312 (a month earlier) and C-35001 (a month later) detailed other transactions that your tipster failed to mention.

CPAs. They are called "public" accountants, but they work on a fee basis for various clients and hence are generally thought of as "private." Do not ignore the possibility of getting information from them, however—particularly if you have documents that raise questions about an activity they have audited. Certified public accountants are professionally licensed; they are watched by the Securities and Exchange Commission and by state examiners. They have reputations and licenses to protect. So if something looks fishy about a transaction, talk to the CPA who handled it.

To protect his actions and recommendations, he may show you some interesting documentation.

Inspectors general. Somebody with that sort of title works in most large bureaucracies. He is supposed to report only to the chief honcho, but word of his activities and copies of his reports get around. Clark Mollenhoff found a brief reference to such a report about the Department of Agriculture in a congressional committee report. He did more checking with sources, then used the information to penetrate the "I didn't know" defense of an assistant secretary. The assistant secretary claimed "things weren't that bad," Mollenhoff says. "He knew there were some problems there and they were studying them." Mollenhoff dropped some unsettling remarks about facts in the inspector's report, an underling's lying, a Chicago Board of Trade hearing, and advised him as a lawyer that he ought to know something about due process of law. The flustered target became really upset at this point and had to admit that yes, he had been warned of trouble in the commodities market months before it cropped up in public view.

Regulators. In recent years, federal agencies have begun to require more public disclosure of financial structures, insider dealings, proposed policy changes, interlocking directorates, and the banking and holding-company connections of major businesses. The SEC has become a popular checkpoint for serious reporters of business and consumer affairs, and the Federal Trade Commission has a good relationship with the press. Other federal agencies range from responsive to antagonistic, but all eventually answer queries under the Freedom of Information Act. As for the powers, policies, and attitudes of state commissions, they vary so widely that it is impossible to generalize about them.

Courts. Court records are among the best with which to build personal or corporate profiles. You know the general organization of courts in your city, county, and state, but perhaps you have not spent much time in the files of probate court, labor-relations court, federal bankruptcy court, or (in the federal system and in some states) the tax court. Don't deny yourself. Checking the indexes of all these courts is basic. Look not only for the names of target persons but also for their wives, parents, and children. No, you are not planning to visit the sins of the father on the sons or vice versa. You are going to check for ruses and dodges. "Do you know what the most common aliases are?" Bob Greene once asked me. "The maiden name of a man's wife or mother." Greene's point is worth remembering in checking, among other things, hotel registers and in deciphering strange-sounding names of dummy corporations.

Bill Farr illustrates the alias axiom with the story of a minor public official who was improperly buying property in two counties near Los Angeles. Farr ran through the grant deed, grantor, and grantee files and came up with nothing. But Farr had also built a personal profile that included a membership application in which the official had listed the names of his parents. "I noticed the maiden name of his mother, and it rang a bell," Farr explains. "On several of these properties, there was a transfer to someone with that last name...he was buying these things, using the maiden name of his mother." Farr also emphasizes the value of checking applications for government licenses and permits with licensing agencies. "People know that there is either perjury involved, or you could lose your license by not giving full disclosure," so they generally answer questions truthfully, he says.[7]

Almost everything in court records, of course, is sworn to before a judge or a notary. And almost everything officially introduced into court records is privileged against libel actions. Depositions fall into this category, and investigative reporters learn to love them. Usually well before a civil case goes to trial (or even if it is not going to trial), opposing attorneys take depositions. Fascinating stories, told by witnesses under oath in the attorneys' offices, go into court files and become part of the public record.

"They often read like a soap opera," says Stanley Penn, who browses in court files the way scholars do in libraries. "Somebody is accusing somebody of doing something wrong. When you read all of the stuff through... this often provides a good hunk of the piece.... With the names you find there, you call up other people and put more flesh on the story."

As Penn and many others point out, general reporters seldom look at depositions unless they have been tipped that one is particularly significant. Hence, the investigative journalist can mine them virtually unmolested and get sworn, attributable material that he might never extract in direct interviews.

Many other courts are repositories for source-material files:

Probate Court: Wills, trust agreements, and executors' reports are filed here and may tell where your subject got his money.

Equity Court: Equity records can tell whom he sued (or was sued by) while doing business.

Divorce Court: How much did your subject have when he and his wife split?

Bankruptcy Court: What resources did he have when the deal went sour?

United States Tax Court: If your subject, after bankruptcy, got going again and made it big, he might have gotten into an argument with the tax collectors. If he pressed his claim in the U.S. Tax Court, he had to file detailed information on such items as income, outgo, depreciation, travel expenses, donations and contributions, cash flow, and debt. Not only are such numbers fascinating, but as in all court records, and names of others (creditors, debtors, partners, bankers, suppliers) pop up as potential sources.

David Nimmer and Stephen Hartgen relied heavily on court records when they did a series on influence peddling in the Minnesota legislature in 1970. They traced various forms of influence being used by lobbyists on legislators: special prices on stock, low-priced land, and uncollected loans.[8]

One more word about institutional records: for every page of official summary and report, there are probably 100 or more pages of logs, daily activity reports, production reports, time sheets, and similar working papers. Ideally, you'd like to see all 100 pages, but you'd never get your story done. Think of these working papers, however, when you find gaps or conflicts between interviews and official records. The *Boston Globe* Spotlight Team had a tip and a lot of circumstantial evidence that Judge Francis J. Larkin had tried to pay money to Gov. Francis W. Sargent in an effort to obtain promotion to a higher court. To resolve the conflicts, Steve Kurkjian went to the guardhouse outside the governor's home and checked the log kept by state policemen. It showed that the judge had indeed visited the mansion on two different evenings, and on one evening had shoved an envelope full of cash and addressed to the governor into a patrolman's hands. The logs helped refresh several official memories.

"PRIVATE" RECORDS

Think, now—what other groups besides government agencies keep records? Businessmen do in order to comply with laws, to collect bills, to audit and analyze their operations, and sometimes just because they are fussy. Trade associations do out of a need to organize and disseminate technical, political, commercial, or educational material to their members; to develop prestige, and even to satisfy the egos of their officers and managers. Churches keep records, too; so do civic associations. But getting to those records presents a separate and ethically thorny set of challenges.

Before you enter the preserve of "private" records, read the law and visit your company lawyer. You may find that laws about business records are written mostly in terms of protection of trade secrets, and that criminal prosecution or civil recovery depends on proof of damage to a business. But also read the current law, both federal and state, covering the general topics of "privacy" and "trespass." They will tend to dampen your gumshoe aspirations. Then talk to your editor and teammates about your problems and plans for acquiring documents that are not on public file.

Problems and Approaches

Don't pretend you don't have an ethical problem. You do. You must decide how important the story is, what people will think of your use of private records, and what methods are feasible to get the ones you want. In my own thinking about these questions, I am influenced by the ethical bases from which my target operates. Is there evidence that the target is breaking or bending laws and as a consequence operating to the disadvantage of my readers? Is my target lying to my audience (not just to me as a reporter; I'm used to that, and it's my problem) or manipulating the machinery of government? What are the practices of the world in which he operates? Ethical violations on his part do not motivate me to break the law in pursuit of my story. But they do motivate me to try harder to get the proof I need. I try to resist self-righteousness. I try to weigh all the alternatives, knowing that in about 90 percent of cases, I don't even have to bend standard business ethics to get information. None of the six score of veterans I interviewed for this book admitted ever breaking a law to obtain information, so they're not much help. How would you prepare for getting "private" information?

Assume you have a reputation and performance record for preserving confidences. You have demonstrated great discretion about not publishing information that may embarrass someone personally and is not essential to your story. Now consider all the avenues through which the information must flow and find sources along those avenues. Even confidential information is often distributed in multiple copies within an institution, so try several sources if you have them. Do not ask them to steal records. Tell them you are interested in getting information about a transaction or event. Then wait.

Let us say you are interested in obtaining financial information about a particular target. Every successful reporter has at least one banking source. He knows that there is an efficient grapevine of precise information within the industry. He visits his source and chats about the general subject of shaky real-estate promoters. He drops the names of several promoters into the conversation; eventually he will tell his source he's interested in Franz-Josef Snerd, a promoter. He will share with his source some of the information he has picked up. He wonders if Snerd has borrowed any money recently, and what sort of net worth he showed on his financial statement.

A few hours to a few days later, this reporter will have his information, unattributable to any source. But it may be complete enough that he can scour other, public, records and virtually replicate the figures without fear of contradiction.

Essentially the same kind of approach—although usually much less fastidious—is used in getting information from investigators for law-enforcement agencies. If there is one common trait among investigators I have talked to, it is that about 90 percent of them have very close private contacts in law-enforcement agencies—in several levels of the local police department, at the sheriff's office, the state police, the FBI, and the city, county, district and state attorneys' offices. The growth of "privacy" laws covering release of investigative reports has not appreciably changed these relationships, and I doubt if it will. We will discuss working with sources in Chapter 4.

One source that may be less helpful than he used to be is the telephone company official. The Bell companies had their share of trouble with exposure of executives' political slush funds in the post-Watergate era. They also went through a major to-do about giving law agencies secret access to long-distance call records and such. So some telephone officials are now less cooperative with reporters.

What about credit-card billings? Are they private? Bob Greene can get information from some card companies. Some companies often want to use *Newsday's* morgue. "If they won't provide us information, they don't get to use our morgue," Greene explains.

There are commercial credit-information companies, of course, that sell their services to business clients, always labeled "confidential," "for use of clients only," and so forth. Your newspaper probably subscribes to such a service. If it doesn't, you may want to suggest it. But be chary about using any such information without verification.

Numerous trade-association newsletters are also labeled "confidential," "for members' use only," or similar words, usually put there as a defense against libel claims. Oddly enough, there seems to be some difference in the eyes of the law between giving false information about someone in 10,000 copies of a "confidential" trade newsletter and giving similar information in 5,000 copies of a newspaper.

Finding Insiders

When trying to secure internal institutional records, the kind that don't flow through avenues like those described above, look for a disaffected insider within the institution. He or she may be a middle-level functionary who was passed over for promotion or was recently fired. He may be a supervisor whose conscience is aroused by what he considers unethical or illegal practices within the firm. Occasionally, such a source will present himself to you because he has been impressed by one of your stories. Sometimes, during preliminary interviews in the research phase, such a person gives signs or words of willingness to help you.

At times it is best to be rather open in your search for information. If your source is concerned that a leak can be traced back to him, your open inquiry to several people will ease his mind. If a given record will pass through half a dozen hands, he knows the chances of its being traced to him are much reduced.

Secretaries can also be helpful insiders. "Always be kind to secretaries" is a rule so old that I cannot attribute it to anyone. But it works. It does not carry any implications of illicit relations or even improper suggestions. It is simply a working principle: people to whom you are kind will sometimes do favors for you.

Public-relations people? Yes, on occasion. Many of them started in newspapering, and many long to return to it. They, too, have a grapevine. Dick Gibson put it this way: "They're human beings who know a hell of a lot of what's going on. . . . . . . Some will tell you not only things about other companies, but also about their own."

Not only in public relations but in virtually every division of an institution, the best place to find a sympathetic contact is around the middle of the organizational ladder. The junior clerk may not have access to the records you want and is likely to be scared of being caught. The senior official has been schooled for years in taciturnity; his ability to accept and follow company goals has been a big factor in his promotion. The middle-level person in his thirties—particularly if he has been stymied in his career—knows the system, has access to information, and sometimes has enough personal security to survive the loss of his job. As a person nears middle age, he is likely to have worked out his own principles, which do not necessarily follow institutional policies.

You need to think about human relationships and motivation. What is important to this prospective source? What line of argument will most likely appeal to him or her? You should watch for their "body language" in responding. A shrug, a gesture, a smile of sympathy when key questions are asked, may be an indication of cooperation.

The question of how to develop and motivate sources will be dealt with more thoroughly in Chapter 4. In the context of "getting the record," however, be guided by the principle of protecting your source and reducing his or her risks. The best way to do this is to be sure you have combed both the official—that is, governmental—records and the less official—the libraries, the trade press, etc.—records thoroughly. Some specialized types of records will be discussed further in Chapters 11 and 12.

For general records search, then, these are the major guidelines:

- Get the whole record, not just notes or excerpts.
- Evaluate each document's validity and possible weaknesses.
- Compare and contrast similar or overlapping records—in other words, "triangulate."
- Build and maintain a workable system of record keeping for yourself.
- Get to know the people who keep records, and learn their systems.

- Know the laws covering public access to records; help protect and extend the public right of access.
- Don't break laws to get nongovernmental records.
- Persist.

Not until you have done these things at the start of a major project should you begin to undertake significant interviews.

4
Talking
and Listening

LEARNING TO INTERVIEW

HOW DO YOU find out what's going on? By asking people.

What do you call the process of asking questions and getting answers? Interviewing.

What's the best approach to investigative interviewing? To paraphrase a popular saying: any way that turns them on.

In any interview situation, remember:

- Preparation
- Control
- Information

The professional reporter spends his whole career developing and polishing his interview skills. In college, he studies psychology, sociology, and survey methods to learn about motivation, bias, and interviewer-interviewee interaction. Early in his career, he uses trial and error. He questions other reporters. He reads other writers' stories to deduce how their interviews worked. If a colleague taped an interview, he borrows the tape and plays it back, analyzing the success or failure of particular lines of questioning. Before any significant interview, he sits down with a colleague and tests different lines of questioning—working to get his questions in the right order, to anticipate what turns the interview may take and how he will respond to them. Gradually, he develops mental reflexes so that he can interview anyone, anywhere, any time, and obtain usable information. He develops the self-control to ask challenging questions under pressure without losing his cool and without letting the interviewee dodge the questions.

And he *listens* to what the respondent is saying. After all, the purpose of the interview is to obtain information. "The first thing I'd ask a guy who wanted to be an investigative reporter," John de Groot says, "is to get himself into a good sensitivity session so that he can learn how to listen to people. Hear what the guy is saying." As city editor of the *Akron Beacon Journal* at the time of the Kent State killings, and later as a reporter for the *Miami Herald* and the *Philadelphia Bulletin,* de Groot became known for getting people under pressure to talk to him. His whole approach was based on letting such people know he was concerned about what they had to say.

Don Barlett puts the message this way: "The biggest trap most reporters fall into is not asking questions, but making statements."

Jim Steele, Barlett's investigative teammate at the *Philadelphia Inquirer*, also emphasizes the purpose of investigative reporters' interviews: "Their mission is to get information and not to try to impress people with how brilliant they are."

It's true; the unskilled investigator does not listen well. Too often, he is looking for answers that fit his preconceptions or investigative assumptions. If such answers are not forthcoming, he may become impatient or angry, which causes him to lose control of the interview. He may become discouraged and break off the talk, never having heard the tip or clue his respondent provided. Sometimes an interviewee is afraid for his job or his status, so he cannot give the appearance of cooperation. He may be trying to preserve "deniability," that wondrous Watergate suspension of conscience. But at the same time, he may be hinting to the reporter where to obtain the information he wants. "You'll have to ask somebody else about that" is an answer experienced reporters take seriously. Often it is a signal: go to such-and-such an office or look in such-and-such a file, but don't tell them I sent you.

Preparation: A good interview involves knowledge of the background of your topic—obtained through base-building. A well-prepared reporter has detailed knowledge of the elements of his story, accumulated through documents and notes of previous interviews. Further, he has knowledge of the aspirations, achievements, failures, fears, and motives of the person being interviewed, obtained through building a personal profile as described in Chapter 3. Finally, preparation includes making lists of questions, then screening and rearranging them in an order intended to extract neutral, factual information before more controversial questions of opinion and motivation arise. Such planning also entails careful phrasing of critical questions so that answers to them are truly responsive.

Control: Solid preparation for an interview results in its being controlled by the reporter. Control includes being courteous and restrained while asking the most pointed questions, and refusing to be disconcerted by angry counterquestions or challenges from the interviewee. Establishing control begins with the kind of grooming, dress, and demeanor that can cause the interviewee to regard you as slightly enviable. If, for example, you have to interview the chairman of a corporate board, a person born to money, schooled in the Ivy League, and borne on his journeys in a Rolls Royce and a Learjet, you may achieve your enviable status simply by appearing as an independent, well-adjusted person who is not caught up in the same competitive net of conspicuous materialism. Control is further achieved by motivating the interviewee through flattery or fear, and through demonstrating mastery of the subject matter. Mastery is best shown by the content of your questions, not by self-adulatory statements. And control is maintained by causing the subject to talk when he doesn't want to (by not asking a follow-up question, so he feels impelled to say more) and to stop talking in irrelevancies (by pointing out that he hasn't answered your original question). When it appears that the subject is taking control, you may regain it by asking an unpleasant or unexpected question that causes him to stop in surprise or fear.

Information: Careful listening is the best way in which to secure information. As the interviewer, you analyze each answer against your framework of independent knowledge and of the answers the subject has already given. If the answer does not fit the framework, ask your question again in slightly different words, preceded by a phrase such as "Do you mean that...?" or "In other words...." Or simply ask: "What does that mean?" Answers to such questions will confirm and solidify your understanding of what the subject has said.

Think of preparation, control, and information as we discuss categories of interviews. Remember the diagram in Chapter 2—the part about multilevel, spiral, cyclical interviewing? The idea is to start around the edges and work in toward the heart of the subject.

THE SOURCE

"There is one cardinal rule you have to live with," Jack Tobin cautions the investigative reporter. "If you deal with people [sources] in public places or in public positions, you have to keep their identity absolutely consecrated. Because once you burn [that source] you will burn every other guy in his line of communications, and pretty soon you cannot get to first base.'' An investigative reporter, Tobin adds, is only as good as the people he knows. ''You have to have direction. Otherwise that big mountain of paper that comes spewing off that Xerox machine will bury you.''[1]

Tobin was speaking of the subtle, complex, and sometimes dangerous relationship a reporter enters into when dealing with confidential sources. Some very good investigative reporters say they work without confidential sources. Barlett and Steele, for instance, have developed and refined the ability to analyze mountains of documents efficiently, and have achieved remarkable impact with stories based entirely on documents and attributed quotations.

Still, the overwhelming majority of investigative reporters work closely and regularly with unattributable sources, for exactly the reason Tobin states. A good source can tell you where to find the chink in the protective wall around your target. By the same token, of course, he can steer you away from places he doesn't want you to go. When he does, he is, to some degree, managing your search for truth. This risk is a subject of constant controversy among reporters. It calls on the reporter to exercise careful professional judgment in order not to be trapped into serving the source's ends without also meeting the needs of the reporter's audience. It places an extra burden on the reporter to confirm the source's information from independent, disinterested records and, where possible, from on-the-record interviews with other participants in the story.

A source is different from a tipster. A tipster is a more or less casual contact who gives you a piece of information about something he is not involved in and asks to be kept out of the story. A source, on the other hand, gives you information and assistance under an explicit agreement that he or she is never to be identified in connection with that information. A tipster is essentially a gossip; a source is an expert with whom you have established mutual trust.

You don't even think of your expert as a source until you have proved he is about 90 per cent accurate in the information he passes along. And you do not think of him as a source if he deals only in information that you can get from the public record. Think of him as a source only after he has told you things other people are trying to keep from you—things your reader wants to know but can't find out for himself. In other words, a source is someone who secretly helps you be an investigative reporter. And keeps his (or her) skirts clean.

Questions and Judgments

It is this last sentence that gives you, the thinking reporter, trouble. It means that you have to take risks the source will not or cannot take. It means that you have to make judgments about ''greater good'' and ''significance" and "being used." And it means that you must check everything a source gives you—very carefully. A source can be mistaken. A source can be biased. A source can be using you to get at somebody. Or a source can be pure as the driven snow. As George Bliss says of his Pulitzer Prize (1968) stories about the Chicago Sanitation District: "What I found over there were a few honest people and a lot of crooks, and I used them all. I can go to one trustee, I have something on him, and he'll blow the whistle on the other trustee to get me off his back. . . ."

Sources are rarely all good or all bad. David Burnham recalls that one of his best leads came from "a little lawyer who represented a lot of corrupt cops, a kind of a nice guy, even though he was an evil person essentially. His heart was maybe one-third in the right place." The lawyer, for his own reasons, told Burnham of a secret police report which showed that a district attorney had dropped corruption charges against a policeman even though he had the ironclad supporting evidence he needed. The story became an important part of Burnham's systematic report on official apathy toward police corruption.

And sources, no matter how good, can leave the reporter with mixed feelings about being used. David Kraslow tells of an experience most veterans have had: "Face it, there are stories planted with you simply because you have the reputation for doing this kind of reporting. If someone has information that could do in a rival and thinks he can plant it and get away with it, he will do so. A public officeholder who had been a source of mine was determined to do in a good friend of his who had become fairly prominent. He was aware of some activity of this other party which was totally improper. So he leaked the damn thing to me, set me on a trail. It was implicit that I would have to protect him as a source and go after his friend of many years.

"I got the story. It was a perfectly legitimate story. The accuracy was there. It was in the public interest . . . but to this day it is a bother to me. I was used . . . and this man to this day has gone totally protected. That's a tough call to make."

At the other end of the spectrum is the source who is literally self-sacrificing. A secretary working in a Maryland direct-mail firm began talking to reporters about suspicious things she was ordered to do in behalf of the firm and its part owner and major client, the Pallotine Fathers. She provided information to the *Washington Post* and the *Baltimore Sun,* both of which carried several stories over a period of several weeks. After less than two months, her boss traced the leak, fired her, and threatened to sue her for a million dollars in damages. In a story in the *Post* later, she explained: "I felt that if I kept quiet I would be compromising my values. . . . I felt I had seen an abuse [of donated money]. . . . I don't consider myself a crusader at all. . . . My conscience wouldn't let me sit back and not do something about what I saw."[2]

Such experiences should constrain the reporter who works with a relatively "innocent" source to consider what will happen if the source is uncovered. The secretary conceded she would have fired an employee leaking information, but the reporter using such a source has to balance with his own conscience whether the continuance of evil outweighs the consequences for the innocent.

Another ethical question in dealing in sources is the temptation and pressure to swap information with undercover law-enforcement agencies. If a reporter is willing to pass along unpublishable information to the police, the district attorney, and the FBI, he may get from them information he would not otherwise come by. Little of it will be attributable, much of it will be uncheckable, and all of it will be damaging to someone the authorities want to nail. How far should a reporter go in trying to manipulate—or in being manipulated by—law-enforcement agencies? Is it okay, for instance, to publish from "reliable official sources" information you know was obtained by an illegal wiretap and thus cannot be admitted in evidence?

There is a wide range of opinion on the question of "use," and exceptions to virtually every position. These are a few reactions from some of the investigative reporters with whom I discussed the matter. Regarding Mollenhoff's comments, it should be noted that he has worked closely with members and investigators of congressional committees.

Bob Greene: "In the first place, an investigative reporter has a cop mentality. Anybody who says he doesn't is full of crap. You're an investigator; the cop's an investigator; you think in investigative hypotheses. When you start working on somebody, you say he may be innocent, he may be guilty. And as more proof comes in, you become more convinced he is guilty. No matter how hard you try, you start seeing more things as evidence of guilt than of innocence.... There's no question that you get into a police mentality. Investigators are investigators—newspaper investigators, CIA investigators.

"Now, do you become a cop? Well, no, you shouldn't.... That's up to the team leader, the editor, to constantly be monitoring.

"Police can give you help. You take that help. The underworld can give you help. You take that help. You analyze that help. You verify that help, which is the key. [Do you trade with them?] Sure. Not quid pro quo necessarily, but you will trade. You've got something that is on the record [available for later publication] and they've got something [and so] you swap. If it's a bad law-enforcement agency that you know is corrupt, well, you're not going to give them anything. If it's what you consider, in your own experience, a good law-enforcement agency, going for reasonable aims, then give it to them.

"We are part of society. We cannot stand there and say we are not part of the total societal process of the United States, any more than youngsters can sit on a university grounds and say that the laws of the United States do not apply there because it has some sort of sanctuary like the Roman Catholic Church of old. We are all moving within the process.... We move into a terrible danger area when we try to set ourselves up outside of the societal necessities.... Sooner or later the public is going to turn on you and we're going to lose whatever advantages we have.''

Clark Mollenhoff: believes he has a responsibility to confront public officials with evidence of irresponsibility when he uncovers it, although he says he has been criticized for taking such action. ''Your investigation is not done as long as there are outstanding responsibilities of public officials.... That includes the oversight committees. You go to the oversight committee and say, 'Here are my stories.' If you're publishing out in Des Moines, you have to take them the stories.... You are facing the committee chairman with the responsibilities that he has.... You go to the chairman and say, 'Now what in the hell are you doing about this? This fellow has lied to you under oath. Are you bringing him in?' Then you write your story.... You say all those things that he's done, if [the chairman's] not going to bring him in, and [you] point out that [the chairman] is an ass because he's not fulfilling his responsibilities.

''It's an advocacy of solution.... When I went to Bobby Kennedy with the initial labor-racket investigation and the Hoffa thing, nobody complained about that.... This has something to do with whether it's liberal or conservative. And I don't care whether it's liberal or conservative, both sons of bitches should be treated in the same way.... I don't know where you draw this line. The place I draw it ... I go to the people with the responsibility.... If he's going to take action, okay. If he's not going to take action, then you escalate it, you get into the position of putting the case before the people ... and that's really all it amounts to.''

Ed Pound: ''You know that they're using you, but you're also using them, and it's a beneficial arrangement. Obviously, if a source in the federal government gives you a piece of information...[it may be] because he can't get the U.S. attorney's office jacked up to prosecute. And that's happened —I know that going in. For instance, on the racetrack scandal, I know I received information on certain politicians because certain of my sources were trying to light a match under the U.S. attorney's office. [It] was laid out to me that way. They wanted to see this publicized...I like to be aware of those things. I don't like to be used if I can help it.

''Ninety-nine per cent of the people I consider to be valued sources are people I've dealt with for years and I just know that these people are not going to screw me, because if they screw me, I'm going to screw them.''

Edward R. Cony: ''We're very cautious about that kind of a relationship. There are a lot of dangers in getting too close to any organization....

There's always a danger of being used. We are very sensitive about not becoming law enforcement, for instance, a part of any government agency. That isn't saying we wouldn't take information which might be available. I think a lot of people don't realize that an awful lot of information is on the public record if you know where to get it. And you don't have to be that cozy with sources.''

Avoid the Single Source

Decisions about how far to go in attributing information to unnamed sources are usually those of the reporter alone. The main reason reporters must assume this responsibility is because many sources do not want even his editor to have the information. In such circumstances, the reporter's reputation and personal integrity are at stake. As Jim Polk says, the reporter is responsible "for the truth of every word. It does no good to come back later and say, 'My source was mistaken.' ''

Because relying on only one source is risky, veteran investigators like Bill Lambert decry the story based on a single unnamed source. The reporter, therefore, must get confirmation, not from other unnamed people, but from records and from attributable sources. Letting the person under investigation respond in the key interview to what unnamed sources are saying about him is vitally important to the validity of the story.

To summarize: plan and work to get information from all kinds of people and from all kinds of records; use your judgment about what is true and fair; avoid being overly influenced by any single person. The truth is elusive; don't be hobbled or steered in your search to get it.

THE EXPLORATORY VISIT

Interviews on an investigative story may occur as early as the base-building phase. Such preliminary exchanges are, by their nature, exploratory. You have developed a general assumption, and are beginning to test it. You are dealing with a person you don't know. You may have to go back several times, so a primary consideration is to establish sincerity and competence. The thing you don't want to do is frighten or threaten the subject.

Consider his status. Seek the most comfortable setting you can. Generally, this means on his or her turf: office, company lunchroom, neighborhood bar, evening at home—or if his or her spouse is a problem, your home.

If you phone ahead, phrase your request in general terms. "I'm interested in the background of Topic A," in one approach. "I hear you are an expert on Topic A," is another that allows the subject some self-flattery.

Using the name of a mutual acquaintance may help put him at ease. You may have to do a good deal of selling of yourself, particularly if the subject knows or thinks you specialize in investigative work. In general, do not say things like, "I'm trying to get to the bottom of the highway department scandal." Make your approach positive and let the subject believe he can help you do a good job.

I avoid telephoning ahead if there is a good chance of finding the person in. Even if I don't get in the first time, I'll get to see things and meet other people. I may establish a connection with his receptionist or secretary. I may meet one of his associates who will tell me something about the personality of the person—and carry back a good impression of me. Almost certainly, I will get an appointment for another time or find out when is the best—that is, most relaxed—time for him to see me.

If you don't get in to see him, don't take a refusal too easily. Sit down and wait, or get up and wander around. While you are waiting, you may pick up some literature from the reception-room table; you can see who enters and leaves his office; you can get some feel for how things around him work. Often you'll get a brief chat with your person, followed by an appointed interview.

Two Objectives

When you do get in, you have already written on your note pad or engraved in your brain a number of questions. But normally, don't plunge into them right away. You are beginning a relationship that may become quite complex, so spend some time getting acquainted and letting your subject become comfortable with you. You are, in Jack Anderson's phrase, beginning to "baptize" a potential source,[3] and you want him to have confidence in you. Talk about mutual friends, ask about his family, his business or profession, places he has lived or traveled, the things that are on his mind such as seasonal trends, the coming election, competitive problems, professional issues. You are trying to do two things:

- To learn his strengths and weaknesses, his relationship with others involved in the issue under investigation, his attitude toward the matter at hand. Knowledge of these matters will help you phrase questions that appeal to self-interest.
- To establish yourself as a person of professional competence.

At this early stage, follow up hard on only one or two questions (not key questions just yet). What you principally want to do is demonstrate an ability to control interview situations and show that you are not going to let him snow you. "Why do you say that?" is a good question to ask several times in an exploratory interview. "What does this line in the budget mean? Why does this agency (company, institution, union) do things this way?"

It is good to let the subject know that you have talked to others and have read something more than newspaper clippings. Citing some primary document—a professional or technical journal, congressional testimony, a court transcript—can establish your competence.

But don't try to overawe your subject. "Don't forget to ask the dumb questions," is an injunction Mel Opotowsky repeats frequently to reporters. Dick Gibson also regards "stupid" questions as a useful device. "You disarm people that way," he explains. "They will probably tell you more than they really wanted to, on the theory that you really don't understand."

Here, too, is the time to try the studied silence. Look your subject straight in the eye as he answers a question—but don't rush to ask your next question. Don't try to feign doubt or cynicism. Just wait. He will probably say more, and it may provide lead to more information.

If in doubt, however, avoid playing psychological games in this first interview. It is far better to gather information, to get clues about where the bodies are buried, to see where the road is leading. Always be sure, before you leave, to ask for other sources of information. Ask for copies of letters, policy statements, working reports, memoranda. Ask for the names of others who may have more detailed knowledge. Try putting up a straw man (a consumer organization, for instance) and see if he tries to knock it down. If he does, that organization should be the next stop on your interview list.

Why People Lie

In any interview, you have to realize that the respondent will not be telling the whole truth. He will be protecting himself. He will try to steer away from ideas or information that may reflect unfavorably on his colleagues, his institution, or the people he respects. You accept this as part of human nature. But in investigative work, you must also face the prospect of being told bald-faced lies.

"I think people lie more than they used to," Ben Bradlee says. "I really do. [Twenty-five years ago they] would emphasize things that shouldn't be emphasized, try to throw you off the track, but the outright lies were rare as hell. I think that's the ultimate shock of Watergate: the lies, layers of them.... As a reporter today you have to move the possibility that somebody's lying to you higher up the list of things that might be happening."

People don't always lie out of basic dishonesty, John de Groot asserts. "Most people I have dealt with in government who have lied to me have done so out of fear," he said. "Fear of being found out about something they did, which they did out of fear and insecurity."

De Groot's point is that the reporter must understand the feelings of the person he is interviewing. People are rarely all good or all bad—a realization that comes slowly to most young reporters who have been brought up on cops-and-robbers newspapers and television. When it finally does come to them, they are better able to deal with the ideas of accepting information from convicts and dishonest businessmen and of spotting and screening lies told them by respected people such as ministers and civic leaders.

By the time you walk out of the exploratory interview, you should have:

- Knowledge of how the person fits into the overall situation and how he feels about the people involved in it
- Some documentation, even if fairly superficial
- Specific places to look for more information
- The person's respect, which may be based on fear, professional admiration, or even altruistic interest in what you are doing
- Some idea as to the person's truthfulness

What do you do now? As soon as possible—the same day—type up your interview notes. Specify what is on or off the record, attributable, or background. Include a description of the setting, notes on who else was present, and a paragraph or two of your impressions. Proofread the memo, then index and file it carefully and logically. You may not see it again for days, and you want to be able to understand it easily when you do.

THE ESTABLISHED CONTACT

An established contact is a person—either within the target institution or with close connections to it—whom you know well and who may be able to provide attributable information and records. You are, in effect, going to play on your friendship with this person, who is more than a tipster or a confidential source.

Relationships with an established contact can be sticky. Avoid painting yourself into a corner through a hasty promise to go off the record. Until you are sure your friend is "clean" of whatever misdeed may be occurring (and it's very hard to be sure of that), you can't conscientiously promise anything. Every reporter has to face such dilemmas and make judgments he'd rather not make about his friends. As an operating reality, he often has to weigh degrees of involvement or culpability. If your friend is a mere functionary who follows orders that he knows are wrong, perhaps to protect his job (and his family), he may be viewed as a victim of the system being investigated. It is easier to forgive him than the second-level executive who takes part in the major decisions at a salary of $100,000 a year plus stock options. You may not like what you find out about either one, but it is realistic to recognize the difference in circumstances and motivation.

"The idea of maintaining this pristine purity [as a reporter] that so many people talk about is just preposterous," Lambert says. "It ain't there.... Certainly you have to make little compromises.... You can't go in with a meat ax and lop off the head of every guy who commits some minor transgression." You try not to compromise on matters of "substance," Lambert adds. He recalls a piece he wrote for *Life*, pointing out that a respected U.S. assistant attorney general, and an established contact of his, had misled a congressional committee about his knowledge of connections between organized crime and a congressman. "There was quite a flap," he says. "I caught a lot of hell from the Justice Department.... But a fact is a fact. I felt the guy was a friend of sorts, but I just felt I couldn't ignore it."

Deals and Decisions

The temptation always is to make a deal with the lower-echelon person. You may in effect give him "immunity" in exchange for his assistance. In that case you have chosen to make him a "source." The choice should be considered carefully. Even if the idea comes up early in a conversation, don't do it on the spur of the moment. Give it a day or two of thought. Think of other ways of getting information without this person. The more deals you make, the less freedom you have. By agreeing to block one line of investigation, you are depriving your readers of your best skills.

In most cases, thank goodness, the established contact is simply a straight (or uninvolved) shooter who can handle your questions as a duty that falls within his field of competence. Even so, there are still decisions to make:

- Should you sketch out for him the investigative assumption and ask his help in putting the pieces together? Obviously, if he is disinterested, this has advantages. But if he has an interest you don't know about, it gives him the chance to obfuscate, warn others, and generally make your job harder.
- Should you ask only specific questions and ask for specific documents and records? This keeps him out of active involvement in the story (which he may well prefer), protects him against recriminations, and to some degree protects the story against leaks.

- Or should you use him only as a checker, a touchstone against which to test information and theses? This relationship is the one Bernstein and Woodward had with their famed "Deep Throat." It can be invaluable, but as those reporters have since written, it can lead to misunderstandings.[4]

Weigh the pros against the cons in any given case and make your choice with care. The limits are fairly obvious: if your story is based entirely on unattributable sources, it will be sharply challenged or ignored; if it must rely solely on quotable persons, you may not get the facts you need. Usually, the best course is simply to ask some test questions and see how your contact reacts. If he divines your intent and volunteers more information, you may be home free. If he seems skittish and less helpful than usual, play your hand closely. End the interview with some word or gesture that you didn't think much of the story idea anyway and then look elsewhere among your list of informed contacts.

In any case, you are wise to maintain a professional distance from your established contact. Sure, you may buy him a dinner or a beer, and sure, you may bring up your general subject of concern ("Isn't it a shame how little the public cares about this ripoff?" "Don't you get concerned about how Boss Sneer throws people aside?"). But never should you become personally involved unless you are prepared to offer your well-placed friend blanket immunity from investigation, past, present, or future. And remember, if you do, you could be setting yourself up for a shock when somebody else hands you his secret ledgers.

ENEMIES AND FRIENDS

"The good thing about talking to someone's enemies first," Tim Leland says, "is that they give you all the dirt they have on him and more, and they don't tip him off."[5] Not only the *Boston Globe* Spotlight Team, which Leland once headed, but others place "enemies" high on their interview lists.

Enemies can include a number of types: ex-spouses, business competitors, former employees, former bosses, political opponents, ambitious political associates, neighbors, creditors, debtors. As you build a personal profile of someone from records, you will see such possibilities for interviewing enemies emerge in court complaints, bankruptcy petitions, divorce decrees, news clippings, magazine articles.

So you talk to these people. Generally, do not even say you are thinking of doing a story on the person in question. You can go back later, if the facts dictate, and ask the enemy for quotable opinions. But at the beginning, just bring up the target's name, get the enemy talking, and don't take many notes. As Leland says, you will get "all the dirt and more."

Your first job is to sift out the "more"—to find out what is fact and what is opinion. Keep in mind, particularly when you have not told the "enemy" you are doing a story, that probably less than half of what you get is true. Check neutral records and other people's recollections of dates and events. Especially guard against rumor and opinion that build up around a person who is strong and active, as your target will likely be. Apocryphal anecdotes imbed themselves in mythology about such a person. They must be checked.

The other major problem is screening out what is relevant to your story. It is easy—oh, so easy—to learn surprising, titillating, or shocking things about a person. You must use discipline and discretion to decide how much of this information—if any—belongs in your story.

At the same time, do not overlook friends. Hardly anyone is all good or all bad. The manager who had to fire 50 people in order to keep his plant open may lie awake at night wondering how those people will get along. The politician who rakes a percentage off every insurance deal may be sending the money to his aged grandmother in Ireland. The insurance agent who supports the politician through kickbacks may also serve on charitable boards where he has many friends.

Everybody has friends with whom they share their secrets, their feelings, their ambitions, their fears. Most people enjoy talking about friends who are powerful, famous, or fearsome. They will know things that help you understand your subject. They may interpret his actions much more knowledgeably than his enemies did. They may provide anecdotes that give balance to the story. Bob Greene tells of a long-standing policy with the *Newsday* teams: "If the guy's the worst thief in the world, we'll also publish a little profile on the guy saying that he does some nice things. Even if we have to dig to find out, for instance, that he pets his dog."

EXPERTS AND INNOCENTS

In translating almost any major investigative subject into the language of your audience, look for outside experts who can help define the norms and standards of a given profession, business, institution, or life-style. You may have to go out of town to find a disinterested one, but not necessarily. Any major university will have faculty members who know the literature and practices of your subject.

In our investigative piece on Boys Town, for instance, we sought out experts in the fields of child care and fund-raising. The late D. Paul Reed of the National Information Bureau provided information on accepted standards in reporting the finances of charitable institutions. Daniel Dowling of the National Child Welfare League gave some guarded help in relating current child-care trends to those in use at Boys Town. Two local professional fund raisers (off the record) helped us estimate what might be Boys Town's return from mailing 33 million or more letters each year. Such information will help you understand your subject. Later you may use some of it in sidebars to help your audience understand what is out of kilter in the situation you are exposing.

The Value of Associations

The good news about this category of interview is that there is a national association of almost everything, and it has several to hundreds of staff members who are experts in their fields. Often, you can call up the association cold, talk to a secretary, and be steered to the leading technical expert. Once you have established bona fides with that person, you can get a batch of publications in the next day's mail describing the national trends and showing specific figures, yardsticks of performance, and accounting and reporting standards against which to check the local subject. The first inquiry to the association should be couched in general terms in order to obtain the most complete framework of information. After you have digested it, go back with more detailed questions.

Which brings up the bad news: the expert may start to leak the story. Most national associations, for example, are funded by institutions such as the one you have under study. The expert in New York to whom you are talking may have gotten drunk at the Las Vegas convention with the very guy you are investigating. So accept the possibility that within days if not hours, the investigatee is going to know that you called association headquarters. It's a risk you have to take at some stage. One defense against this risk is to invert the line of questioning, letting the expert believe you are working on a story sympathetic to hometown business interests, for instance. Even so, the hometown interests will likely hear about it. There will come a time—if your investigative assumption is borne out—when you don't care if the target finds out he's being investigated. It helps increase the psychological pressure on him.

Always look for associations and institutions that are not funded by the local target. These groups include consumer organizations and agencies; purely technical agencies that live on foundation money, and the Siwash University Agency for the Study of Topic A. These institutions are often valuable repositories of hard-won facts and specialized bibliographies. Some have computerized information banks. If you discuss your goals with them, they may be able to whip out a special factor analysis or financial study from their data. Occasionally, they may embarrass you (and save a lot of time) by providing sophisticated studies (already published) that utterly perforate your ambitious hypothesis.

The staff people almost certainly will be interested in learning what you know about their topic. So you have a quid to exchange for their quo. Often it is advantageous for both parties to keep this exchange information confidential.

The Value of Proximity

People involved in a questionable activity without being accomplices are innocents. They are the clerks and secretaries, the draftsmen, the mechanics, the orderlies, the bookkeepers. It is easy, but not wise, to categorize them as "little people." It is better to think of them as your most ubiquitous helpers.

Their value is in their proximity to the target and their relatively neutral view of things. By having friends among innocents, you can pick up accounts of conversations, minutes of meetings, detailed knowledge of the way things work inside the target area. Bernstein and Woodward did some of their best work in extracting knowledge from innocents in the headquarters of the Committee to Reelect the President.[6]

Some are more innocent than others, certainly. Each prospective innocent must be approached with care. The best strategy is to appear low key and friendly and not too strongly opinionated. Especially, do not look at such a person as a stereotype. Take the time to get acquainted and to find out what is important to him or her: family, job, bowling, fishing, drinking, education, money, honesty, security, or climbing the conventional ladder of success. As much as possible, let the innocent do the talking; you will usually find out more that way than by interrupting frequently with questions about when, where, how. Many people who are inexperienced in dealing with reporters are either frightened or resentful of their presumed arrogance and aggressiveness. You are used to interrupting the double-talking politician, and he is used to having you do it. But in talking to most persons, such conduct borders on insolence.

Problems and Relationships: At times, the innocent may be generally responsive but afraid to "get involved." He doesn't want to be put on the spot with his boss; he doesn't want his information used to wreck an agency and wipe out his friends' jobs. The best approach in such cases is to present the most convincing arguments—arguments that you really believe in—about why it is important for the public to learn the things the innocent already knows.

A different problem is the innocent who wants to be too involved, too cooperative. He or she wants to play cloak and dagger. He or she may try to answer questions too completely, going beyond what he or she knows. He or she may make wrong assumptions, based on incomplete information and misunderstood messages. Your job is to be visibly receptive but inwardly resolved to check, to compare, to contrast.

In general, avoid formal interview settings that will make your subject uncomfortable. Try just to run into the person at the coffee machine, in a café, on the loading dock. It is important to build a relaxed relationship so that you can go back again and again to check other clues.

As these relationships develop, the innocents will sort themselves out. Some will become helpful, others will fade into the background. You can test them by asking for specific information: How many people were at the meeting? Can I see that report? What did the boss say when he got the phone call? Who should I see to find out more than that? If your innocent demurs, taper off the contact. If he or she comes up with solid answers, you may begin to upgrade that person to the status of source.

If an innocent supplies what he claims is solid eyewitness knowledge of an illegal act, and if you may have to depend on him as your sole proof of that point, it is a good idea to ask him to make an affidavit and sign it in front of a notary. Signing an affidavit is serious business for most people. If your innocent refuses, you may lose him and perhaps the story, but that is better than losing a libel suit or printing wrong or exaggerated information. And even though the affidavit may be attacked in court, the fact that you obtained it tends to show you used caution in preparing your story.

To be successful with innocents, you have to deal with them as individuals of varying morals, motivations, and methods. Some may nurse secret grudges against people above, below, or around them—want you to "get the bastard." Some don't want to get involved. Some don't care. So you may have to talk to 25 or 30 to find four or five who can provide usable information.

TELEPHONE INTERVIEWS

Ma Bell, Uncle ITT, and their collateral relatives have provided you a device that is at once a boon and a bane.

Advantages: The telephone spans continents and oceans with its magic beeps. It demands answering. It lets the interviewer build his own image, often larger than life, in the mind of the interviewee. It is cheap compared to the air fare, taxis, hotel bills, and time involved in getting a few hours of interview time in New York, Washington, or Los Angeles. Used lavishly, the long-distance call may even impress an interview subject with your determination to get the facts (the impression quotient is inversely proportional to the interviewee's annual income). When a person doesn't want to talk to you, the telephone can pursue him. His wife or secretary (though not necessarily his kids) will usually at least relay messages. And if you catch him at home after his evening martini, he may be more relaxed and talkative than at the office.

Disadvantages: The phone can cause the interviewee to develop a negative image of the caller, particularly if the latter has a thin voice or halting or unclear speech. Because the aural message is not reinforced by gestures or facial expressions, it can easily be misunderstood. Calls are often screened through operators, receptionists, assistants, and secretaries (or, at home, wives and children). When you are in a hurry, the line is always busy. Many home telephone numbers are unlisted. Worst of all, the phone can be hung up and then left off the hook.

A general rule: do not use the telephone to interview significant people whom you have not met. "Significant" here means not just "big" or "important" people; it means people you expect to quote, people who don't like you, people you hope to develop into sources—and, of course, key interview subjects.

Take the time to go see such people. Usually you will get far better communication and more information than in cold calls on the telephone. Once you have had a good face-to-face visit with someone—even a hostile person—it is much easier to get further information on the phone.

There are, to be sure, many exceptions to the rule. One occurs when you want to reach someone who is ill, recently bereaved, or facing sudden or unwanted publicity. In these instances, the apologetic phone call often works best. Abrupt or persistent questioning will not only get you nowhere, it may cut you off from contact with friends or relatives as well.

Gambits

There are times when a person you want to see during business hours is not actively dodging you, but is actually busy. Until you are sure he is dodging, keep trying him at the office and leave messages indicating the call is urgent. "I am working on a story about him" is a line that gets attention from most secretaries. If that doesn't work, call the person at home, either early in the morning or in the evening. If he or she has an unlisted number, check your profile; unlisted numbers show up in places like voter registration records, license and club membership applications.

When the recluse finally does answer, your challenge is to attract and keep his attention. You need his attention until you can make him answer one or two questions, after which you can go into a more relaxed conversational mode. Usually, this means a carefully thought-out opening with a few key words in it. For example:

"Mr. Doe, I need to know more about the deal you made with Mayor Roe. He says you and Ace Grinch met in his office to decide the price of the city's new police cars. This is Williams of the *Sun*."

That took just nine seconds. I didn't mention my name in the first phrase because I didn't want him to hang up. It may work. It may not. The odds are that he will make some kind of answer, which gives me a chance to mollify him:

"It's important that we talk more about it. I don't want to take somebody else's word. How long have you and Ace Grinch been working together?"

Another type of opening, one that Art Petacque favors, goes like this:

"Wow, Mr. Doe, I'm glad I finally got to you. I'm working on a story, but it's not the kind of thing I can talk about over the phone. Can I come over and see you?"

The point is to be reasonable but keep asking questions. If you apologize, you are giving him reason to hang up without regret, muttering about your intrusion. So keep moving and try to turn the call into an appointment to sit down for a face-to-face talk.

The ultimate phone call, of course, is the kind Woodward and Bernstein were forced to use often in covering the Watergate story: the formal "denial" call. Common in fast-breaking stories, it also has its uses with recalcitrant cases in the story expected to cover weeks of development. Thus:

"Mr. Doe, I want to read you a story [or several paragraphs of a story] we are publishing today. I have been trying to reach you, and I'd still be happy to come over and see you now if you'll talk to me."

An entirely different situation is the long-distance call to a person you don't know but who presumably will not be hostile. The challenge is to establish mutual trust within a few minutes and to keep the person on the phone even when his secretary, lawyer, and accountant are all demanding attention at the other end.

Regardless of the phone company's urgings not to do so, I find it most effective to make such calls person to person. Two reasons:

- If you call station to station through the interviewee's switchboard, and if he is not at his phone, his PBX operator may never come back on the line to take your message.
- A person-to-person call may make a stronger impression. If his secretary answers, she is more likely to put you through.

When the call goes through, keep the approach friendly and relaxed. Take a few moments to let him get to know you. If someone else referred you to him, by all means use the other person's name. If possible, flatter the interviewee a bit and then background him on what you are doing.

Do not rush him. Ask questions slowly and clearly. Ask follow-up questions from two or three directions. "In other words, Mr. Doe, you mean...." or "What does that mean?" or "I want to be sure...." are good phrases.

This is sound practice because of the lack of reinforcing nonverbal communication. Unless you know a person well and unless both are talking from the same level of understanding, it is easy to misinterpret short statements over the telephone.

CIRCLING AND SHUFFLING

"Circling" is the application of "compare and contrast" to the interview phase. It is a matter of taking a bit of information from one source and running it back around your circle of contacts for refutation or confirmation.

"Shuffling," a term used by Les Whitten, implies building from a single bit of information. It involves "shuffling" around to other persons who may have been involved in the transaction, levering an additional tidbit from each until a complete picture emerges.

Activities that represent circling and shuffling are important aspects of investigative reporting. Their importance is evidenced by the fact that any time you have a tip that more than two or three persons are part of a significant transaction, you have a pretty good chance of reconstructing the event in detail—and of getting more information.

The shuffling procedure for getting more information requires patience, judgment, and guts. Here is the way it would work in a transaction involving seven or eight people. Pick the most salient feature of your tip and play it for Participant A. Then ask him a series of questions about it. Don't ask him to defend or justify it—just to talk about it. Even if you get only one clear quote or exchange (say between Participants E and H) from him, don't try to pin him down. Go instead to Participant B and replay the tune, dropping in the exchange between E and H. If he confirms, press him for other details. If he refutes, ask him, "Well, what *did* happen between E and H?" If his response overlaps the response from A (perhaps he agrees with the meaning of the exchange but not with A's quote), go on to Participant C. By now, you are no longer fishing. Instead, you are asking for clarification and expansion. By the time you talk to E you should have enough detail that he has to respond.

Until the pieces begin to weave into a solid pattern, avoid naming others you have talked to. But once the pattern is clear, change tactics and start presenting as much rich, attributed detail as you can. This switch in approach will usually jar reticent participants into adding details in order to protect themselves. Make at least two trips around the circuit. Go back to

Participant A with your more substantial story, and he will likely come through with details clarifying his own position. Then revisit Participants B, C, D, and so on.

THE KEY INTERVIEW

The key interview (some call it the target interview) is an essential part of any planned investigative piece: the interview with the person or persons directly in control of whatever you are writing about—the person you are bringing to account before the public. If you work according to plan, it is usually the final interview. It has two purposes:

- To let the target comment on or refute the information you have and the assumptions you believe this information proves.

- To obtain additional information.

It is, invariably, a hostile interview. As a rule, you are dealing with a person who is tough, worldly, and experienced in dealing with media. Except in rare instances, he knows approximately what you have found out and whom you have talked to. He has briefed himself fully, has gone over the problem with aides and advisers, and has chosen strategy and tactics designed to knock you out of the box. So be prepared.

Making the Appointment

Your first consideration is to do everything reasonably possible to obtain the interview. A simple refusal, transmitted over the phone or through an intermediary, is not sufficient excuse to say the person "could not be reached for comment." Try personal confrontation. Try going to his home. Try talking to his lawyer, his closest friends, his fellow members of the board of directors about getting to see him. Bear in mind Denny Walsh's general advice about going to see people rather than calling them on the phone for interviews: "I want to make it uncomfortable if not impossible for the person to avoid seeing me."

Ed Pound and his colleague, Tom Moore, had some difficulty making an appointment with Stanley Kusper, the Cook County Clerk in Chicago, who was known as a tough customer. When Moore called, Kusper said he didn't know if he cared to be interviewed by the *Sun-Times*. Pound tells his story:

"I called Kusper and said, 'Look, Stanley—and he said, 'Watch your mouth, Mr. Pound, I don't like to be called Stanley.' And I said, 'Well fine, Stanley, I don't like to be called Mr. Pound. Stanley, we investigated Tom

Keane for damn near a year and he never gave us an interview, and we repeatedly asked him for an interview. I thought you, Stanley, had more balls than that. I thought you had guts, but I guess maybe you don't.' And he started arguing with me, and he finally said, 'Well, I'll think about it.' He called me back about two hours later and granted the interview."

That's an extreme case, valid for the likes of press-wary Chicago pols. In most cases, persistence and courtesy work better. When Bill Lambert was preparing his exposé for *Life*, which eventually caused Supreme Court Justice Abe Fortas to resign, he finally resorted to a registered letter asking him for an interview. It didn't work, but Lambert could then write the piece with a clear conscience.

Some people think that by refusing to see a reporter, they will block publication of the story. At that juncture, remember David Kraslow's advice: "The only way I've been able to get people in that case to talk is to convince them that ... we got [had information] from other sources, and he [the target] would wind up getting the worst end of it if he didn't cooperate. At least by cooperating ... he would be sure that his version would be covered."

Assuming that one of these ploys work—most likely the courteous— your next major decision is on the structure of the interview. Think first about how well you know the person, what he thinks of you. Is your factual case complete, or do you need significant new chunks of information from him? Where will the interview be held? How much time will you have? Thinking about such things will help you decide whether to take a hard, soft, or intermediate approach.

Preparing for the Meeting

Remember the early stress on preparation, control, and information? Preparation is vital, both your control of the interview and the information to be gleaned depend on your preparation. Begin by working with the person who will accompany you on the key interview. A second person is essential for corroboration of whatever exchanges take place in the interview, and for tactical purposes that will become clear later. If he is a member of the team, he will be up-to-date on your files and plans. If not, you will need to brief him and rehearse the interview. Dick Lyneis was one of several reporters who told of having a target make false accusations against him after an uncorroborated key interview. Lyneis's editors at the *Riverside Press-Enterprise* stuck with him, but Lyneis also adopted a policy of double-teaming all key interviews thereafter.

In preparing for the interview, first reread the entire file, making notes of information yet to be obtained and of "why" questions to be asked (for example, "In light of these facts, Mr. Doe, why did you take the action you did?''). Classify the questions. Place the neutral, information-gathering questions early in the interview outline, then lead into the ''why'' questions. Finally, review the phrasing of critical questions so that they are clear and that answers to them cannot be evasive.

I have always liked to script the key questions and then go through them orally with an experienced colleague. I want the colleague to try giving incomplete or evasive answers so that I can be prepared with follow-up questions. Such an exercise helps to weed out weak questions and to refine the order in which to ask the questions. Obviously, I can't plan for every turn the interview may take, but I can usually identify and correct basic flaws in the approach and in the questions.

Bob Greene and his *Newsday* colleagues start by writing a master chronology. They merge dates and descriptions of pivotal events into a summary that may run two to five pages. They also write a synopsis of facts from each major topic file, which in turn becomes the basis for a general synopsis of the story as they see it. Theirs is a compare-and-contrast process that, as Greene has often said, makes ''the files do your investigating for you.'' It brings out links and patterns that may not be visible in any single file. It also helps the reporter decide which, if any, copies of documents he will take with him to show the person being interviewed.

'Hi, How Are You?'

Unless special circumstances—a shortage of time, an extremely hostile opening by the subject—indicate the need for a hard approach, plan to open the interview with a courteous, brief, general statement of what the story is about. Avoid any accusatory remarks that might make the interviewee more tense than he already is. Your first goal is to get him talking. The more freely he talks, the better your chances of getting him to answer the difficult questions later.

''I try to tell the guy at the outset that I don't understand the things I've been hearing and tell him my mind is not made up,'' says John de Groot. ''I want to let the guy talk. The mistake I've made, and I've known other reporters who worked for me who would, because of their own fear, stick religiously to a set of questions. As soon as the guy started to slow down his answers they'd ask the next question right away, rather than letting a guy just talk on and on. They should be quiet, not saying anything. Silence is one of the best questioning techniques I've ever learned. Ask a guy a question, let him answer it and then remain silent. He starts to answer it further, and answer it again and then answer it some more.''

Bob Greene puts it this way: ''Our interviews are very low key. We're not district attorneys and we shouldn't be playing district attorneys. We're not playing for a jury. We'll say something like, 'Hi, how are you?' and make some pleasant small talk to begin with, and then maybe, 'You've probably heard that we've been doing some work. We have some allegations. We have been doing a good deal of digging. We don't know if the allegations are true. If they are true, we would like your explanation as to the reason. If they're not true, we want you to show us where you can that they are not true. And we want to do this thing in as total fairness as we can.''

Control Techniques

Almost always the subject knows he has been under investigation, Greene says. He may already have called the reporter to ask what is going on. If he has called, the reporter has assured him that he will be interviewed before any decision is made about a story. With that, tension begins to build for the interviewee. And now, if the reporter is well prepared, he has control of the interview and is in position to obtain answers to his questions.

"I will have the key date lists with me," Greene says, "and everything else. I may say, 'Now on August 23, we understand, you sat down with Joe Doe and talked with him about this event.' And the man will say yes. And I will pull out a copy of a warranty deed, and say, 'Now on such-and-such a date, this deed was made over to you....' Of course, this kind of questioning frightens and impresses them because you are so precise."

Lou Rose explains how such an approach can cause a subject to provide information without even realizing it. Rose was investigating a scheme by which a political payoff was made after St. Louis agreed to purchase a plot of land adjoining its airport at an excessive price. "So I took that man [who sold the property] out of the records," Rose recounts. "There was not one thing that I did not know about that man for the past twenty or twenty-five years: his financial history, his personal history, his interest in horse racing, his driving records, his traffic violations. I went into his office and I had a stack of records.... We began talking, and he said, 'Well, I started in business—' and I said, 'Oh, yeah, you started in business in 1929,' and he looked surprised and said, 'Right.' And what really shattered him was that I said, 'I see you're interested in horses,' and he said, 'Yes, here's this picture of my daughter,' and I said yes, and named his daughter and told him what event was pictured there and what ribbon she had won.

"He was stunned; there wasn't anything he knew that we didn't know. Little things like this began to get to him, and I pulled out these zoning maps and talked about the history of the case. And I began asking questions, very simple ones, and I said, 'Let's see, Mr. So-and-so handled this land deal for you.' And he said, 'Right.' And then I said, 'And the city paid you a quarter of a million dollars,' and he said, 'Right.' 'And then you paid So-and-so $83,000.' And he said, 'Right.'''

Shortly afterward, Rose finished the interview and wrote a story about how a crony of the mayor had received $83,000 for helping the investigative target arrange the land sale at an inflated price. What the target didn't realize until after the story had been printed was that Rose had never been able to obtain proof of the $83,000 payoff until he (the target) confirmed the figure out of his own mouth. It was one fact that Rose had not been able to document.[7]

Rose's reward—the answer to one crucial question—followed naturally from careful planning and from his resulting control of the interview situation. That should be your aim as you lead the subject through relatively easy questions to which he can give simple, nonargumentative answers. Among these should be some questions designed to stimulate his ego, to get him talking about himself, his family, his business or other interest. If an ego question turns him on, let him ramble for a while—and *listen* to what he is saying. Occasionally, his meandering response will answer questions you hadn't thought of; about as often, it will suggest new questions that you may want to ask later.

If the target does prove talkative, it is fairly easy to lead him into questions about factual points. If a particular fact is essential to a later, harder question or to a point of your assumption, ask for it when the target is relaxed and talkative and before you move into the tough questions. It may be impossible to get the information later if the subject becomes angry and decides to throw you out. If you have done your homework, the factual questions should be relatively few. If they can be phrased as simply refining or confirming knowledge you already have, they should also help build in the interviewee's mind an impression of the depth of your research.

Confrontation

The fact-finding stage leads naturally to the confrontation stage. When you first sat down, you told the subject: "We are looking at the subject of municipal purchasing practices." Now you want to make the definition more specific: "Okay, let's talk about the desks and chairs you have been selling to the city." Obviously, this warns the subject that a tougher question is coming, but he has been expecting trouble anyway. Your warning simply increases tension for him in a courteous way.

Face it: you are literally trying to outmaneuver your target. You want to keep control, which includes maintaining your courtesy while increasing the pressure. Throwing an unexpected, accusatory question may give him the opportunity to say, "None of your damn business—get out of my office." That response may make one piquant quote, but it will also deprive you of better quotes and a better understanding of the story. Delay the recriminatory rhetoric as long as possible. Often, it is wise to ask just one or two nerve-racking questions, then veer off to another topic for a while.

"Frequently, when you're dealing with a really bright person, you'll ask him a series of questions that will lead to the $64 question," Greene says. "Sometimes I'll go ahead and ask the $64 question. Other times, since he sees where I'm going and he is now anticipating and making up his answer, I will suddenly jump off and start another line of questioning. And in the middle of that, when his mind is occupied with new questions, I'll come back to the $64 question. It gives him too much to handle."

As your questions become more specific, start showing documentation. If you have a document to refute one of his statements, show it to him. Similarly, if you have an on-the-record quote from another person, use it at the time when it will be most likely to confound him. The point is to catch the target in contradictions and lies. Even if the contradictions are so minor that you don't intend to write about them, it is usually to your advantage to point them out.

There is, of course, danger in carrying this tactic too far. Going into a third-degree grilling may literally confuse the target into giving mistaken answers or may cause him to make up answers.

"If I can point to something that contradicts him," Al Delugach says, "I'll point it out, but I will usually not try to pressure somebody into changing their statement. I feel there is a certain theory of fairness involved. He has a right even to lie, and to have the lie recorded as his position, or his equivocation. I won't third-degree anybody. I don't really try to pressure somebody when the question goes right to his own guilt or innocence. I do have this feeling about self-incrimination, that a person can't be reasonably expected to incriminate himself. I think there is a lot of bad reporting done on the basis of pressured questions and answers."

Delugach's point is well taken. Greene phrases it a little differently:

"If the guy lies, it's my technique not to confront him with the lie. It is to ask him that question again. I will ask him that same question three or four other ways so that there is no question at all that he didn't understand the question. Then I just let it go. I put his answer in the paper, and I print the document that contradicts him.... Your job is to give a fair, factual report to the public, not to entertain yourself.... That guy may be frightened and he may have a good deal of animosity toward you, but there is no real necessity for you to have animosity toward him."

Experienced reporters tend to agree that in nine out of ten cases, neutral, persistent questioning will obtain more information than an impassioned, sledgehammer inquisition. Marcia McQuern of the *Riverside Press-Enterprise* suggests using a tone that says, "Please explain it for me. I'd love to believe you." But, she adds, the interviewer must not quit when the target gives a false answer: "You move on until he is backed against the wall. As the interview goes on, they get more and more nervous, more and more out of control.''

Shifting Gears: If the conversation becomes too heated and if the target begins to refuse answering questions, shift gears. Let your partner take over the questioning for a while. Let him be easy and friendly. Some people call this maneuver the ''Mutt and Jeff technique.'' One questioner pursues a hard line and presents a skeptical ear. The other breaks in, perhaps even remonstrating with his partner, and asks questions in a friendlier tone. The interviewee welcomes the change, and may tell the second questioner things he wouldn't tell the first one.

''One of the reasons Gene (Ayres) and I conduct interviews in tandem is because our basic interviewing techniques are totally different,'' says Jeff Morgan. ''I use sort of the giggle and cough technique.... I'm really embarrassed to have to ask you these horrible questions, you honorable citizen.'' Gene, on the other hand, is a man who can fall back on a Missouri accent and lull somebody into a false sense of security that he's dealing with a yokel. Ayres has a number of degrees and speaks perfect English when he finally says, ''Gotcha!''

This diversion also gives the target two people to worry about. Ayres and Morgan further refined the technique once when they gave their interviewee a geographical problem with which to cope. While talking to a young man standing in the driveway of his home, one of the pair would wander out of the young man's field of vision, so that he couldn't see both reporters at the same time. Morgan recounts: ''So when Gene was going to nail him with a real tough question, he was literally coming out of left field. It had a startling effect. We didn't do it consciously, but when we were talking about it afterward, we realized it had worked.''

Steve Kurkjian describes working with Gerard O'Neill, who became chief of the *Boston Globe* Spotlight Team after Tim Leland was promoted: ''It's great with Gerry. He's six two, a tough-looking guy. I'm naturally mild-mannered and I like to soothe the target down. It has worked to our advantage a lot of times. Gerry will wrap the guy around and the guy will get very hostile and won't answer a question, and I'll say, 'Well come on, we know it's not all your fault....' ''

Another advantage of double-teaming is that while one reporter is carrying the questions, the other can sit back and analyze the answers. If he spots a fuzzy or inconsistent answer, he may break in with a series of questions that bursts the bubble. Kurkjian recalls questioning a fire chief about improper political activity. One minor aspect, perhaps not worth a story in itself, was that the chief often used his official car for private errands or to take his wife shopping. When he denied it, Kurkjian challenged him with dates and times of misuse that the *Globe* reporters had observed. ''We broke him on a minor angle, so that when it came to the bigger questions, he might say to himself, 'Well, Christ, these guys do have it.' "

Registering Indignation: There are times when the interviewer, while keeping his temper under internal control, needs to let the target believe he has become indignant about being lied to. Such indications of displeasure are best used when dealing with an experienced public figure—an elected official or a top-level bureaucrat—who is clearly accountable and who is trying to avoid his responsibility. Clark Mollenhoff often uses such controlled indignation when he hears a target evading a question. Mollenhoff uses phrasing like this:

"This is a serious problem and I want to know the answer. I asked you this question and I want to know your response. I want to take it down very carefully, because you are going to be held to it. You've got a responsibility under the law; now what's your explanation? I am going to take it down and I am going to read it back to you so we don't have any quibbles about whether I'm quoting you properly."

Under such questioning, Mollenhoff says, the evasive bureaucrat "sometimes backtracks. If he is in a tight enough bind, he probably says just about what he has to say. But you don't have to trick them to get answers. I don't believe in taking people out of context. I never take advantage of a guy who simply slips. If he says something unusual two or three times, that's different."

Learning from Others: One further point about questions: wherever you can, observe and talk to experienced questioners. They have learned a lot of common-sense applied psychology. Trial lawyers are experts at developing lines of questioning, though their purposes are generally different from yours. Their tactics are basically designed to "crack" a witness, to break him down—questionable practices indeed for the reporter who is only trying to get information. What is interesting and useful to observe, however, is the skill with which such questioners absorb and analyze answers, then ask specific challenging questions designed to find weaknesses in the witness's story. This ability to think clearly in the midst of a series of questions and answers is worth your study.

Results

Even after using combinations of all questioning techniques, the reporter must still expect to come away from most key interviews with little more than formal denials or at best "no comment" responses to his crucial questions. "Most of the time, I view it purely as journalistic exercise," says Kurkjian. "He [the target] is going to be quite leery of giving us any angle, giving us much of anything at all. I am very rarely surprised—either by something he gives me or something he takes away from me."

That "something he takes away from me" is the ultimate disappointment of the key interview. It occurs when the target supplies documents or other irrefutable proof that the reporter has been on the wrong trail. Ed Pound describes an instance of this kind:

"We had a situation where one particular firm had a monopoly on one phase of the Chicago Housing Authority business. They had three or four million dollars worth of business in three years; they were underbidding everybody by hundreds of thousands of dollars, then specifications were being changed after they had won the job, this sort of thing. We went to the guy running the company and he just blew us out. He could defend everything. For example, there was a change order that permitted a fellow to use aluminum instead of steel on window guards. . . . We had an architect go out and give us an evaluation, and he thought this was going to save . . . hundreds of thousands of dollars. So we went in there very confidently and the guy pulled out one of these pricing books and showed us that aluminum is a hell of a lot more expensive then steel. So yes, it happens. . . ."

It happens most often to the inexperienced reporter who has not prepared properly. When it happens to a veteran like Pound, he doesn't let it shake him. He simply reports "no go" to his editor, and goes on to the next job, a little wiser but no less confident. "I've always enjoyed key interviewing more than anything else," Pound says. "You've got to be convinced when you go in that you're able to handle it, and that when you get it, you're going to be fair with it."

TAKING NOTES

Except in the full-dress key interview, don't take too many notes. Most people get nervous when they see you scribbling their words down. Keep good eye contact with the subject. A fairly common trick of veteran reporters is not to start writing when the subject makes a startling or unexpected revelation. Instead, they keep the subject talking for a few moments. At some less tense time, they make a few key-word notes. Later, after the revelation has aged a bit, they may go back and review it, taking more notes as necessary.

Learn to memorize the key points of conversation without taking notes. Work at this, and test yourself in non-story situations. There are times when the appearance of your pencil and pad will stop an interview cold. So be prepared to work without them. Andy Alexander and Keith McKnight have done so with great success in double-team interviews. They learned that after the interview it was best for them not to talk about it until each had sat down at his own typewriter and written his best recollection of both the major facts and the important comments. They explain that if their notes didn't agree, they would either throw out the uncertain point or call back later to clear it up.

Jim Polk tells of interviewing a prime grand-jury witness in a case involving "shuffling money around" in Alabama politics: "I sat and drank with the witness for three hours, and he opened up because he thought I knew more than I actually did. I picked the right amount of money out of the air, and he thought I knew everything.... I didn't use a notebook, but I went back to the hotel and wrote notes for the next hour.... It's not too hard. You memorize the key facts, and then worry about the quotes. You get the basic facts and maybe two or three quotes you're going to use—one-sentence ones."

When you do take notes, do it as quickly as possible. In fact, learn shorthand. It isn't hard. I taught myself and have, more than once, used such notes to back down a politician who was crying "misquote." The main advantage of shorthand is that you don't have to spend as much time writing; you can keep the conversation flowing.

Reiterating: always transcribe all of your interview notes on the typewriter the day you take them, without fail.

Tape Recordings

The tape recorder is not a good instrument to use on a nervous grand-jury witness of the kind Polk was interviewing, but it can be useful in key interviews. There is a great deal of anti-tape mythology among pencil-and-paper reporters. They believe the machine scares interviewees even more than a note pad. I held the same attitude for a long time, and I suppose it was valid in the 1950s when recorders were bulky and more of a novelty. But in the 1970s, I began to use tape more often, and found it didn't hamper most formal interviews.

I was fascinated by a survey compiled by the Public Relations Society of America in 1974 for the Associated Press Managing Editors. The PRSA questionnaire was answered by 470 national figures in business, politics, public relations, education, and labor. It indicated that:

- 53 per cent felt they had been misquoted within the previous year.
- 83.9 per cent of these claimed newspapers had misquoted them. Less than 20 per cent blamed radio or television.
- 69.6 per cent *favored* the use of tape recorders for in-person interviews in order to avoid misquotation.

As the report noted: "The response suggests that wide use of tape recorders might help build credibility for reporters and newspapers."[8] It certainly suggests that many of the people you will deal with in key interviews and expert interviews will not be intimidated by the machine.

The tape recorder can also serve as a reference—and for the target, too. Bob Greene says that when a *Newsday* team goes in for a key interview, "we invariably ask to tape record the interview and suggest that he do the same thing. We do not rely on the tape recorder as the principal instrument. We take notes as any reporters do in terms of answers to the key questions. We use the recorder only to clarify notes or for the exact quote."

So learn to use a good, unobtrusive hand-size cassette recorder. Be prepared to spend $125 or more for it. Be sure it has a digital counter. Use best-quality C-60 or C-90 tapes. The C-120 tape is very thin and snarls easily.

Yes, there can be problems in using a tape recorder. The batteries can run down if you don't put fresh ones in before an interview. The microphone will pick up unwanted noises such as the tap of a pencil or the rap of knuckles on a desk. A single microphone may not pick up the voices of two persons on opposite sides of a desk. Therefore, if you do use a tape recorder, make pencil notes also. And pick quiet places—not noisy hotel coffee-shops—for your interviews. Look out for defective fluorescent lamps, whose buzz can ruin a recording.

It isn't necessary to make a typescript of every tape. It takes an expert secretary four or more hours to transcribe a single hour of taped conversation, even using earphones and a foot pedal. The best policy is to play the tape after you get back to the office and make careful notes (including the counter reading) of the spots that contain key quotes, then file the tape carefully until it is time to write your story.

Before you think about making covert recordings (either by bugging your own phone or carrying a microphone in your brief case or purse) be sure about the laws on eavesdropping in your own state. As long as you identify yourself as a reporter and simply use the recorder as a stenographic device, you should have no serious problems. But the law does not agree in all states. In general, it prohibits anything that smacks of eavesdropping—listening to others' conversation—without permission.

Because investigative reporting is more than routine daily reporting, the responsibility for accuracy is more severe. Above all, investigative reporting is an intellectual process. Logic—not emotion—must rule when decisions are made, ideas gathered, facts sorted, patterns built, and options analyzed.

Because a source can be mistaken or biased, the reporter must check everything carefully. Truth is elusive, and the reporter is responsible for the truth of every word. Consequently, reliance on one source is risky. The investigative reporter should develop the patience to run information from one source to another and on to another and another if need be.

Interviewing is an art, and good interviewing involves talking—and listening. Ask questions, even what might be regarded as dumb questions. The reporter's objective is to get information, not to impress the interviewee with his own brilliance. Remember that careful listening is the best way to gain information. By combining listening with strategic periods of silence, the source will be encouraged to go on talking, often telling the reporter more than could be gained by firing off questions in rapid succession. Put the subject at ease early in the interview. While this is important in any interview, it becomes doubly so when the session plunges into serious questions or allegations.

For any interview, proper preparation is vital. Only with a solid base of background information can the reporter hope to control the course and direction of the interview and obtain the information he or she seeks. Use the exploratory interview to advantage. Learn the strengths and weaknesses of the interviewee and make this an opportunity to establish your professional competence. Go to *see* a person rather than telephoning. If you must use the phone, use it to advantage—turn the call into an appointment for a face-to-face session with the source.

Before conducting the final interview and confronting the subject with the meat of your questioning, reread the entire file carefully. Plan your questions and rehearse the interview with another person. Double-team the source at this interview by taking along another reporter or your teammate. This technique provides corroboration for what you will learn. Be courteous during the interview. Get the source talking. Remain neutral but persistent. Establish facts that pave the way to a confrontation, using supporting documentation when necessary. Impress that source that you have done your homework and know whereof you speak.

Make full use of eye contact during the interview, rather than hastily scribbling notes. Learn to memorize the key points of conversations. Maintain control of the interview by being flexible in your pattern of questioning, shifting gears to maintain the element of surprise. Allow your partner to help out when needed. At a less tense time in the session, commit the key points to paper and go over them again with the source if necessary to achieve accuracy. Support taped interviews with penciled notes. Later, at the typewriter and as soon as possible after the conclusion of the interview, record the major facts and important comments. Transcribe direct quotes from your notes.

While all this confrontation and drama are going on, be aware that you have some additional responsibilities. Be alert before, during, and after the interview. Pay attention to the color and circumstances that occur accompanying the occasion. Be observant of detail and record these with your notes for future reference. Direct observation is an effective and useful technique for the investigative reporter.

5

Inside
and Undercover

DIRECT OBSERVATION

COMMON SENSE tells the investigative reporter that direct observation is the best way to get the facts. It is the best way to get information unfiltered by others' biases, faulty memory, or incomplete records.

In a sense, direct observation is like making a snapshot. A reporter goes to the site of a public occurrence. He listens to the speeches and estimates the size and reaction of the crowd. At the scene of a disaster or crime, he counts the bodies, paces off the skid marks, talks to witnesses, notes the actions of the people, looks inside the wrecked cars for whiskey bottles, surveys the charred ruins for signs of arson.

Perhaps the snapshot analogy is not sufficiently apt. For rather than making snapshots, the investigative reporter is drafting the script for a full-length documentary movie. He must not consider just the given moment but more extensive actions. He must describe the strategy, tactics, ambitions, misdeeds, reasoning, and motives of antagonists in one subplot of the continuing drama of human existence. To do so, he may have to become part of the action.

The *Boston Globe* Spotlight Team used direct observation in several ways to tell how a parking-lot operator was fleecing the city. Reporters counted cars in the lot, which was on land owned by the city, and found they far exceeded the number reported by the parking-lot operator, who was leasing the land on a prorated basis. They then parked their cars in the lot and found that they were sometimes given claim checks that had not been date-stamped, indicating that claim checks were being used over and over. Finally, they took photographs of the lot. All of these forms of observation confirmed the fact that the operator was understating his business, and hence was cheating the city out of hundreds of thousands of dollars of annual rent.

In Santa Monica, California, reporter Tom Riney of the *Evening Outlook* was sent out to check on a "skimming" operation at the Department of Welfare. Riney let his whiskers grow, put on some tattered clothes, and established himself as a skid-row habitué. He got on the relief rolls for a week in order to prove how the racket worked: the skimmer simply bought social-service vouchers from welfare recipients anxious for quick cash at half price, then turned them in to the county to collect full value. It was the baggy pants that got Riney the story, not the trench coat.

Experience tells the investigative reporter that for some types of observation he will learn more if he keeps his press card out of his hatband and doesn't drive up in a company car with "Daily Tribune" painted on the door. When people know you're a reporter, they tend to act differently. They will clean off their desks, sweep the dirt under the rug, even tidy up their language. If they have been beating prisoners or patients, they will hide their whips, and the whipped, until the reporter leaves. Some will strain to please the reporter. Some will make up answers to questions rather than admit they don't know. Others will clam up, claiming they can't remember what happened thirty minutes earlier.

To avoid these results, the reporter may have to resort to "inside" work, to role-playing, to dealing with informants, or to covert surveillance. Before undertaking this type of action, however, investigative reporters should ask themselves a number of questions in order to choose the safest, least offensive and most productive course. Here are examples of such questions: What information do I need? Can I get it through records? through interviews? through direct, open observation? Have I exhausted these possibilities? When I identify myself as a reporter, will the person or institution I am examining tell me the truth? Is the information I am seeking crucial to my readers' understanding of a significant abuse? Do my readers care? Do I need to conceal my true identity in order to find out the truth?

The answers are never chiseled in stone. Nor are they found in the Bible or the Boy Scout Manual. The reporter must work them out with his editor, his colleagues, and himself. He must decide whether he believes in situational ethics. He must decide whether circumstances do indeed alter cases. If he cannot do that, he should probably give up his investigative ambitions, because he will find the experience too frustrating. He will never be able to go into the trenches and find out what the daily battle of life is really like.

SITUATIONAL ETHICS

Two words are most often invoked in discussing undercover work: "morals" and "ethics." The word "morals" derives from the Latin *moralis,* which means customs and folkways—in short, the ways in which people or communities act toward one another. In modern dictionaries, definitions of the two words refer to principles of right and wrong action, good and bad character, of actions based on inner conviction. Moral actions, says Webster's Third New International, are those "sanctioned by or operating on one's conscience or ethical judgment ... of or relating to the accepted customs or patterns of social and personal relations." The Random House Dictionary calls morals "principles or habits with respect to right or wrong conduct," and speaks of ethics as "a system of moral principles ... the rules of conduct recognized in respect to a particular class of human actions" and as "that branch of philosophy dealing with values ... with respect to the rightness and wrongness of certain actions and to the goodness or badness of the motives and ends of such actions." The Third says "ethical" may suggest "conformity to a code or to the conclusions or considerations of right, fair, equitable conduct."

Situational ethics have been around for a long time. In short, they relate to the idea that what may be "wrong" in one situation may be "right" in another. Whether the reporter likes the idea or not, he is unrealistic if he pretends it does not exist. The people we encounter every day deal in situational ethics that are generally not very rational. An editor deals with them every day—rationally, it is hoped—as he decides whether to carry a story about the sexual behavior of an errant schoolteacher or to pursue a tip about corruption in the police department.

Whatever he calls it, the investigative reporter applies situational ethics when he decides to go "inside" or "underground" to get his story. Certainly the actions he takes must be acceptable to his conscience and his ethical judgments. He is concerned with "right, fair, and equitable" conduct by persons and institutions that impinge upon his readers' daily life. He is also concerned about maintaining his own personal integrity and morality while uncovering the actions and motivations of others. If the reporter is going to find out something that people less moral than himself are trying to conceal, he must use imagination, guts, guile, and, yes, sometimes deception, to do it. If he has a low threshold of indignation, he is going to be as aggressive as his conscience will permit him to be. He may not have much fun going underground, but he may finally decide he must do so to do his job.

One quality the investigative reporter must guard against is self-righteousness. He must guard against the "cop mentality" that Bob Greene speaks of. He must, while doing inside work, commit himself to understanding the external forces and pressures that explain the person or situation he has under observation. He must be a passive observer, not a *provocateur* or a modifier of what he is observing. He must not, in other words, be manipulative or selective in his observation—any more than he should be myopic. It would be foolish to take the risks of going underground and emerge with a less than honest report, or one that nobody cares to read about. For this reason, the early stages of feasibility and base-building are highly important: they give the investigative reporter the opportunity to understand the norms of the subject he is investigating.

Once the reporter identifies what society expects of its institutions, he can better diagram its malfunctions. He will have a model against which to measure reality. Before going into the gutter to face a real or metaphorical beast, the reporter wants to know that the stakes, including the mental and moral strain, are worth the effort. He cannot engage in sophistry to avoid the questions. He does not want to use innuendo to say or imply things that cannot be proved. He does not want to dissemble, to play a false role or to ask others to do these things unless he can see clear rewards for his readers as a result.

TEMPTATIONS AND PERILS

If, after weighing the stakes and risks, the investigative reporter decides that some kind of covert or inside activity is needed, the reporter should then impose controls on his own discretion and judgment. He should work with his editor on determining a reasonable path to obtain pertinent information. In adopting this course, the reporter is willingly imposing constraints on his predictable tendency to go too far. Constraints also include seeking as much corroborative evidence as possible. He keeps "discretion" at the top of his checklist. He does not expect to publish everything he finds out. For both ethical and pragmatic reasons, he avoids such temptations as:

- Deception for its own sake—that is, playing secret agent for kicks.
- Entrapment or provocation—that is, inducing or encouraging others to commit illegal or immoral acts in order to fatten the reporter's story.
- Self-hypnosis—that is, imputing evil motives in everything he sees to persons he is covertly investigating.

Obviously, the investigative reporter must also guard against committing either a crime or a violation of someone else's civil rights. He should consult with a lawyer who specializes in publications law. Laws vary from state to state, and those covering the right of privacy in particular have recently been under extensive legislative and judicial review. There are, however, five major kinds of legal perils about which the investigative reporter should be aware:

- Burglary is a felony almost everywhere. In most places, you are guilty of it, if you overcome the slightest obstacle (such as turning an unlocked doorknob) to enter a place with intent to take something that is not yours.

- Trespass can occur if you enter a private place without permission of the owner or inhabitant. Some lower courts have held that reporters trespass when they accompany policemen or firemen inside a house where a crime or fire has taken place.

- Larceny, in varying degrees, occurs if you take something of value that belongs to another.

- Impersonating an officer can have serious consequences. Not only is it a crime, it can also open a reporter and his publication to civil suit from the victim of impersonation.

- Invasion of privacy is usually a civil matter, though some federal and state laws also carry criminal penalties.

Having weighed and discussed these perils with his editor and attorney, the reporter should then consider the precise mechanism through which he will undertake covert observation.

VOLUNTEER SOURCES

There are still other perils. Anyone who voluntarily becomes your source is usually trying to use your journalistic clout—your ability to get a story published—to achieve a personal end, one that he cannot accomplish on his own. Rarely are his motives pure or altruistic. Indeed, he may even be a double agent or a *provocateur* trying to set up a situation that will reveal the reporter in the most unfavorable light. Reporters Bill Anderson and Dick Cady of the *Indianapolis Star* learned this object lesson in 1974 after witnessing what an "informer" told them was an illegal payoff to a policeman. The informer then told the county prosecutor that Anderson and Cady had tried to get him to bribe the officer; the reporters were indicted,[1] but later cleared of all charges. The volunteer source was part of a plan by city policemen to undermine the *Star*'s credibility; the paper had been engaged in a yearlong exposé of police corruption.

Less threatening, but no less false and frustrating, is the volunteer who bamboozles the reporter for selfish reasons. In 1975, in more than ten columns of its own space, the *Los Angeles Times* admitted it had been

tricked into spending some $15,000 (including several weeks of expert re-
portorial time) escorting a volunteer source first to Hong Kong and then to
Bangkok for a promised meeting with the missing Patty Hearst. After the
whole misadventure was exposed,[2] the source, one Michael Casey, even had
the audacity to send the *Times* a bill for $500 in daily "consulting fees."

Conversely, the volunteer source can be solid gold, altruistically
motivated, and the only person who can get the information the reporter
needs. The *New York Times*' exposure of the Tweed Ring and Tammany
Hall in 1871 began when a disenchanted bookkeeper turned over his secret
ledgers to a *Times* reporter. In 1974, an executive of Combustion Engineering, Inc., walked in on Jonathan Kwitny of the *Wall Street Journal* and
delivered copies of documents describing a series of contracts the firm had
made the previous year. While public investors had bought Combustion
Engineering stock at rising prices in 1973 on news of $565 million worth of
new orders announced by the company, thirty-six Combustion Engineering
officers, directors, and other insiders were selling their stock at good prices.
The documents handed to Kwitny showed that the publicized new contracts
(actually only letters of intent) carried unusual warranties, penalties, and
cancellation clauses that could hurt the company's profitability. Before the
Journal published the story, of course, it checked many other sources—
Securities and Exchange Commission filings, Atomic Energy Commission
spokesmen, other Combustion Engineering executives—to be sure that
what the volunteer had handed over was authentic and significant.[3]

THE RECRUITED INFORMANT

Paid informants are trouble. The risk in using them almost invariably
outweighs the possible payoff. Newsmen learn this lesson anew every time a
major story comes along. During the height of the search for Teamsters
union boss James Hoffa, an ex-convict named Clarence N. Medlin first
tried to extract $200 and air fare to Miami from the *Fayetteville* (N.C.)
Times in exchange for information leading to the recovery of Hoffa's body.
Spurned there, he sought out Patrick O'Keefe, a journalism teacher at the
University of North Carolina who had previously worked for the Associated
Press. O'Keefe went to editors of *Harper's* magazine; they paid him a $700
advance for an article and suggested he take Medlin over to CBS News. The
network paid O'Keefe $1,000 for Medlin's interview on "60 Minutes," then
another $9,000 for uncovering the story. A network crew rushed off to Key
West, following Medlin's directions, to search the ocean for Hoffa's body,
and Medlin rushed off to New Orleans to try to sell his story to the weekly
Figaro and the *Times-Picayune.* The FBI finally arrested him for obtaining
money under false pretenses.[4]

The Paid and the Unpaid

Sometimes a tipster, anxious to sell you information, will give it away if properly motivated. Al Knight of the *Rocky Mountain News* recalls that a disgruntled executive secretary came to him in 1973 with information about a private detective who had been hired by ITT to spy on Dita Beard, onetime ITT lobbyist whose confidential political memo (published by Jack Anderson) showed a connection between ITT's promise of a campaign donation and a favorable anti-trust settlement that had embarrassed the Nixon administration. Knight told the woman the *News* was interested, but would not pay for information. "You'll just have to take it somewhere else," he told her in the friendliest and most sympathetic tone he could muster. "She came back in about half an hour or 45 minutes," Knight recounts, "and said, 'Okay, I'll tell you what I can and you can check the rest.' " Knight and Richard O'Reilly then spent two days placing phone calls to the East Coast until they found an ITT security official who confirmed that the detective had been hired.[5]

There is in the minds of most newsmen, of course, considerable difference between paying for inside information and buying dinner or drinks for an informant who has delivered usable information. For the reporter, the old political definition of purity may be the most reasonable one: don't give an informant anything he can't eat, drink, or smoke in a single sitting. And certainly, most editors and reporters do not count tips to bellboys, hack drivers, bartenders, or waiters—people who derive their living from tips—as bribery or paying for information.

The most dangerous kind of informant is the one who has a vested interest in providing reports in dribs and drabs. He makes certain a steady supply of payments is forthcoming—and that information that might contradict the reporter's investigative assumption, and hence kill his golden goose, is not divulged. This kind of recruited informer is of no value to the reporter in backing up his story. And if the cash-for-information deal is ever exposed, the reporter's credibility is badly damaged.

The recruited, unpaid, informant, on the other hand, can be invaluable. The unpaid recruit has agreed, at the reporter's request, to obtain information, such as accounts and observations of nonpublic meetings and other activities within a secretive organization. Al Delugach and Denny Walsh used this kind of informant in reporting on corruption in the steamfitters' union in St. Louis in 1966–1969. In this instance, the unpaid recruit proved to be the best way in which to find out how union officials were using members' dues to make illegal political contributions, to take over an insurance company and pay themselves agents' commissions, and, in general, to subvert trade-union ideals. To get both specific information and leads about records to search, Delugach says, "we found and cultivated some dissident members who really couldn't afford to have it known they were talking to us. This was a pretty rough outfit. They were able to tell us what happened at union meetings, what kind of assessments were put on, and that these policial assessments were not legal.'' The reporters, of course, could have tried burglarizing union offices, bugging telephones, or seducing secretaries, but working with informants was by far the soundest course.

What if the informant brings you documents from the secret files of the target institution? Les Whitten, associate of Jack Anderson, says he will take them.

On that point, Bob Greene reasons this way: "I'm going to take the same position as Whitten. I didn't ask them to do the stealing.... I'm probably receiving stolen goods, but I am only holding facts. I'll go through the loopholes. I go for the technicalities. Why play pious? I won't tell an informant to steal papers because then I am committing a crime, and I'm as bad as the people I'm writing about. ... I will not go to the point where I conspire with somebody to steal a document.... I might indicate, 'Boy, I'd sure like to get a look at records like that,' which is just one step this side of saying, 'Will you get them for me?' ... You're going to be walking the tightrope sometimes, very carefully...."

It is, incidentally, not always a crime to possess pieces of paper. From a criminal standpoint, some monetary value must be established in order to prove larceny. Still, issues of trespass and privacy are to be considered in holding secret papers. As Greene says, on this question the investigative reporter walks a tightrope.

Obviously, a reporter should not recruit an informant who does not want to be recruited. The reporter must be especially careful not to threaten the informant with exposure if he refuses to cooperate; to do so would be to flirt with extortion. The informant must be convinced that the public good and his own interests will be served by working with the newsman. The thoughtful reporter does not want the kind of plea-bargaining or "protection" leverage that police and prosecutors have when they turn a suspect into an informer. What he does want is an informant who will help because he believes that to help serves the community's best interests. And he wants the informant to know all the risks involved, and to protect himself against either taking unwarranted chances or fabricating information in the hope of obtaining rewards.

Protection

The reporter must also have a firm policy about what to do should he be called before a grand jury or investigative agency seeking to learn the identity of his informant. If his state has a reporters' shield law, it may provide some protection. If there is no such law, he must have the backing of his editor and publisher. The reporter must also have worked out plans to protect files, notes, and documents from subpoena—perhaps by placing them in the custody of another person just before the story is published. If the story is a significant one, he can expect some such form of legal retribution to be invoked, if only for its publicity value to the aggrieved target. The reporter must find the legal technicalities that will provide maximum protection for himself and his informant.

The best method to adopt for the protection of an informant is to think about whether his information, if published, can be traced back to him. There are ways in which to obscure the trail. When Keith McKnight and Andrew Alexander of the *Dayton Journal Herald* were investigating misfeasance in the Ohio Bureau of Vocational Rehabilitation, they faced this problem. A source brought them a copy of a document that had been routed to him. Alexander describes their response:

"Take the document and put it on so-and-so's desk tomorrow morning when nobody's there. So-and-so will pick it up and say, 'What the hell is this?' And he'll tell somebody else. Perhaps he'll duplicate it. And then two or three people know about it."

In dealing with more open contacts, the reporter can also ask guarded, tangential questions about the same topic on which his informant has provided data. If the open contact seems willing to talk, the reporter can then lead the discussion until it has covered enough ground to encompass what the informant reported. Using this variation of the shuffling technique in a series of interviews shortly before publication, the reporter can effectively cover a trail leading back to his informant.

A chancy but sometimes necessary procedure to follow in protecting the informant is to "wire" him with a concealed tape recorder or small radio transmitter. If the informant is participating in conversations that are to be recorded, he may not be eavesdropping in the legal sense, but merely taking notes. The reporter should, of course, always discuss any such plan with his editor and lawyer before undertaking it.

Whatever method you develop for working with a recruited informant, your major risk is in effecting the transfer of the information. Scheduled calls between pay telephone booths are often used. Regular mail contacts are relatively secure. If the informant also happens to be a friend, a fellow church member, or a bowling-league buddy, the contacts are easier to arrange.

Depending on how highly placed the informant is, he may have to use diversionary tactics to maintain his credibility. George Bliss recalls going to cover a Teamsters' union meeting and finding himself the direct target of a blistering verbal attack from the main speaker, who was one of Bliss's best informants. "I thought I was going to get lynched," Bliss recalled. "I called him that night and said, 'Pete, what the hell are you doing?' He said, 'I thought they were getting suspicious of me.' So I told Pete: 'Well, you're putting up too good an act.' "

THE LEGMAN

A legman is a reporter on a loose leash. He gathers information by settling in where his antennae tell him tantalizing information lurks. Some, but not all, legmen do not write well but have a genius for searching out stories. Many investigative reporters believe one of the best methods for gathering authoritative information is to get right inside a target organization where they know what to look for and how to record and relate it accurately. The *Boston Globe* Spotlight Team and others have used legmen particularly for investigations of consumer swindles.

Reporter Bill Jones got a job as an ambulance driver and wrote a Pulitzer Prize series about it for the *Chicago Tribune* in 1970. Five years later, he became assistant managing editor. As a result of Jones's inside technique, the paper's task force was formed in 1970 and operated under a succession of directors. The legmen exposed systematic vote fraud in Cook County (another Pulitzer effort, directed by George Bliss). And they have uncovered the operations of fast-buck dealers in franchise sales, bill-collection agencies, career schools, money-grubbing nursing homes and private hospitals. The task force also unmasked abuses of city-patronage jobs, police brutality, and a full range of other misdeeds of the kind for which Chicago is famous. (One suspects that competition among the *Tribune, Sun-Times,* and *Daily News* simply exposes more hustlers than the relatively leisurely operation of monopoly papers in other cities.)

Virtually all of the *Tribune's* efforts have called for reporters to become legmen and spend from several days to several months inside target organizations. The success of the vote-fraud series, for example, pivoted on Bliss's ability to get reporter William Mullen into line for a patronage job in the election commissioner's office. Mullen remained in the office nearly a year He observed, listened, took notes—and fed his colleagues information that enabled them to monitor and photograph currupt polling places, then to develop documentary proof of falsified registration and voting records. The *Tribune* and the Better Government Association worked together on several other kinds of original research to corroborate and flesh out Mullen's leads. For instance, using addresses on the voter rolls, they mailed out questionnaires and found many of the addresses to be nonexistent, confirming their suspicions about the high percentage of dead or nonexistent voters.

Details...

Pam Zekman, a member of the original *Chicago Tribune* Task Force and its director for more than a year, says legmen should not remain at their undercover post too long. "We try not to stay in a company or an institution past what you would call the training period, because then you may get yourself into the very misdeeds that you are exposing." In applying for jobs, task force members use their own names and try to fill in application blanks accurately up to the point of saying they work for the *Tribune*. They use each other's names as personal references. "You do this to find out if they check references," Zekman says. "Part of the story on nursing homes was that they hired us on the spot. They didn't check a single reference...." In being interviewed for a job, "you say as little as you can," says Zekman, in order not to be caught in lies. Because most task force members have worked several inside jobs and have also done nonjournalistic work while attending college, they can pass most screening tests.

"When we were starting on the bill-collector series," Zekman recalls, "a couple of agencies put our people through little tests. Our guy was being hit with this test cold and didn't know what to expect. They gave him an index card on a debtor and said, 'Okay, find him.' Well, you know, if you're a reporter, you go to the criss-cross directory, you call the neighbors, you know all the ways to get information on the phone. This bill collector just sat there with his mouth open, and pretty soon he hired our guy."

Once inside, the *Tribune* reporter is expected to put in a full day on his or her pseudo-job, then trek back to the newsroom every night and write a detailed memo on the day's activities and observations. If there is danger of being discovered, the reporter may arrange to do the transcribing elsewhere, but the cardinal rule remains: make a *daily* record and keep contact with teammates. When the inside assignment or job-training period nears its end, the *Tribune* reporter simply fades away. He may tell the boss he doesn't like the work or has obtained a better job. Occasionally, he simply doesn't show up.

For the *Tribune's* collection-agency story, Zekman got a job as an agency receptionist, work that made it easy to make notes about what went on. She observed collectors impersonating policemen, claiming warrants had been issued for the arrest of the debtors, posing as attorneys and saying their furniture would be sold and their homes taken, and threatening a foster mother that she would lose her child. Some time later, the task force won an award for another project and the *Tribune* carried a story naming its task force members, Zekman among them. She had, of course, used her right name to get the receptionist's job. Still, she went to the pseudo-job the next day, "and it was worthwhile because I got to see them take money from a debtor after they'd laughed among themselves that he didn't owe any. They just pocketed the money and I was able to witness that.

"However, in the middle of the day, the owner of the agency got a telephone call and went rushing out. The secretary said, 'Where are you going?' He said, 'I'm going to get a paper.' I asked another bill collector what was going on, and he started singing the *Tribune* jingle that had been on television: 'You've got a friend at the *Tribune*.' So I just took my notes off the desk, went to lunch, and never went back.

"That afternoon about 4 o'clock I got a call at the *Tribune* from him [the boss]. He said, 'This is so-and-so,' and I just said, 'Well, can I help you?' He said, 'I think you just have,' and hung up." What Zekman helped to do was to influence the passage of legislation regulating collection agencies. As a result of her stories, three of four agents of the company pleaded guilty, and one was convicted.

Bill Crawford, another *Chicago Tribune* Task Force member, once filled out an application to work for a fly-by-night "trade school." As he was doing so, he heard a salesman in the next room talking to the sales manager.

"Is the *Tribune* cool?" the salesman asked.

"What do you mean?" countered the boss.

"Well, last year I was selling franchises and they came out with one expose after another and drove me out of business."

Crawford suppressed a smile, turned in his application form and successfully completed his job interview. He knew something about fast-sales pitches, because he was one of the reporters who had worked for the franchise promoter the previous year.

The legman may learn things he might never discover by interviewing others. Late in 1975, for instance, Bill Gaines worked as a janitor in von Sollbrig Memorial Hospital, the only for-profit general hospital in Chicago. As later *Tribune* stories detailed, he "found himself summoned [by hospital staff] into the operating room as many as six times in a single week, often in soiled clothing, to assist patients. . . . [He] saw nurse's aides routinely used to awaken patients after surgery and return them to their rooms, a violation of state regulations that require them to be attended by a registered nurse and released by a doctor. . . . At von Sollbrig, he found, there was only one orderly, an unpaid, untrained 16-year-old who within three days on the job was working as an assistant in the operating room. He bragged to a *Tribune* reporter and to his parents . . . that he was 'really into some heavy surgery.' "

Gaines also noted other facts, such as that the names of fifty persons were listed as "staff doctors" on a large display board. When the *Tribune* checked those listed, however, it could find only forty-seven of them.

Furthermore, of the forty-seven, only eighteen said they practiced at the hospital.[6] Theoretically, this kind of information might be obtained through careful interviewing, particularly if the reporter is guided by a disgruntled source. Practically, it is much easier to get the information, and it is much more authentic, if the reporter writes about conditions in such an institution from his own experience.

...And Drawbacks

There are, understandably enough, drawbacks to inside work. It cannot always be carried through, for instance, and there are times when some of its results are best left unspecified. The legman activities of Zekman and Susan Schwartz in two different hospitals are illustrations.

Zekman worked as a nurse's aide in 1973 when the *Tribune* was exposing bad nursing homes. Two years later, she used this experience to get a similar job in the von Sollbrig hospital. "They decided they would hire me and let me work the floor with a licensed practical nurse," Zekman recalls. "She would be my supervisor and watch everything I did, and then when they hired enough nurse's aides they would put me through a regular two-week orientation. But then the LPN got sick one morning and I was left by myself. They wanted me to take blood pressures and do things this LPN would do. I didn't go back to that job. Some of these people were very sick people, and if something happened to them. . . .

"Sometimes you have to curb your enthusiasm," Zekman says. "You know if you do these things you'll get a hell of a story, but you just can't do it. You just have to draw the line."

Schwartz of the *Seattle Times* played the role of a depressed person in order to get inside a mental hospital. But here, too, the inside work involved problems. As she relates:

"How much was I, in writing that story, going to talk about the patients? Inevitably somebody's going to recognize—and people did recognize—who I was talking about. Not naming names is not an answer to these things, because the patient's friends are going to know who that is. If you can write at all, you are going to describe this person sufficiently well. To make this vivid, I was actually telling details of people's very bizarre behavior. That is not kind, really."

It can also be dangerous if the person being written about—almost certainly a private person under the *Gertz* rule—chooses to sue. This factor must be weighed carefully in writing a story based on inside observation.

Other drawbacks to inside work include the heavy expenditures of time and money—and the rare but real danger of direct retribution from the target if the reporter's cover is stripped away. In general, it is best to get into and out of an undercover situation as quickly as possible.

Remember, too, that inside work must be supported, corroborated, and fleshed out by other kinds of research. In Cleveland, for instance, Christine J. Jindra and George E. Condon Jr. followed a series of leads to get to the office of a doctor who was selling prescriptions of Quaalude to young people. Their story in the *Plain Dealer* reported:

> "Who referred you here?" [one of two receptionists] asked.
> Condon replied, "Nick," a fictitious name.
> "Nick who?"
> "I don't know," Condon said. [The receptionist] laughed and moved on to the next question.
> "Are you over 21?"
> Condon said, "I'm 21, but I don't have any ID."
> This response momentarily stymied the receptionist who looked to the other girl for advice. Condon said, "Surely, I must look 21?"
> "Well, no you don't," the brown-haired receptionist said with a laugh. But [the first receptionist] went on with her questioning.
> "What's your name?"
> "George Edwards," the reporter said.
> [After Condon gave a fictitious address and paid $15 to obtain a prescription:]
> "Have a good time at the holidays," she said. Then, her smile broadening, she pointed to his prescription, winked, and said, "You will."

The story went on to detail a similar experience for Jindra on another visit, though she was even more evasive than Condon had been, and said she was only twenty years old.

Less thorough reporters and editors might consider these two cases sufficient for the expose but the *Plain Dealer* didn't. The reporters checked seven pharmacies in the general area and found 118 prescriptions written by the same doctor in recent months. They went further; they tried to find the purchasers of the drugs. After checking fifty names, they found that more than thirty were fictitious.[7] Subsequent stories detailed cases of other doctors' abuse and produced strong corrective reaction from the medical profession. The additional research corroborated and made more credible the two experiences of the reporters. Unsupported, the story might have died a quick death.

IMPERSONATION

Exactly why people—newspaper readers—view a legman as different from an impersonator is hard to determine, but they do. The differences seem to be in the public's perception of intent. Readers tend to admire and support the reporter who spends time—days or months—playing the fictitious prisoner or mental patient or cheating salesman or corrupt precinct worker in order to report authoritatively. Yet readers also tend to scorn a reporter who poses as, say, a credit or insurance investigator in order to get information that would not knowingly be given to a reporter. The body politic—the people as a whole—has decided formally (and properly, I think) that it is a crime to impersonate an officer of the law. But is it a crime to receive volunteered information from someone who mistakes you for an officer of the law?

Bill Farr of the *Los Angeles Times* had such an experience while checking on a public administrator. The administrator was believed to be appropriating property from estates that the law charged him to preserve and protect. Farr found that the official had written to a widow in another state saying that because of liabilities against her husband's small estate, his office had been forced to sell her husband's Cadillac in order to meet the bills.

"The truth of the matter," Farr once told a seminar on investigative reporting, "was [the deceased] had made all but one last $167.17 payment. [The administrator] made the last payment and had the car transferred to his [own] wife's name.... The reason we were able to find out was ... [that I went to the financing company] to ask them [how much was owed], thinking they would not tell me, but they mistook me for an investigator from the public administrator's office ... I think it is very bad to misrepresent who you are. I will admit to you, however, that I did not clarify then who I was, after he made the mistake, and he provided the information."[8]

Or consider the situation of Art Petacque of the *Chicago Sun-Times*. Shortly after the mass murder of eight student nurses in 1966, Petacque, led by investigative instinct, took to the streets, looking for people who might have clues or knowledge of the killer. "You have to go out and dig yourself," he says, "You do the same job the police would do. Every morning," Petacque says, "I would get up and play the role of the investigator working for the state attorney's office. I'd get out and knock on the same doors they did.... On one particular day I went to the rooming house where [Richard] Speck [the killer] had stayed. I knocked on the door and a woman answered. I said, 'Has the state attorney's office been here today? She said, 'Yes, sir. There were two men here and they left about twenty minutes ago.' I said, 'That's too bad. I'm making a follow-up investigation.'"

Whereupon Petacque proceeded to ask the woman what she and the other men had talked about. "I didn't say if I was with the attorney's office or the post office or anyplace else," Petacque notes. "I imagine she assumed. I would use that technique right along. Every day, for the first edition, I had one big headline scoop and the other guys were waiting for the state attorney to make some kind of announcement."

Should an investigative reporter use impersonation at all? The reporter has to live with himself, and his paper has to live with the fruits of his deception—and the reaction to it if it is discovered. One variation on Petacque's technique, described by another reporter, is the business card which says

Paul N. Williams
Investigations

488-8310

and nothing else. I am told (I wouldn't know, because I have never used one) that the "investigations" card has a magical effect simply because many people get a thrill out of talking to a private detective. Is a card like this one deceptive?

While you ponder the question, ponder also the reliability of information obtained through such a ruse. If presented to people who believe their information will be held confidential, it will produce at best a mishmash of knowledge, opinion, gossip, and impressions. It would be not only unfair but professionally foolhardy to use information gained by a ploy and to attribute it either to the person who had been duped or to vague sources like "neighbors" or "close associates." The absolute maximum evaluation a reporter should give information under misleading circumstances is "interesting; to be confirmed elsewhere."

Certainly any questioning by ruse should, for both moral and pragmatic reasons, be conducted with one goal: to verify or refute the leads suggested by the unwitting informant. "Is there any record of that?" is an appropriate question to ask after the informant has made an allegation. "Did you observe this yourself; Did anyone else see it? I take my responsibility seriously, and I don't want to make a report to my superiors that would damage this person unless I can probe it conclusively."

I would impose one further control on the business-card approach: have you tried straightforward, open questioning? In adopting a gumshoe mentality, we sometimes forget that the majority of people are as willing to talk to a reporter as they are to a private or governmental detective. Unless they have a direct personal interest that would be hurt by talking about others, most people are excited about being interviewed. So it is only after an experienced reporter has been rebuffed in an open contact that I would consider sending another person in under cover.

SURVEILLANCE

Any reporter on the police beat learns some of the secrets of surveillance. He learns that only rarely does a law exist against watching a person or an activity—as long as he does not eavesdrop on private conversations or break into a home, office, or other private place. He learns about the use of an innocent-looking panel truck to conceal a photographer armed with telephoto lenses. He also learns that police use exotic equipment—like sensitive directional microphones—to pick up conversations hundreds of yards away. And if he hasn't learned all the secrets of surveillance first-hand, there's the nightly television show to fill him in. The tube was never remiss in filming yarns about cops, FBI agents, and spies who tape small mikes to themselves or informers so that details of an impending drug deal or garroting can be relayed.

From observations and from conversations with detectives who have sat for hours on fruitless stakeouts, the reporter learns a good deal about covert surveillance. He learns, for instance, that it is time-consuming and frustrating unless the stakes are high and the information about impending action is solid and precise. He also learns, particularly from the public reaction to post-Watergate disclosures of FBI and CIA activities, that covert surveillance is unpopular, often morally reprehensible, and susceptible to abuse.

The conscientious investigative reporter, therefore, generally avoids surveillance. He never even considers it without also analyzing and weighing the possible consequences. He may decide that there are occasions when surveillance is the only way to get information of crucial importance to his readers. If the occasion does arise—probably only once or twice in most reporters' careers—he elects to do his own surveillance (usually with a partner, a photographer, or both) in order to be sure it is reasonably and discreetly carried out. As always, he discusses it with his editor. And he does everything he can to be sure the surveillance produces solid evidence (like publishable photographs) with minimum risk.

The best kind of surveillance is passive—simply making unobtrusive observations of what many may see but fail to recognize. For example, hundreds of people saw men walk in and out of Sam's Loan Shop in downtown Indianapolis in the five days before Christmas, 1973. So it seems specious to raise moral questions about their comings and goings from a room across the street by reporters and a photographer from the *Indianapolis Star*. They were not only taking photos, they were noting license-plate numbers. They later traced the license numbers to at least twenty-five law-enforcement officers, most of whom had walked into the shop empty-handed and walked out carrying packages. Nearly three months later, after further checking, the *Star* published photos and stories about the traffic. Even so, to make the story meaningful, the *Star* had to rely on un-named "qualified police sources" to say that some of the policemen had received gifts from the pawnshop owned by a man convicted of dealing in stolen goods. And not for another several months were a few of the *Star's* police informants willing to be identified publicly.[9]

During the same year long expose of police corruption, the *Star* used other secretly taken photos. All were pictures of activites that any passerby could have seen. The only questions most editors have about "stealing" photos—taking pictures without the subject's knowledge—or covertly observing their activities concern the invasion of people's privacy and of unduly exposing their own staff to embarrassment.

Reporters observing activities from a distance get only a myopic view that still must be clarified by direct questioning. Surveillance, then, with its ethical problems, is a radical and certainly not a scientific tool—to be used rarely and with caution.

RIGHTS AND ABRIDGEMENTS

I

Congress shall make no law respecting an establishment of religion, or prohibiting the free exercise thereof; or abridging the freedom of speech, or of the press; or of the right of the people peaceably to assemble, and to petition the Government for the redress of grievances.

IV

The right of the people to be secure in their persons, houses, papers and effects, against unreasonable searches and seizures, shall not be violated, and no warrants shall issue, but upon probable cause, supported by oath or affirmation, and particularly describing the places to be searched, and the persons or things to be seized.

IX

The enumeration in the Constitution, of certain rights, shall not be construed to deny or disparage others retained by the people.

These quotations, of course, are from the Bill of Rights. They are the First, Fourth, and Ninth Amendments to the Constitution of the United States, and they should be pasted on the wall above the typewriter of every person who calls himself or herself an investigative journalist.

Before you start thinking about covert work, think about the Constitution. Ask whether your proposed plan will violate "the right of the people to be secure in their persons. ..." As a further control, think about the latter clause of the Fourth Amendment, setting rules for the issuance of warrants. As a matter of principle and practical policy, do not consider taking covert action unless you can make a personal oath or affirmation to your editor describing why you want to take such action and what you expect to find. Prove that you can do the job without violating individual rights described not only in the Fourth Amendment but alluded to in the Ninth.

If your plans for getting a story can pass these tests—and if it is the last alternative in a search for illegally withheld facts of overwhelming public importance—then you can undertake your investigative reporting with a clear purpose. Very few cases, however, can pass these tests. Virtually all of them require you to think in legal technicalities and to rationalize your action according to your perception of the public interest. Taking advantage of legal technicalities does not bother me. The same body of law that allows criminals or corporate executives to escape prosecution because their indictments are not properly drawn or their rights not properly enunciated protects me through its strict and narrow definitions of the elements of criminal acts and intent, and its definitions of and requirements for proof of damages in most civil questions.

Beyond that, conscience—and a strong belief in individual human dignity—are the best controls on irresponsible covert activity.

6
How Do
You Figure That?

COMPUTER POWER

THE MOST ADVANCED mathematical work in newsrooms used to be done with Comptometers on election night. Women, holding pencils crosswise in their right hands, sat punching numbers into the bulky green machines, then writing numbers in columns. Somehow, the results turned out to be reasonably accurate unofficial returns for each precinct in the newspaper's circulation area.

Next afternoon, political writers would study these tables, talk to ward chairmen and state party leaders, then produce impressionistic stories about why the vote went the way it did. Their findings helped to set basic directions of public policy for at least a couple of years. If the blacks in the city, for example, voted for the winning candidate for mayor, it was assumed that the policies he had implied in his speeches and policy statements had become a mandate. Given the deliberate vagueness of most political campaign talk, of course, this assumption might be 180 degrees from the truth. But the mayor wouldn't find that out until he encountered voter reaction later, violent or otherwise.

Today, the computer is in the newsroom, and its presence has been prompted by a change in the attitude of the journalistic hierarchy about the interpretation of numbers. Computers began to influence scientific, industrial, and governmental policy as early as the 1940s. They reached wide acceptance among academics in the 1950s and '60s, and even began to help politicians plan their campaign strategies. Television networks and wire services began to use them for national and regional political analyses in the early 1960s, but only a handful of newspapermen were visionary enough and resourceful enough to obtain the technical training and facilities for local use of computer power. By the mid-1970s, however, publishers in droves began to find it profitable to install integrated computer systems for bookkeeping, billing, classified advertising, purchasing, circulation control, typesetting, page layout, and numerous other non-editorial functions.

This computer revolution has now spread into the newsroom as reporters begin to find the computer an exciting tool that can assist them in their work. In addition to its well-known ability to tabulate surveys, it has been tested for such tasks as sorting and patterning webs of influence, tracing complex transactions, and merging information obtained from diverse sources. Because the potential of the newsroom computer has yet to be exploited, because once-revolutionary concepts are being outmoded almost daily, and because sophisticated discussion of survey methods and computer applications comprises a sizable body of literature in itself, this chapter can cover only a few cases that represent the broad concepts and general issues concerning the use of computers in journalism. The reporter will have to read more deeply—and keep himself current with new literature—in order to use fully the computer power that has become available to him.

Before the investigative reporter begins to use computers, however, he must provide himself with a good grounding in the general use of numbers. He must know how to analyze public budgets and corporate balance sheets and how to check quantitative measurements made by social scientists, legitimate ones as well as fakers.

The Challenge

The understanding and routine use of mathematics, at least to the level of college algebra, is assumed as part of the investigative reporter's background. He may not have done much more than pass the subject in school, but once he has tried to analyze a bureaucrat's budget presentation or work his way through a pyramid of corporate self-dealings, he finds he must either sharpen his mathematical skills or return to writing light features.

Jay Harris, professor in the Medill School of Journalism, Northwestern University, has phrased the challenge this way: "In many important areas there has been a quiet shift in the foundation of language from verbal to numeric. The language and vocabulary of most institutions, and thus the foundation of their decision-making processes, are more numeric/scientific than verbal/intuitive."[1]

With the advent of the inexpensive pocket calculator, rote skill in arithmetic has become less important than conceptual ability. The reporter is freer than ever before to break down, massage, and rearrange numbers that have been presented as holy writ by others. He now has the tool to check the validity of statistics presented by social scientists, public officials, and corporate executives.

When the investigative reporter is faced with someone else's numerical presentation, his first question must be: do these numbers tell the truth? He must go on to ask other questions: What is the bias of the person or institution presenting the figures? Do their statistical claims have any relevance to my readers? If a corporation changes its accounting method this fiscal year, why should I accept its comparisons of profit and loss or value per share with last fiscal year? When a professional sports promoter pitches the city to build a new stadium, do his projections of income and expense tell my reader the true share of the full cost that the promoter will pay in rent?

The reporter who thinks of questions like these has built his own base of knowledge of accounting principles. He is able to sit down with his pocket calculator and develop his own pro forma statement from the reader's viewpoint. He now has the basis not only for checking records but for conducting key interviews with those who use numbers to persuade.

BUDGETS AND REPORTS

Frederick O'Reilly Hayes, budget director of New York City in the late 1960's, has offered some insights into budget analysis in an article for *Columbia Journalism Review*. People who issue public budgets, he points out, usually talk about "compared to last year." According to Hayes: "This approach has obvious limitations. Usually the increases . . . account for only 5 to 10 per cent of the total budget, and reductions are even smaller. . . . [If we] only look at these pluses and minuses, we are accepting on faith the other, larger part of the budget: for example, our attention might be directed to a police chief's request for ten additional detectives and a proposed 5 per cent pay increase—but not to the uses of the 900 officers already on duty. Like an iceberg, the largest part of the budget escapes our gaze."

Hayes cites the example of the Department of Sanitation's marching band, which survived Mayor John Lindsay's first budget-cut efforts. This band of sanitation employees played on even after the police and fire department marching bands had been converted to voluntary, off-duty groups simply because the City Council restored its funds. As Hayes describes it: "The [sanitation] band had strong supporters and was a small item in an annual budget of $5 billion to $6 billion. [So] we in the budget bureau decided to discuss the band in terms of cost per performance in the next year's budget. The cost, as I remember, was computed at $2,900 per performance, which was a meaningful figure to councilmen; it clearly indicated to many of them that the band was a luxury. . . . It was eliminated."

Hayes emphasizes the importance of thinking creatively about measurement and comparison of unit costs. The person who presents and advocates a budget (or any other set of figures) is naturally going to do so in the way most favorable to his own cause. The reporter must look for ways in which to test the budget presenter's premises.

"The 'divide and compare' strategy takes time, effort and information," Hayes points out. "But it need not be done comprehensively; a reviewer can pick his spots, concentrating on areas of greatest importance. . . . It need not be done all at once, since the executive budget is usually before the city council or state legislature for one to three months."[2]

Governmental budgets, Harris adds, "reflect priorities, trends or responses to extragovernmental pressures."[3] The investigative reporter who is trying to measure the influence of a given lobby can sometimes use the statistical approach to advantage. He may find clues for its influence by tracing the amounts spent by government over several years to serve the lobby's interests.

Threads leading to the forces behind both corporate and governmental budget decisions may hide in several places: the offices and advisers through which the document traveled on its way to the chief executive, the style— frantic or reasoned—of the public presentation, and the reactions to portions of the budget. Reporters themselves can find help in understanding budgets from their newspaper's accountants and tax attorneys and, by translating the budget into human terms, can present important insights to their readers.

Analyses and Calculators

The reporter will face many other types of number analyses. In 1974-75, when Jim Risser of the *Des Moines Register* started examining the export of grain in the New Orleans port area, for example, he found indications that official reports filed with the federal government by grain-elevator companies were false. To check this theory, Risser sat down with a desk calculator and went through three years of monthly reports filed by one company. The reports dealt in several different kinds of shipments: barge loads, boxcar loads, hopper-car loads. He had to find out what factors to apply these different loads in order to arrive at a common denominator: bushels of grain.

Risser then calculated the number of bushels shipped in and out of the elevators over a period of three years in order to be certain the figures were meaningful. To have done it for a shorter period would not have accounted for such factors as month-to-month carry-overs and seasonal variations in activity. He did the calculations by fiscal years (July through June) and then checked himself by calculating calendar years. When he got through, he had proof that more than 18 million bushels of grain had been embezzled. The operators, with the collusion of government inspectors, had been short-weighing outgoing shipments destined for foreign countries, then selling the grain to others.

To solve another kind of number-analysis problem, Bill Farr had to give himself a quick course in bookkeeping. He was checking the possibility of racketeering in the office of a public administrator (an official who man-ages the estates of persons who die intestate in California).

"I spent three weeks in a public administrator's office looking at files and found nothing illegal, literally because of my lack of ability to under-stand double-entry bookkeeping," he explains. "I went to a college and bought an accounting textbook and spent all night reading it, and then all of a sudden I understood."

The incident re-emphasizes the importance of "compare and contrast" in checking records. The public administrator had been divorced. A check of his court file showed he had an interest in a corporation that built dune buggies. When Farr cracked the so-called double-entry bookkeeping system, he found that Volkswagens belonging to estates processed by the adminis-trator kept disappearing. As any southern Californian knows, a dune buggy begins with a VW chassis. "We were able to show that [the corporation] was where the VWs went," Farr says. "They were literally running a used-car lot out of the public administrator's office."[4]

In more complicated situations, the reporter should seek the help of experts. It is often available in the newspaper's business office where there are specialists in accounting, tax laws, and rules of government agencies. When Jeff Morgan and Gene Ayres of the *Oakland Tribune* suspected that President Nixon was avoiding income taxes, they got the *Tribune*'s ac-counting firm to develop a set of pro forma tax returns for Nixon. These returns were based on figures the White House press office had released in conjunction with the President's land dealings in Florida and California. The statements confirmed Morgan's original hunch—the one referred to in Chapter 1—and became the peg for a series that was widely copied in other papers.[5]

HYPOTHESES AND PROCESSES

What we have discussed so far, however, is only the application of creativity, imagination, and everyday arithmetic to visible questions. More elegant problem definitions and more exotic deductions are available with proper hypotheses processed through more sophisticated machinery. These definitions and deductions involve:

- Merging data from diverse sources
- Analyzing larger masses of data than have heretofore been available
- Sorting by verbal factors rather than numerical in order to build patterns
- Defining "social reality"

Many investigative problems require sorting, grouping, and patterning bits of information. If there are more than a few possible combinations to study, the analytical work quickly becomes mind-boggling. If, for example, you are trying to trace the flow of a payment between two of thirty-five state senators, the single-dimensional arrangements of those senators involve more than 1,100 possibilities. If the payment could have flowed through other hands—in other words, if the facts may be interrelated from any of several angles—the challenge becomes too much for most minds. Writing down the possibilities or evaluating them mentally takes too much time. The story idea fails at the feasibility stage. The card-sort machine, the computer, or both are tools that bring it back within the realm of feasibility.

Finding Patterns

The other single most important reason for using these mechanical aids is to build your story on a broad base, a pattern of impropriety, rather than on a single case that may be no more than an aberration in the conduct of a single person in a system or institution. Every reporter, for example, is continually exposed to tips and rumors that a judge has taken a fix in a given case. Any reporter who has tried to substantiate these tips has found that he needs doubly corroborated, crisply photographed, and tape-recorded evidence in order to even begin to get his readers' attention. The legal system (rightly, I believe) allows great latitude for judges to make the critical choices regarding sentences versus probation, the degree of intent, and the likelihood of recidivism in deciding the fate of a defendant. In my experience, the majority of citizens tend to side with a judge who invokes his legal rights in defense against a reporter's claim that he did wrongly in a single case.

But if analysis of 100 cases handled by the judge shows wide divergence from the norms or the spirit of the law, the reporter is on much stronger ground. His readers will be in a better position to understand the issues and make their feelings known.

COUNTING, SORTING, AND CROSS-TABULATION

To study a case such as a hypothetical one involving, say, an investigation of Judge Grimm, the countersorter works fast enough, and is much less expensive than a computer. You feed it a thousand cards on criminal cases and ask it how many were heard by Judge Grimm. In a minute, its digital meters tell you. To find out how many of those criminals Judge Grimm put on probation, you run the sorted cards through the machine again. How many of Judge Grimm's probationers committed crimes later? The machine will tell you quickly.

In each of these steps, you are measuring the frequency of one variable at a time. Each time you get an answer, you write it down. After you've gotten several pages of answers and several stacks of cards, you need to stop and decide what it all means. You may have to do some algebra on your calculator to check the probability of such combinations being the result of pure chance, or to compare Judge Grimm's record with that of other judges or with national averages. If you decide to make similar checks on six other judges, you soon run out of time, patience, and the mental capacity to handle all of the data. That's when you may need a computer.

The ability of the computer to cross-tabulate several variables represents a major expansion of the reporter's intellectual power. In their analysis of criminal justice in Philadelphia, Barlett and Steele compiled some 100,000 bits of information on 1,034 persons accused of crimes. They then cross-tabulated the information in numerous ways through a computer program set up by Knight correspondent Philip Meyer. They came up with checks on the variations in the handling of cases by white and black judges, Republican and Democratic judges, white judges in cases where the accused was black and black judges in cases where the accused was white. They found variations between the conviction policies of judges who had been public prosecutors and those who had not, in the sentencing practices of different judges, and in the follow-through activity—or lack of it—by the prosecutors. In more than a score of other interesting ways, they were able to measure performance against claims—in short, to tell how things really worked in Philadelphia's Criminal Courts.

The resulting series, which ran in 1973, was titled "Crime and Justice," and it has been widely cited as a model for reporters interested in factual method. One of the less-noted benefits of the project from the reporters' viewpoint was that its statistical solidity enabled them to write their story clearly and dramatically without having to use excessive qualification and attribution.[6]

On a similar scale, the Paddock Newspapers, a combination of dailies and weeklies in the northwest suburbs of Chicago, executed a study of drunken-driving cases in their circulation areas. Al Messerschmidt, Toni Ginnetti, and other reporters on occasional assignments worked for nearly fifteen months to gather data on some 1,500 cases in which motorists had been charged with driving while intoxicated (DWI). Messerschmidt and Ginnetti worked with Dayton Nash, data-processing manager for Paddock, to modify a computer program (originally developed for circulation purposes) in order to analyze their data. They eventually came up with a series of five stories showing among other things that:

- More than two-thirds of the defendants escaped conviction for DWI.
- The escape rate varied from 82 per cent for the most lenient judge to about 50 per cent for the "toughest."
- Jail sentences or significant fines were levied on only 6 per cent of those convicted.
- Drivers who refused to take breath-analysis tests managed to keep their licenses in nearly one-third of the cases, in apparent contravention of the state's "implied consent" law.[7]

Pitfalls

After it was over, Messerschmidt and editors James Vesely and Robert Casey, who had supervised the project, explained some of the things they had learned. They are worth thinking about because they are typical of so many beginning efforts in the use of computer technology.

First, learn the records-keeping system you are working with. "We were thumbing through thousands of pages of documents," Messerschmidt says, "before we learned that if we had gone to the clerk [of court] and simply given him the traffic-ticket number, we would have found all the information we needed."

Second, observe your target scene thoroughly to learn what you need to measure. "We were taking statistical information [without] knowing what was happening in the courtroom," Messerschmidt explains. "If we had observed some of the basic procedures in court, we might have had a better idea about how one thing related to another, about how we were going to code some information for the computer and whether it was necessary to code it at all."

Third, test your analysis format. Barlett and Steele routinely develop a form for each project and then field test it on a few cases. Invariably, they make modifications on it before putting it to massive use. Look at how the information you gather will be presented in the computer printout, says Messerschmidt. "We should have had the column showing final court date next to the column showing initial date. We didn't have the town of residence column next to the town where the arrest took place. When you are trying to compare how many homebodies are arrested, you need this display."

Fourth, know your computer's capabilities. Messerschmidt and Ginnetti wanted to determine the average length of time between arrest and final disposition of each DWI case. But only after they recorded the starting and ending dates by month, day, and year did they learn that the computer couldn't make accurate calculations from data in that form. Processing manager Nash had to work and rework his program several times in order to adapt it to the reporters' data. The whole effort, in short, "was a three-month project that took fifteen months to do," Messerschmidt says.

Casey refuses to be dismayed by the experience. "It was the first time, and yes, we had some problems," he says. "But we'd never been able to correlate material like this before." Adds Vesely: "The traditional ways we have of accumulating information don't necessarily apply to the computer. You really need to enter into a partnership with those [data-processing] people."

Computers can also sort things by key words. The possibilities this offers for revolution in the traditional newspaper morgue are being further explored every day. The *New York Times* and many other newspapers' current libraries, indexed and cross-referenced, are available in the computers of a few large public and university libraries, and other newspapers are computerizing their own morgues. The same capability that permits a library to scan several million volumes for the words "investigative," "reporting," "power," "crime," and so forth (as the Ohio State University libraries did for me while I worked on this book) can be applied to scanning records for the names of key operatives (accountants and lawyers, for example) in a series of complex land-use maneuvers. Or the computer can pierce webs of corporate security by connecting common factors in several hundred transactions.

Many large law firms and law schools now use computer systems for studying legal problems. One, known as the Lexid System, not only can call up cases by key words (such as "gag order") but also can give an attorney the legal history of all cases heard by a given federal judge. It can present this information simply as one-paragraph listings of the plaintiffs, defendants, case numbers, dates, and lawbooks containing further details, or it can seek out all the cases the judge heard on a particular point of law and provide his opinions and reasoning about it. The implications of this system for journalistic research are obvious.

PATTERNS

Properly instructed and fed, a computer may warn its user of new trends in the consumption of goods, in political attitudes, or in the expenditure of public money. Stephen Isaacs of the *Washington Post* utilized this capability in 1975 when he studied the spending patterns of committees of the United States Senate.

"From looking at the report of the Secretary of the Senate for a week or so," Isaacs explains, "I realized there was no way, short of spending a year, to unravel what the figures held. By listing expenditures chrono-logically . . . the Senate effectively obfuscated the pattern. I ended up coding [on punch cards] every bloody figure in the book myself."[8]

Before making that decision, however, Isaacs checked one committee's expenditures by hand arithmetic. When he found a pattern of abuse, he felt justified in using expensive computer time to finish the analysis. Three months later, he had material for a seven-part series that added up to about five full newspaper pages of information that included these highlights (quoted material is Isaacs'):

- Many of the Senate committees and subcommittees were "being routinely and sometimes illegally diverted" from their stated pur-poses. A number were "being used to help re-elect their members," and a few were "being used to try to further members' ambitions for higher office."

- Of 190 days of committee hearings held outside Washington, "85.3 per cent, or 163 days, were held in home states" of members of com-mittees sponsoring the hearings. And all of this favorable home-state exposure and publicity went to just 40 of the 100 senators.

- One senator, Democrat Henry M. (Scoop) Jackson of Washington, controlled staff budgets "totaling $1,901,970 a year, a sum that is probably unprecedented in the U.S. Senate. . . ." Of the 80 persons on the staffs of the two committees he chaired, Jackson controlled the appointments of 63. Appointment of the other 17 was parceled out to 11 other members of Jackson's committees, while 12 members had no say. This meant that, with the additional help of his personal staff (budgeted at $388,416 a year), Jackson was able to produce volumes of material that advanced his image as a presidential can-didate.

- Two subcommittees headed by Massachusetts Democrat Edward M. Kennedy were authorized to spend $590,900 in 1974. One of the sub-committees held one day of hearings on the three bills referred to it during the 93rd Congress. The other committee had no bills referred to it, and held two days of hearings. Of the 33 staff members assigned to the subcommittees, only 13 actually worked in their offices. The others worked for Kennedy or other senators.

- "Sixty-three members of the U.S. Senate have not converted a single committee employee into a personal staffer. . . . Fifty-seven members . . . have co-sponsored a resolution that would authorize committee staff for all those who do not now have it."

One major benefit to Isaacs in using the computer was the discovery of unexpected patterns. He had expected, for example, to find that Senator Jackson would control large numbers of committee staffers. But he was surprised to find that Washington's other senator, Warren Magnuson, also had considerable influence: 56 per cent of all the travel money spent by his Commerce Committee, for example, involved his home state. Magnuson also had "put a number of his old associates on the committee, at salaries ranging up to $35,910 a year."[9]

Isaacs' project demonstrates three of the computer's advantages:

- By unraveling, sorting, and then rearranging data according to several variables, it performed a task that would have been literally impossible to do by hand.
- By relieving him of much tedium, it gave him time to conduct extensive interviews with scores of senators, committee staff members, and outsiders.
- By building on a broad base of factual data, it obviated much of the criticism a reporter can expect if he relies solely on hunch, tip, and judgment to select "typical" examples.

A Fitting Form

An earlier, pioneering example of computerized investigation was done by Jay Harris and Ralph Moyed at the *Wilmington Evening Journal.* Leslie E. Cansler, Jr., managing editor, has told how, in the spring of 1971, executive editor John G. Craig, Jr., decided "to throw the spotlight of publicity" on the city's heroin trade and "put the weight of the *Evening Journal* into the fight" against it.

Craig marshaled six veteran reporters, challenged them to report the scene in depth, and gave them two months to do it. Two months later, he rejected their stories as "superficial, run of the mill." He sent them back and once again was disappointed. Finally, he pulled off all of the reporters except Harris and paired him with Moyed, an experienced political and investigative reporter.[10] After several days of conferences, a new guideline emerged for putting the story together. Harris designed a set of forms and an information grid for computer use. He and Moyed worked up fifty typed pages of description and instructions for use on special information forms. They acquired data from thirty-seven agencies in the local, state, and federal justice systems plus the Internal Revenue Service. Data was also taken from public directories and from the newspaper's own morgue. Gradually, they got the information punched on data cards and merged into a computer's memory.

On the basis of all this information, the two reporters began building patterns. They traced the routes by which heroin flowed into the Wilmington metropolitan area. They built detailed personal profiles of the leading sellers of heroin. They documented the inability of the criminal-justice system to cope with the traffic. They were able to write with assurance that "jail is a reality for only about 2½ per cent of heroin users in Delaware" and that "narcotic rehabilitation programs are inadequate." They mapped locations and then photographed the specific sites, intersections, and buildings where heroin was marketed regularly. In the last article of their three-part series, they gave names and addresses of more than a dozen active heroin pushers and published a map showing thirteen major centers of heroin trade in the city and its suburbs.[11]

With the publication of the third story a special Heroin Line was opened which received 42 calls in its first 24 hours of operation. Police and drug counseling services were flooded with calls. On June 30, Delaware Governor Russel Peterson ordered a vigorous prosecution of persons listed in the article and asked that police and newspaper personnel sit down and exchange information. The main supplier cut off supplies to heroin users named in the story, and Delaware's Senator J. Caleb Boggs asked Attorney General Richard G. Kleindienst to "take a careful look at the situation in Wilmington" and called for permanent assignment of Bureau of Narcotics and Dangerous Drugs agents to the state.

LEARNING HOW

How can you get and use all of this expanded intellectual power in day-to-day reporting?

The journalism student can take courses in college that make him familiar with sampling, statistics, and the principles of computer programming. He should learn the techniques of simple card-sort and complex cross-tab methods. He should learn how to design, test, administer, and analyze simple questionnaires. If he is serious about applying this knowledge to investigative reporting, he will try analyzing existing programs, then write some of his own programs in order to analyze something new and interesting. For example, he might analyze the university budget, the school's hiring policies, rumors of "old school ties" influencing the election and promotion of faculty members, or the frequency with which the university awards contracts to firms in which its trustees have financial interests.

In his introduction to the *Data-Text Primer,* Hugh F. Cline says: "I would strongly recommend that students have at least one course in statistics, including descriptive statistics, inferential statistics, non-parametric statistics, and correlation. . . . If the students have had an additional course in multi-variate techniques, covering regression, analysis of variance, and factor analysis, they will be able to understand all of the material [necessary to use Data-Text].[12] Data-Text is a fourth-level computer language, one that permits the user to converse with the machine in simple scientific words. It obviates the need to describe a complex series of computations in an arithmetic language.

While beginning to learn these new disciplines, the student reporter should also read standard texts and current periodicals. He must read *Precision Journalism,* Philip Meyer's landmark book, and more recent works such as *Handbook of Reporting Methods* by Maxwell McCombs, Donald Lewis Shaw, and David Grey.[13]

The journeyman reporter who finished college before the 1960s has several options about how to make up lost ground. Reading Meyer (and the books Meyer recommends) will help him converse with social scientists and computer experts. By reading newspaper trade publications, he can watch for short courses and seminars being offered under various auspices. The veteran can also develop contacts with public computer specialists. The nearest large university probably has several types of computers and dozens if not scores of Ph.D.s or doctoral candidates who can earn professional or academic credits by working with a reporter to analyze a new social problem. As long as the collegiate researcher is free to publish his own findings (usually months after the reporter has printed his story), he can be most helpful, providing not only theoretical experience but expensive computer time.

Expert Help

I once had a mildly investigative piece handed to me by Prof. Ralph Todd at the University of Nebraska at Omaha. While we were chatting about another subject, I learned Todd was studying variations in real-estate tax assessments in Omaha. After I told him I saw story possibilities in his project, I had to do little but wait about a month for his computer printouts. He broke down the printouts by sectors that roughly matched the circulation areas of the four core Sun Newspapers. His tables, which we translated into maps, showed that homes in the old (eastern) half of the city were being assessed at much higher percentages of market value than were homes in the newer and more affluent (western) half. In short, the rich were getting richer and the poor were getting poorer. Our reporters spent no more than twenty hours of complementary research on the story, interviewing county officials, real-estate brokers and community-club spokesmen for comments and explanations.[14]

Another use of university computer power was made by the Dubuque, Iowa, *Telegraph-Herald* in 1975. Reporters Jack Brimeyer and John Mc-Cormick worked with experts at the nearby University of Iowa and Prof. Byron Scott of Ohio University, a specialist in studies of physicians, to poll doctors in the Dubuque Health Service Area on some of their personal views (see page 131).[15]

Similarly, though not always so freely, the journeyman reporter may get help from a governmental computer operator whose duties include answering questions for the public. Many offices now use computers tied to video screens to call up records from their files. When Mick Rood of the *Sun* staff undertook a story on ownership of ghetto housing, he learned the simple codes needed to operate this function. If you have ever spent a day trading land ownership—going through two or three indexes, then looking in big hand-written ledgers for information that is not quite alphabetically arranged—you can appreciate the saving that Rood enjoyed by punching a few keys on the video console.

Official Mistakes

Irritants have been known to develop, however, in connection with "official" computerized information. Sometimes an agency puts records on computer tapes or discs—and then wants to charge the user for printouts. Don Muhm faced this problem when he set out to check the operation of a disaster-loan program for Iowa farmers. It was only after the *Register* and *Tribune* agreed to pay the Department of Agriculture nearly $900 that Muhm secured a list of persons who obtained loans and grants for replacement of livestock killed by a severe spring storm.

The list turned out to contain "all kinds of errors and discrepancies," Muhm recalls. "I took the lists over to the state Farmer's Home Administration office. The state director started screaming right away that they were inaccurate. I said, 'Okay, then, I'm writing a story that says we paid $900 for bad information from the government.' He said, 'Well, now, just a minute.' " After the state official agreed to cooperate, Muhm got a story that showed abuse by some farmers of the disaster-relief program.[16]

"Are government computer tapes a public record?" Philip Meyer asked when I mentioned the Muhm case to him. "If so, we should be able to get a copy of the tape and do our own analysis for a lot less than $900. I contend a record is a record whether it is written with ink or polarized iron oxide."[17] I agree with Meyer. Yet I can also foresee a period of frustration and irritation for reporters and others who seek to inspect and copy public records from computer tape at a reasonable cost—as federal and most state laws say they should be able to do.

Neither the public nor reporters should allow the bureaucrats to put them off. George Hahn of the *Cincinnati Enquirer* refused to be sidetracked after he discovered that at least seventy persons had been falsely arrested in eighteen months because of faulty data in the Hamilton County (Ohio) regional computer information center. His discovery indicated that about one in every 514 warrants entered in the data bank was incorrectly recorded.[18]

YOUR OWN COMPUTER

Once his newspaper has installed its own computer system, the investigative reporter begins immediately to take problems to his in-house programmer. He watches and listens as the expert shows how to record information in a form usable to the key-punch operator. Gradually, the reporter learns to think of ways in which to use the computer.

Reporters on the *Minneapolis Tribune,* for example, have learned to gather and analyze large amounts of data for investigative purposes. The *Tribune* got its own computer in 1967—after receiving university computer help in the 1960s to build a 100-precinct model of the state of Minnesota for election analyses. Peter Vanderpoel and the late Frank Premack used the company computer in 1973 to develop information about plea bargaining in Hennepin County courts.[19] They were able to do it quickly enough to have their stories overlap with the running wire copy about the plea bargaining of Vice President Spiro Agnew. At the time, Agnew was bargaining his way out of a possible trial on evidence of illegal political kickbacks in Maryland. The Premack-Vanderpoel series (and others done subsequently by other newspapers) owe much to the methodology pioneered by Barlett, Steele, and Meyer.

New Paths

The paths bordered by computers are open for further exploration by any investigative reporter. To enter them requires, primarily, planning and thoughtful study of the records and procedures surrounding the target. The exploration of campaign financing, for example, is an ideal subject. The *Roanoke Times* tried it after the 1973 gubernatorial election in Virginia. Editors and reporters combed records kept in several locations concerning the financing of the campaigns of Miles E. Godwin, Jr. (the winner) and Henry E. Howell (the loser). More than 13,000 data cards were used to record more than 130,000 bits of information. The data included: the name, address, and city of each contributor; the geographical region within the state from which the contribution was reported; where out-of-state money came from; which of numerous "front" committees received the contributions. They found that more than $300,000 was spent by committees other than the candidates' principal organizations.

Forrest M. Landon, associate editor, and C. Vaughn Porter, computer-services chief, designed the program, which produced data to support twenty stories, four tables, a map, and an editorial. The data showed that Howell got much of his money from unions, and that 55 per cent of the labor money came from outside the state. They also showed that Godwin got major support from business interests, much of it given by individuals as the *Times* suggested, "to dim the spotlight of public attention forced on them through the state's contribution-disclosure law."[20]

The development of a file for a single project invites further refinement. As *Louisville Courier-Journal* reporter Jim Herzog suggests, the paper's computer system might accommodate full public-record profiles of all candidates for office. "We'd like to go into the county where they came from and check all of the records and vital statistics, deeds, lawsuits, and so forth," he says. Developing files of business, political, fraternal, and familiar affiliations could eventually help reporters trace links that might not be apparent to the lone researcher pouring through paper records scattered in dozens of places.

"We are relying on horse-and-buggy techniques that were created back in the 1800s," writer Jack Tobin declares. "The big boys don't do it that way. They have the best accountants, they have the best computer people, the best legal people. . . . You are trying to combat them with a pencil and a piece of paper. What has got to happen in the world of journalism is that we have got to have a data bank."

Drawbacks and Dilemmas

"The big boys"? Our own "data bank"? Speculation like Tobin's brings the reporter, his editor, and publisher hard against a number of ethical considerations. Most of the mass media of the 1960s and '70s has either reported critically on or editorialized actively against governmental networks designed to merge and compare data from computers in governmental units. They have been opposed to the mising of data from the Federal Bureau of Investigation, the Internal Revenue Service, the Bureau of the Census, the Veterans Administration, the Central Intelligence Agency, the Department of Commerce, the Department of Health, Education, and Welfare, among scores of other agencies. One plan for such a network, to be called Fednet, was blocked in part by the reporting of Seth Kantor of the *Detroit News* in 1974. Kantor wrote about a General Services Administration plan to gather personal information on people across America by hooking federal agency computers into a massive network. He quoted concerns about dangers in years ahead when future generations of computers could snoop into individual lives despite federal protections set up to ensure the right to privacy. "On the surface," Kantor wrote, "FEDNET is being set up by the GSA for its own needs and for the Agriculture Department as a leasing client." GSA officials promised that FEDNET would not pry into private lives.[22] The specter of Big Brother looms large in such arguments. What, if anything, is different about the efforts of individual media to build similar, private networks? Would such efforts be less reprehensible, less invasive of individual privacy, in the hands of the privately owned and (presumably) publicly accountable media than in government hands? Answers to questions like these are not within the scope of this book, but that does not mean they should be ignored.

For the present, more pragmatic perils in connection with the computer confront the investigative reporter. One is the danger of computer hypnosis or loss of perspective. Meyer and others point out that because computers can do so much so fast, reporters and editors may become afraid to question their "findings." Jay Harris has written: "The journalist is in danger of holding the computer in awe and adopting the proposition that whatever the computer says is incontrovertible fact. As the journalist works more regularly and closely with computers . . . he is in danger of losing touch with the people and the reality that the people constitute." He may also overrate the importance of "each statistical gyration, each individual finding, each percentage" fed to him by his beloved machine, Harris warns.[23]

Reporters working with computers and seeking simplistic answers may fail to measure, or even to recognize, all the variables that affect whatever it is they are trying to measure. They may fail to consider whether pure chance might have produced the same result. Inexperienced reporters may fail to heed Meyer's constant warning: "Beware of small differences" in statistical tables. They may not be aware that computers can make errors quite independent of their programs, and that such errors are, in Harris's words, "virtually undetectable." Particularly if the error begins early in a chain of computations, the final result may be a picture that is far from reality. As Meyer points out:

> . . . [S]ome statistical programs have been discovered to contain flaws or limitations which produce computational errors . . . [found only] after the programs were in use for several years and learned journals had published papers with substantive findings based on the inaccurate statistical manipulations. Roy W. Wampler of the National Bureau of Standards tried a mathematical problem on twenty different computer programs and got nineteen different answers—some of them not even close to the right answer. The chief flaw was rounding error. Some of the calculations required very long numbers—

longer than the storage capacity of the computer could accommodate—and dropping off the excess digits threw the results badly out of line. The problem had a historical basis: programmers worked from textbook formulas designed for desk calculators. But a man with a desk calculator could see when a rounding error was likely to be a problem and allow for it. The computer did its rounding out of sight and plodded mindlessly ahead, spewing out wrong numbers to unsuspecting users.[24]

SOCIAL REALITY

By far the best-tested application of computer technique to news work is the statistical analysis of sample surveys. Pre-election predictions and post-election analyses have become almost standard fare for larger newspapers. Each year, social scientists and reporters go a little further in thinking of ideas to count and measure, and of the ways in which to interpret the results. As they do, they are helping to define "social reality," a concept of Harris's that is beginning to win acceptance. The reporter who can measure social reality may help in the future to forestall such damaging political mistakes as the massive American intervention in Vietnam—or even an unpopular and costly new freeway route through his own hometown.

The concept of social reality depends on your acceptance of the notion that the mass society is a force with a life of its own, quite independent of its formal institutions. "If a politician changes his position on an issue we learn about it through the media almost immediately," Harris writes. "If the society changes its position we learn about it through the media years after the shift begins—if we learn about it at all."[25]

One reason for this time lag in recognizing social change, Harris suggests, is the resistance of the institutionalized media. Liberal young reporters become worried middle-aged editors, some of whom may become conservative old publishers. Experience and media mythology tell them to be wary of those who proclaim change, particularly if they are not formally constituted in groups of the kind with which ruling institutions like to deal. Failure to recognize changing social reality has caused the political demise of more than one officeholder, and it has caused the disappearance of many once-healthy print media in the latter half of the twentieth century. Extensive research suggests, for example, that Americans changed their position on the war in Vietnam after the 1968 Tet offensive. But it took seven more years, after the death of hundreds of thousands of more Americans and Vietnamese, and incalculable financial and social losses, before the war was finally terminated. The point is that social reality had long since shifted—and neither the media nor the political leaders realized it.

The Politicians

Local politicians are as capable of ignoring social reality as their national congeners. More than a few did not discover until the 1970s that public opinion no longer supported the automatic extension of multilane freeways, at ever-increasing per-mile costs, willy-nilly through established neighborhoods. To determine reaction to, say, midtown freeways or freer ways mid-town, the investigative reporter can begin to develop small-scale measurements of local opinions and attitudes. As part of his base-building process, the findings may help him determine what course to pursue in his major research. Or they may convince him and his editor that social reality accepts certain types of conduct that the reporter and editor regard as scandalous.

Editors and reporters of the Knight Newspapers began defining social reality in 1967. Meyer, fresh from his Nieman year at Harvard, directed a special study for the Detroit Urban League, which was published in the *Detroit Free Press* a few weeks after the July riot. With carefully trained black interviewers, a fifty-six-item questionnaire, and a random-sampling method, the *Free Press* reported findings that contradicted much of conventional wisdom about why people rioted and how black people felt about "the system."[26] The survey was later included in the report of the National Advisory Commission on Civil Disorders (the Kerner report), and won a Pulitzer Prize for the *Free Press.* Sixteen months later, the newspaper did a follow-up study in Detroit,[27] and the *Miami Herald* did a similar one among blacks in its city.[28]

The *Free Press* also gave an impressive demonstration of the uses of computer technology in analyzing social reality when it reported on a special election held in Michigan's Eighth Congressional District on April 1ː, 1974. The seat had become vacant when Gerald R. Ford resigned to accept appointment as vice president, replacing Agnew. The district had been safely Republican for forty years; indeed it had elected Democrats only three times in seventy-four years.

The special election came as the Watergate-cover-up was being exposed, but before Richard Nixon's active role in it had been proved. Nixon himself went to Michigan to campaign for James M. Sparling, Jr., against Democrat J. Bob Traxler. The whole nation, it seemed, was watching, trying to learn the political effects of the Watergate scandal.

But there were many complicating factors in the election. If Sparling won, would it be because the district was such a bedrock Republican stronghold that the vote was meaningless? If Traxler won, would it be because of Watergate, because of rising unemployment, inflation, the energy shortage, or because of some unidentified local issue? Would people be voting on the basis of party loyalty or on the basis of personal sympathy or antipathy toward Richard Nixon?

Meyer and his associates developed a simple self-administered questionnaire which they handed to every tenth voter in selected precincts as he or she left the polls. While the election judges were counting the ballots—which gave Traxler a 51.4 per cent victory—Meyer and his associates were analyzing their questionnaires through a statistical technique called multiple-regression analysis. It can show the varying degrees in which several factors may affect an outcome such as a voter's decision.

Five days after the ballot totals were registered, the *Free Press* reported:

> If the special congressional election . . . had not been so close to income-tax time, the Republican might have won instead of the Democrat.
>
> [The Knight Newspapers] analysis shows that President Nixon's tax troubles had an extra impact on the voters, over and above the displeasure they were already feeling because of the Watergate scandals. . . .
>
> Although the voters were upset over many of the policy issues . . . they did not swing toward one candidate or the other on these . . .
>
> Voter concern about the Watergate scandals . . . accounted for 36 per cent of the variation in the way people judged the president . . . When the tax issue was added to the equation, the two issues together—Watergate and the Nixon tax problems—explained even more of the variation in attitudes toward the president—a total of 43 per cent. This means that the effect of the income tax problem was an add-on to the president's unpopularity. It made people mistrust him who had not already been made distrustful by Watergate.
>
> No other issues produced any of this cumulative effect. . . .[29]

Four months later, a group of journalists at Meyer's seminar at Northwestern University tried another social-reality study. Twenty-three of them, reporters and editors, surveyed 411 randomly selected eligible voters in the same Michigan district. Another election was coming up, and they were curious to see if, after Nixon's resignation, the Republicans might have regained some of their historic strength. After conducting telephone interviews, they analyzed their data and found that Traxler's support had grown. He had picked up sixteen per cent of those who had voted for Sparling in April. Further, they discovered that "the Watergate effect" was by far the strongest factor in Traxler's strength.[30] Their findings were borne out in the November election.

The *Dubuque Telegraph-Herald* survey, mentioned earlier in this chapter, was an effort to measure attitudes of an institution—the medical profession. Reporters Brimeyer and McCormick sought to measure not only specific facts about physicians (age, years in practice, workloads), but also some of their moral and ethical views. They developed a four-page questionnaire and sent it to 169 physicians in the nine-county Dubuque Health Service Area, which also reaches into Illinois and Wisconsin. One hundred thirty-one physicians responded, providing so much information that the university computer spewed out 812 pages of statistical findings about them, their community activities, their views about government and other "outside influences," their workloads and the general state of health care in the service area. The information enabled Brimeyer and McCormick to write, in the first of their seven-part series:

> We need doctors. And we need more of them here. . . .
> Our doctors are short-handed and overworked.
> They're older than average. . . .
> Our doctors are becoming more specialized. . . . They're closing the curtain on the country doctor. . . .
>
> Each of our doctors practices an average of 62 hours a week. That's considerably more . . . than the [national] average 51 hours. . . .
>
> Our doctors each see an average of 198 patients a week. Nationwide, the average [is] 137.
>
> This area has one direct-care doctor for 1,423 people. The nationwide rate is one for about half that many. . . .
>
> The situation is illustrated by the remark of a southwest Wisconsin general practitioner: "We're killing ourselves for our patients."[31]

As an example of investigative reporting, the main value of the Dubuque survey was in demonstrating ways in which to penetrate not calculated and hostile secrecy but inadvertent secrecy that occurs when one segment of the society becomes essentially closed to outsiders.

What corroboration did the researchers have that the average doctor did indeed work 62 hours a week? Only that in a scientifically conducted poll, you build in some checks and bases for calculating the percentage of error response in relation to the total population. Edward Menge, professor of political science at Ohio State University and a member of the staff of the Behavioral Sciences Laboratory where many polls and surveys are conducted, says, however, that "you have to take what you get. If you start second-guessing your results, you get into difficulty."

The Social Scientists

The Dubuque survey also touches on a problem noted by Harris: how can the reporter check the claims of social scientists who say they have discovered new truths about people's attitudes? Harris has suggested a danger that reporters will identify too closely with the social scientists. He urges that the journalist must not be content to look only at the "summary and recommendations" of a survey, but to check the methodology. "The social-science community should not be afforded the luxury of telling the journalist what is important or what is fact," he writes, "nor should the journalist rely on him to so do."[32]

Menge cautions: "When investigative reporters use surveys by social scientists for stories, they should make certain they are using complete results, that they are not quoting items out of context, and that they have questioned the original researcher to be sure facts used in the story relate properly to conclusions shown in the survey."

To check the social scientist, the reporter must analyze data critically. A research background is handy, and a computer is nice, but common sense is the best tool of all. To check sophisticated surveys, their significance and confidence levels and sampling methods, the reporter who is investigating the social reality needs to develop technical skill and an understanding of the social-science vocabulary. Until he acquires that skill, his best bet is to seek out not one but several neutral sources in the social-science community and then apply common sense. If he finds major flaws in a supposedly significant survey, he should consider designing and conducting a survey of his own to check the first one.

The Dangers

Any self-designed survey effort is dangerous. Careless design and an unwittingly biased interview technique can lead to disastrous results. The act of surveying can itself change people and their ideas, resulting in what social scientists know as the Hawthorne Effect (the testees' unconscious efforts to please the testers) and what the physicists call the Heisenberg Principle (when you measure something, your actions or the effects of the testing device change it). Experienced journalists are aware of these principles when they conduct one-on-one interviews. When they propose, therefore, to conduct scores to hundreds of interviews through intermediaries, they should seek expert advice, then be conservative about interpreting what they find. If they take the proper precautions, however, they will likely have better evidence for their generalizations than they would have had through the old-fashioned "highlight" interviews with opinion leaders or with "typical" persons on the street.

A more pernicious danger for investigative reporters, Meyer suggests, is that "you become so entranced with the tools that you spend all your time enhancing and fine-tuning them and never get around to doing any reporting. The problem most likely stems from the fact that computer problems, quite unlike problems in the real world, can always be solved if you work at them long enough. It can make you develop a taste for computer problems to the exclusion of your real purpose."[33]

7

Getting
the Message Across

THERE IS no formula for writing investigative stories. Good writing is not done by formula. There are, unfortunately, a number of formulas for traditional news writing, and many reporters and editors are unduly influenced by them. The purpose of this chapter is to steer you away from formulas and toward individual solutions of writing problems.

The goal again is planning—planning according to a few general principles. Within these principles, the writer should feel free to innovate as long as he sticks to provable facts.

Clarity is one principle. It requires that your theme, your language, your construction of the overall story—as well as your individual sentences and paragraphs—be easily understood. Clarity implies getting to the point quickly in language that is clear to the reader and carrying the story through to a clear conclusion.

Creativity is another principle. It requires giving careful thought to the tone of the writing. Creativity suggests judicious use of comparisons and metaphors which are strong and effective while remaining factually accurate and intellectually honest.

If these principles seem to pay little homage to the traditional inverted pyramid formula for writing news stories, good. Little homage is intended. Most investigative stories are not traditional "news." They are stories of discovery. They involve piecing together unknown or little-known facts in new ways. They are contradictions of official and traditional views.

By their nature, they are also often overladen with facts. Sometimes they expose unfamiliar schemes and machinations whose vocabulary and processes are alien to the reader. When they deal with the shuffling of money from one party to another through subordinated notes, dummy corporations, blind trusts, debentures, stock swaps, or other arcane machinery, the writer should not assume that the reader understands. When the story involves rezonings, tax abatements or deeds of trust, it needs to be translated not only into words but into images that are relevant to the reader.

GETTING READY TO WRITE

Before beginning to outline a major investigative story, the reporter should write out answers on a piece of copy paper to several questions:

- What is this story about? What am I trying to prove?
- Who gives a damn? Where, among the many interests and *personae* (taxpayer, union member, church deacon, business executive, parent) of my reading public is the primary audience for my story?
- Why will my primary audience care? To which of their interests does the story appeal?

Writing down clear answers to these questions will help the reporter find the voice, vocabulary, and pace that are most familiar and effective to the potential reader.

What Is This Story About?

To determine what the story is about should not be too difficult. Still, it requires a clear appraisal of its point and its features. Only then can it be told with clarity.

A story about a provable crime, for example, one that is defined by law and that threatens the interests of readers, is the simplest story to write. It can usually be told in the traditional inverted-pyramid form because its images and implications are readily perceptible. But a story about a possible crime, one in which the elements of proof are missing or strongly contended, is a different matter. If the suspected crime is against property or is "victimless," it will require careful explanation and interpretation for it to be related to the reader's interests.

If the story is not about a legally defined crime but about the manipulation of a system or institution to the advantage of an individual or group, then the writing problem becomes even more complex. The writer must define terms, establish norms, and explain the effects of the abuse or manipulation. To do so, he must adopt the viewpoint of his perceived audience, and he must be confident he knows his audience even if the story is a relatively neutral "how things work" piece.

For example, writing about the payment of gratuities, finder's fees, consulting fees, or commissions to purchasing agents of foreign governments presents a choice of viewpoints. A common business rationale is that such fees are a necessary means to the end of obtaining contracts; as long as the word "bribe" is not spoken, no bribe occurs. But a more common viewpoint among the mass of citizens is that payment of money to a person who does no work except make a decision in favor of the payer is a bribe, regardless of what noun is used to describe it on the company's books. The writer then is writing about a bribe, and in order to prove bribery, he has to prove intent and agreement. He must provide strong evidence and contemporary documents and testimony from neutral sources proving intent and agreement.

If these elements are not clear, the reporter should ask himself: "What am I trying to prove?" He should try to prove "how things work"—what devices and deceptions (including mental self-deception) are used in making such deals? His story is about the real-life operations of an institution, and he is wise not to assert that the evidence proves anything more.

Who Gives a Damn?

The answer to our WGAD question is not always easy. The church deacon side of your reader may be repelled by the notion of police brutality, but his frightened inner-city resident side may want the neighborhood cop to be aggressive. He is prepared, in other words, to allow the policeman some degree of error in roughing up suspicious-looking persons in his particular neighborhood. The local merchant may bestow free meals or free merchandise on the policeman purely in the spirit of friendship and gratitude. At the same time, however, he is appalled when a multinational corporation provides free travel and legally laundered gifts to a presidential candidate.

To have a real feel for who gives a damn, the writer must be in close touch with his community. Not only must he have many personal contacts, but he must be able to analyze carefully its social indicators. These indicators can vary from election and survey results to crime statistics and consumer boycotts.

It is easy enough to conclude that no one gives a damn. But the investigative reporter who has a sense of outrage will often argue that public apathy is a function of public ignorance. If the public only knew the facts in the proper context, it, too, would be indignant, he will reason. His argument may be persuasive—as long as he has facts. But the facts should be new ones, hard ones, capable of being clearly presented in order for them to be clearly interpreted by the reader.

Old facts warmed over and covered with the gravy of the writer's moral indignation are seldom enough. About those the reader will hardly give a damn. Wisdom on the reporter's and editor's part is in knowing the difference between old and new, between substantive information and impassioned opinion, between who cares (and why) and who doesn't.

Why Will the Audience Care?

The individual reader in your audience will most likely care if the story spells out to him a threat to his (or his family's) person, property, pocket-book or pride. The threat may be as direct as the danger of being mugged on the street or as remote as a rise in next year's taxes or fuel bill. If the threat is even more remote in time or is likely to affect only other people, the typical reader may cluck sympathetically but not be stirred to action.

If you are still determined to tell the story, you will have to puncture the pericardium of private security that most of us build around ourselves. You will have to get close to the reader. One of the best ways in which to get close is to translate abstractions like statistical tables or official reports into personal anecdotes.

The traditional objective lead, by its very concept and design, is not personal. It deals in officially accepted symbolism and clichés that let the reader divorce himself from the action. The objective story processes the violence and injustice of life in neutral, impersonal nouns, and gray, weak verbs in a futile attempt to be acceptable family reading. The investigative reporter, writing from a low threshold of indignation, is not trying to be neutral. He is trying to break through to the reader. So once he and his editor have decided the story is worth telling, he wants to choose the strongest presentation the facts will allow.

Designing the Story

Having gone through these mental exercises (which for an experienced writer takes less time to think about than read about), the reporter should pencil out the *central* line or theme of his story. He should then write only that line in his main story. Within the first few paragraphs, he should make clear what the theme is. Then he should develop the theme, and, finally, he should summarize it. This method for getting the message across is simply the exercise of an old rule of lecturing or public speaking: tell them what you're going to tell them; tell them; then tell them what you've told them.

There may be other tangential angles to the story. There may be a need to fill in the reader with background or biographical material. There may be a need to summarize case law or similar definitive material. As much as possible, the writer should resist stopping the flow of the main story to develop these angles. If he cannot handle the tangential material in a phrase or at most a sentence, he should treat it as a separate piece—a sidebar or short box to be placed close to the pertinent portion of the main story when the page is laid out.

I like to think of the ideal main story as a single, straight tree from which a few branches extend. To get the basic story, the reader simply climbs the trunk of the tree. He may grasp one of the branches (sidebars) momentarily as he starts up, or place a foot on another branch to hoist himself to the top. But his main goal is to get to the top of the tree as directly as possible. After savoring the view from the top, he starts to climb down. He may stop and sit on a branch once or twice along the way. And during a stop, he may examine the branch more closely and study its foliage to determine what kind of tree he has climbed and what its more minute details look like. But after the pauses, he should be able to climb down safely and have a very good idea of what the tree and its view meant to him.

CHOOSING THE LEAD

Often the least painful approach is to avoid writing the lead until after you have blocked out the main narrative. But most writers can't do this. They know too many things are decided in the lead: the limits of the subject, the direction of the writing, the tone, the control. Once the lead is clear, the points sketched out—if only mentally—the rest of the story follows naturally and quickly. In the following pages we will discuss several options: the hard lead that summarizes the main points, the anecdote lead that relates personally to the reader, the soft lead that intrigues, the bullets-and-dashes lead that relieves a story over-loaded with facts, and the easiest of all: "this is the story" leads.

The Hard Lead

The hard lead is similar to the traditional spot-news lead. It tries to summarize in a succinct paragraph or two all of the important information, then lead into a series of paragraphs of progressively lesser importance—the standard inverted-pyramid construction.

For most original investigative stories, the hard lead has drawbacks. Often there is too much important information to pack into a single paragraph. Some of the impact of this information is lost when it is strung out in clauses or phrases. Sometimes the information means little to the reader who lacks technical or legal background.

About as often, the meaning of an investigative story cannot be reduced into a reasonable number of words without danger of distortion. If three or four major statements are packed into the lead, and if there are countering or opposing views about the importance of each statement, the explanatory (or "denial") paragraphs become a confusingly long, disjointed series. The reader is getting arguments about facts he hasn't yet been given. And if he is going to become confused and frustrated before he gets to the corroborating details, he will likely quit reading and the investigator's work will have gone for naught.

Think of a hard lead only *if all* of these conditions prevail:

- There is a single major revelation to be made.
- Its nature and context are familiar to the average reader's perceptions.
- The evidence to be detailed later will firmly support the specific charge or revelation.
- The remainder of the story can be developed in inverted-pyramid style without major concern for chronology or for the development and tying up of subplots.

Relatively few investigative stories meet all of these criteria. Yet an unfortunate number of writers try—usually at their editors' insistence—to fit them into the traditional mold. Here is one that did fit the mold rather well:

WASHINGTON—A policy of apparently illegal discrimination has been discovered in the hiring practices of at least 20 congressional offices through documents obtained by the Star-Telegram.

Job orders from the offices of 19 representatives and one senator, given to the congressional placement office, contain such phrases of racial and religious discrimination as "no minorities," "white only," "no blacks," "white or Oriental only," and "no Catholics."

Requests specifically eliminating certain racial categories recently have come from the offices of Sen. William L. Scott, R-Va., and Texas Democratic congressmen Ray Roberts of McKinney and John Young of Corpus Christi.

Others include the offices of Reps. Al Ullman, D-Ore., newly selected chairman of the potentially powerful House Budget Committee, and Harold Froelich, R-Wis.

A senior Justice Department official, when apprised of the practice, called it "the most incredible, grossest example of overt discrimination" he had seen . . . .

When contacted about the discriminatory job forms on file at the placement office, most of the senior assistants who had called in the job orders disavowed any knowledge of the practice.

However, they generally declined to discuss the specifics.

Stephanie Solari, legislative assistant to Rep. Froelich, acknowledged that the office did not want to employ minorities.

"It's not my policy," she said, "And it's not the congressman's policy. It's just because of the feeling of some of the people in the office whom we don't want to lose."

Senior officials on 17 of the 20 congressional staffs acknowledged that they have no minority members, or no blacks, on their staffs . . . .

Nine of the 20 congressmen whose offices apparently now practice racial discrimination voted for the 1972 amendments to the Civil Rights Act, equipping the Equal Employment Opportunities Commission with enforcement powers—the right to prosecute violators in civil suits . . . .

Eugene F. Peters, executive director of the Congressional Operations Committee, says the placement office tries to "greatly discourage" discriminating requests from the congressmen.

"It doesn't happen very often," he said, but added that the office staff generally puts down what the congressmen want.

He admitted that if a certain congressman says "no minorities" on his order form, the office does not send minority applicants to be interviewed.[1]

By FRANCIE BARNARD
Star-Telegram Washington Bureau
© 1974, *Fort Worth Star-Telegram*

Here is a successful hard lead that uses strong but carefully qualified words to describe a complicated large-scale operation:

WASHINGTON, Jan. 14—A secret White House plan to bend the power of virtually every major federal department to the re-election needs of President Richard M. Nixon was drawn up and apparently implemented in the 1972 campaign, confidential documents showed today.

Copies of the confidential documents, obtained by the Post-Dispatch, indicate that the sweeping plan was drawn up in the spring of 1972 and that implementation was under way by June of that year.

One document—an eight-page memo dated March 17, 1972, prepared under the supervision of Frederic V. Malek, who was then on the White House staff—outlines a number of proposals for increasing the political responsiveness of agencies and seeing that certain federal grants were "rechanneled" for political purposes.

It also includes detailed instructions on how to keep the plan secret and how to shield the White House from responsibility if the plan should become known.

A second document, also prepared under Malek's supervision, is dated June 7, 1972, and represents a progress report . . . [It] claims credit for a broad range of activity, including the return of subpoenaed material to a Philadelphia labor union because the business agent of the union was a Republican supporter and in a key position to influence blue-collar votes.

It also claims credit for getting a $2,200,000 grant for migrant workers in Texas switched from one group to another because the latter was considered more favorable to the Nixon Administration . . . .

The memorandum outlines general actions by the White House to build "a political network in each department."

It said that Malek had met with all Cabinet members except William Rogers, who was then Secretary of State, to outline the program . . . . He had met with heads of key agencies including Action, the Environmental Protection Agency, the Office of Economic Opportunity, the Small Business Administration, the General Services Administration and the Veterans Administration.

At the meetings, the memorandum said, Malek emphasized the need "to make re-election support the top priority" and the need "to respond to requests in this regard . . . ."[2]

By ROBERT ADAMS
A Washington Correspondent
of the *Post-Dispatch*
© 1974, *St. Louis Post-Dispatch*

The Anecdote Lead

The anecdote is a device for puncturing the reader's security bubble. It describes the unhappy experience of a person much like himself, and it quickly makes him aware of a personal threat. In short, its intention is to make him care—immediately.

Chicago Tribune Task Force writers used the technique effectively in describing police brutality. Following the principle of simplicity, they wrote anecdotal leads on each of a series of stories over several days. By the end of a week, they had touched the interests of every age group, sex, race, and economic level. Here are six examples of the anecdotal lead used by the *Tribune*'s task force:

> JOSHIE JOHNSON was sitting on the fender of his car and squinting thru the autumn dusk at a parking ticket when a fist in a black leather glove smashed his nose.

Two policemen with drawn guns watched Patrolman Antonio Francis pound Johnson's face with his black gloved fist until Johnson fell unconscious in a Chicago alley.

When Johnson regained consciousness, he had a fractured jaw, a broken nose, two black eyes, and cuts on his face.

Instead of just a parking ticket, Johnson now faced charges of assaulting a policeman, resisting arrest, and disorderly conduct. The date was Oct. 20, 1971.

JOHNSON, 32, never arrested before in his life, would spend two years clearing his name in court and proving to the Chicago Police Department that he was the victim of a policeman's brutal, calculated attack.

He would lose several days from his auto plant assembly job while his injuries healed. He would lose more days making futile court appearances. Finally, he would get the charges dropped by signing away his right to sue Patrolman Francis in a curious and illegal courtroom bartering system . . . .

In the end . . . he lost nearly 40 days from his job, and his victory was a bitter one.

After months of investigation, the Police Department supported his complaint. It punished Patrolman Francis by suspending him for only two days . . . .

A PART of 14-year-old Claude Bailey's life was destroyed with his first run-in with the police. A promising athlete who had been named most valuable player on his grammer school team, Claude dreamed of playing football some day for Lane Technical High School.

Since a policeman's blow blinded his left eye last May 18, that dream has been laid aside.

This was the first trouble Claude, of 2302 W. Roscoe St., had ever had with the police. In fact, on the night he was injured, Claude hadn't been in trouble. He was mistaken for a suspect for a crime he hadn't committed and for which he was never charged. . . .

POLICE BRUTALITY is supposed to be foreign to a place like Gerald Bauman's Rogers Park neighborhood, especially on a sunshiney Father's Day morning.

Quiet, matronly Harriet Bauman, 36, is not the sort of person one visualizes as a potential victim of police brutality.

And she's usually too busy keeping her $60,000 colonial home and her two children well scrubbed to have much time left over for assaulting policemen.

But last June 17, she was charged with resisting arrest and assaulting Sgt. Edward Flynn of the Foster Avenue Station.

That was after Sgt. Flynn had pulled her out of her house, despite the fact she was wearing only her nightgown and housecoat.

And it was after Sgt. Flynn had chased her across the street and into a neighbor's house.

After, too, he had thrown her across a railing of a neighbor's porch to handcuff her, which he did just before throwing her down a flight of stairs, and addressing her with obscenities in front of her children and neighbors.

Mrs. Bauman's story sounds wholly unbelievable, but witnesses and a polygraph test arranged by The Tribune support it. . . .

JOSE MALDONADO'S problem started last Dec. 18 when his baby was hungry and his wife discovered there was no milk in the house.

It was 8 p.m. and snowing outside, and Maldonado, 23, had already settled into a chair and had four beers.

He was living at 1706 N. Humboldt Blvd., and his wife told him to get in the car and go to the store at North and California Avenues for the milk.

Before he got home the next morning, Maldonado had been pistol-whipped by police in front of his house, kicked in the groin in a hospital, and had his head sewn together in three places.

He also had been charged with assaulting and attempting to elude two policemen and with drunk driving, for which he was eventually convicted and is now serving two years' probation.

At best, Maldonado claims, he is guilty of one thing—double parking. He has witnesses and a police polygraph test to back up his story. . . .

SEVERAL PERSONS witnessed Solomon Marcus being beaten by Patrolmen Joseph Laskero and Timothy McWeeney after they stopped him for speeding on April 6, 1972.

With the witnesses, Marcus was able to beat the charges of battery against policemen when he went to court, but the evidence was of no help when he filed a complaint with the Police Department's Internal Affairs Division against the two policemen.

The IAD wouldn't give Marcus a polygraph test and dismissed his complaint as unfounded. The Tribune arranged a polygraph test, and the results supported his complaint . . . .

AL KASPER, 51, service station operator at 2641 W. 71st St., has seen how the Police Department reacts to complaints of misconduct from both sides of the issue.

He was a Chicago policeman for 10 years and was discharged wrongfully, he says, after he had a run-in with a police investigator.

Last April 12, he went to the department's internal affairs division as an ordinary citizen after he was injured in an incident at his service station. A heart patient who uses a cane because he is hobbled by an old knee injury, Kasper was arrested during a squabble with a customer . . . .

CARL KRAEMER wanted only an apology. Ardale Calvin wanted only $20 to replace a tooth. Charles Dominick wanted a notation on a policeman's record. James Bryant wanted a policeman transferred and disciplined.

All four people were victims of police abuse, they said, and each of them went to the Police Department's Internal Affairs Division sincerely believing they would get some sort of satisfaction.

All they got was more anguish and more trouble, and their anger over a single policeman mushroomed into a distrust and fear of the entire department.

It was this sort of growing public distrust of the department's handling of police brutality complaints that prompted The Tribune to launch a five-month investigation into police abuse.

Reporters talked to hundreds of alleged victims, interviewed hundreds of persons who claimed they had witnessed such incidents, examined thousands of documents, and arranged polygraph tests wherever possible.

The newspaper found that the Internal Affairs Division of the department, responsible for investigating such abuses, continues to be seriously negligent in its duties despite years of criticism . . . .[3]

Jim Steele and Don Barlett faced a writing problem when they completed their massive computer analysis of criminal justice in Philadelphia (see Chapter 6). They had literally hundreds of thousands of facts that they could have presented in statistical and tabular forms—and which would have left readers cold and unmoved. They solved the problem by choosing anecdotal leads to many of their factual pieces. Here is one example:

Angus Williams, a 57-year-old laborer, was arrested in November 1971 and charged with the street robbery of a retired North Philadelphia machinist. For five months he sat in jail awaiting trial, unable to post the $3,000 bail.

In the end, he was acquitted of the charges. And as it now turns out, Angus Williams—who never went to school, who cannot read or write, who had never been arrested before—was indeed innocent. Another man committed the robbery.

That is one man's story.

This is another.

Ernest Jones, a 71-year-old church janitor, was assaulted on the steps of his North Philadelphia rowhouse in July 1971. Two men, James Gay and Jerry Lee Giles, ripped the pockets of Jones' clothing and removed his wallet containing $75.

Gay, 22, an admitted heroin user with a record of seven prior arrests in two states, pleaded guilty to the robbery and was placed on probation. Giles, 19, with a record of at least three prior arrests, was found guilty of the robbery and sentenced to five to 23 months in jail . . . .

Such is the state of the Philadelphia criminal justice system: all too often, the innocent go to jail, the guilty go free or receive light sentences. It is a system that really is no system at all and it has very little to do with justice.

It is a system where some judges work three-day weeks, while innocent men like Angus Williams sit in jail for months awaiting trials . . . .

It is a system where the district attorney cries out in public for stiff penalties while his assistants quietly negotiate pleas and recommend short sentences or probation.

It is a system where hundreds of criminal cases are lost in a court bureaucracy that is staffed by unqualified patronage workers, relatives and friends of court officials . . . .

By DONALD L. BARLETT AND JAMES B. STEELE
© 1973 *The Philadelphia Inquirer*

To illustrate a different problem, Barlett and Steele wrote:

> Within a six month period, two convicted street robbers stood before two different Philadelphia judges awaiting sentence . . . .
>
> One was Alfred E. Smith, 24, a black man from North Philadelphia. The other was William H. Douglas, 19, a white man from Frankford.
>
> . . . Both had prior arrest records. Both had served time in prison. Both were heroin users. Both had been convicted of robbing older victims on the street.
>
> One might assume, therefore, their sentences were similar.
>
> *NOT SO. SMITH* was sentenced to three to 10 years in prison. Douglas was placed on probation. Why the difference? . . .[4]

The Soft Lead

The soft lead purposely avoids conveying startling information. It may seem to be almost a throwaway paragraph. It isn't. The good soft lead is a carefully designed series of sentences intended to:

- Intrigue the potential reader, hinting at revelations to come.
- Guide him into an orderly sequential understanding of the story's elements.
- Provide him (usually) with one or two details of pertinent background.

The writer's challenge is to beguile the reader without confusing him, and to inform him without boring him. The best soft lead normally runs no more than two or three paragraphs. It gives the reader a few dozen words summarizing what is to come and then moves briskly ahead from background to hard fact. The major revelation may be several paragraphs down in the story—but when the reader reaches it, he understands it.

Here are two soft leads from the *Wall Street Journal:*

> Conrad J. Balentine has helped Franklin Electric Co. grow and prosper since he became its president in 1967. So last year, to show their appreciation and discourage offers to woo him away, directors of the Bluffton, Ind., maker of electric motors voted to give the executive, now 59 years old, a 10-year "advisory-employment term" beginning when he decides to retire. That contract, plus his company pension, should provide him with a retirement income of around $100,000 a year, about what he now earns.
>
> "The agreement says I'm supposed to give the company my advice is they ask me and if I'm around," Mr. Balentine explains. "I won't be expected to knock myself out. Like if I'm relaxing at the Jersey Shore, I won't have to scramble back to Indiana to answer a question."

"Actually," he continues, "I think having former executives around to give advice is a lousy idea. If you're not in a business day to day, what can you tell people who are?"

What's unusual about Mr. Balentine isn't his lucrative consulting agreement but his candor about it. The practice of signing on top executives as highly paid consultants after they leave a company is widespread in American business. Just as widespread is the view that such arrangements often aren't what they profess to be and rarely work out well when they are. . . .[5]

By FREDERICK C. KLEIN AND DAVID M. ELSNER
Staff Reporters of *The Wall Street Journal*

SEATTLE—Boeing Co., beginning in the early 1960s, sold a large fleet of jetliners to Pakistan International Airlines. Boeing's salesmen were helped by a local representative under contract to the Seattle company, a Pakistani named Aziz Jamall.

Mr. Jamall's role, according to George Sanborn, a former Boeing sales executive who is currently an American Airlines vice president, was simple: "You've got to have someone on the scene who can assess the attitude of the government (which controls the airline) and the airline," he says. "It saves a hell of a lot of sales trips."

But Mr. Jamall possibly had one other motivation. His older brother, Enver, was a top executive of Pakistan Airlines with important responsibilities for aircraft-purchase decisions. Enver Jamall is currently managing director of the airline, a post that makes him chief operating officer.

Whether substantial payments to Aziz Jamall influenced Pakistan Airlines' decision to buy seven 707 and four 720B jets isn't certain. But at least one former financial officer of Boeing who dealt with Aziz Jamall and who requests anonymity says he assumed the two brothers were partners sharing the commissions. He adds that he decided to tell his story to The Wall Street Journal because "the industry practice was to pay off" in many foreign areas, and he considers it unfair that Lockheed Aircraft Corp. "was taking the fall" for the entire aircraft industry. He believes neither Lockheed nor Boeing was morally at fault because "payoffs are a necessity to compete abroad" . . .

The Pakistan case is important because it is the first detailed example of the kind of problems Boeing, the world's leading commercial jet manufacturer, may have with government investigators. Boeing declines to discuss Pakistan but it has said it hasn't paid any airline official or any government official who could influence purchasing. Further, it hasn't done anything to "condone corruption of governments or customers," Chairman T.A. Wilson said at the annual meeting.

Boeing has disclosed it paid nearly $70 million in commissions to overseas representatives since 1970 on commercial jet sales. The company is among more than 100 major corporations being investigated by the Securities and Exchange Commission, the Internal Revenue Service and the Senate in the burgeoning scandal over foreign bribery. . . .[6]

By HERBERT G. LAWSON AND A. RICHARD IMMEL
Staff Reporters of *The Wall Street Journal*

Bullets and Dashes

To solve the problem of the overloaded lead, one of the best devices is the "bullet" or "dash" construction. This type of lead uses a series of sentence fragments to emphasize quickly several points of about equal importance.

Maxine Cheshire faced the overloaded-lead problem in writing for the *Washington Post* about the uncataloged gifts accepted by the Richard Nixon family from foreign rulers despite constitutional and statutory bans. See how she handled it:

> TUESDAY—On March 28, First Lady Pat Nixon, on the advice of White House counsel J. Fred Buzhardt, removed a stack of velvet jewel boxes from the wallsafe of her bedroom and dispatched them by messenger to the Gifts Unit in the Executive Office Building.
>
> The boxes contained valuable gems given to her and her daughters over the past five years by King Faisal of oil-rich Saudi Arabia and two of his half-brothers.
>
> The gifts, never acknowledged by the White House until the Washington Post was able to verify their existence from other sources in early March, include:
>
> • A $52,400 matched set of emeralds and diamonds (necklace, bracelet, earrings, ring and brooches) presented to President Nixon as a gift to his wife by Prince Fahd during a visit to the Oval Office on Oct. 14, 1969.
>
> • A shoulder-length pair of earrings set with marquise diamonds and cabachon rubies presented to Mrs. Nixon by King Faisal on May 28, 1971, during a state visit.
>
> • A diamond bracelet, containing a watch concealed in the clasp, given to Mrs. Nixon by Prince Sultan in July, 1972, along with a diamond and ruby pin for her daughter Julie and a diamond and sapphire pin for her daughter Tricia.
>
> The $52,400 figure for the set of emeralds and diamonds comes from Buzhardt, who confirms that the President and Mrs. Nixon had the stones analyzed by Gem Trade Labs in New York on Dec. 10, 1969, and an appraisal made by Harry Winston, Inc. on Feb. 26, 1970.
>
> Buzhardt says that he does not know the Nixons' purposes in determining the values of these pieces, nor does he know if the other jewelry was similarly appraised. The evaluations were not made for insurance purposes, he said, because the stones were "never insured."
>
> At least a portion of the jewelry—the diamond bracelet and the pins—had gone unrecorded by the White House Gifts Unit for nearly two years until a reporter began making inquiries. . . .[7]

By MAXINE CHESHIRE
© 1974 *The Washington Post/Chicago Tribune—*
New York News Syndicate, Inc.

"This Is the Story" Lead

Early in my newspaper career, as I was laboring to create an omnibus lead on a feature, a wise old rewrite man gave me a piece of advice: "If you can't think of a lead, try starting the story with five words: 'This is the story of.'" I tried it, it worked, and I have used the device many times since.

When you write "This is the story of . . ." or "This is a story about . . ." you are telling your readers in very simple terms what you are going to talk about. You are preparing them to receive a message about one man's crime, an institution's failure, a public problem, a major business decision. The device is especially useful when the subject matter is new, complex, and framed in values, norms, and issues that are unfamiliar to the reader.

Here is my favorite example, the background of which is further developed in Chapter 9. It also uses the "dash" construction similar to "bullets" to make a series of points:

'Give an account of thy stewardship . . .'
Luke, 16

THIS IS AN ACCOUNT of the stewardship that Father Flanagan's Boys' Home, internationally renowned as Boys Town, has given to hundreds of millions of dollars donated by the American public in the 55 years of its existence.

Never in those years has Boys Town felt constrained to report to its millions of donors how the money was used. Unlike most major institutions which rely on public financial support, Boys Town has drawn deeper into secrecy—indeed has flatly refused questions about finances from donors and newsmen.

This is why the Sun late last year decided to take an in-depth look at the affairs of the institution, perhaps the best-known privately-supported child-care home in America. The Sun dug through public records, talked to persons now and formerly acquainted with Boys Town's operations, and finally confronted Boys Town's leadership with the facts. The facts are that:

—Boys Town now has net worth of at least 209 million dollars, and perhaps much more.

—Boys Town has a money machine that brings in some $25 million a year from public donations and investment income.

—Boys Town increases its net worth by 16 to 18 million dollars a year. This is three to four times as much as it spends to take good care of its boys.

—Boys Town still continues to send out some 33 million letters a year telling Americans it needs their money. . . .

In short, Boys Town has more money than it knows what to do with. It may be the richest city in America. Based on 1970 census figures (993 persons) and 1970 financial reports ($191.4 million net worth), it had net worth of over $190,000 per person. It had net income—after all expenses and after insignificant taxes—of $16,500 per person, man, woman and child. . . .[8]

©Sun Newspapers of Omaha, 1972

Developing the Story

These examples of leads show more about writing the investigative story than just the lead. You can see where the writer is heading: toward proof of the story he is unfolding. Francie Barnard substantiates her lead on page with evidence: what has happened, who is doing it, why they say they are or are not discriminating.

The *Chicago Tribune* series on police brutality, (p. 141), after grasping its readers by the throat, proceeds to prove its case. All the proof is there— the quotes by officials, the records. Reader questions are anticipated and answered.

Note that sentences and paragraphs are short, uncomplicated. The language and presentation never detract from the story. The team had gathered a wealth of information yet sifted out all but the most essential and telling facts.

Jim Polk says the investigative reporter is vouching for the accuracy of every word; he's not "just reporting what so and so said."

"There's always a temptation in writing to over-dramatize, to color the facts a little bit, in some way to make it read a little smoother," says James B. Steele. "But the very nature of a lot of subjects for investigative work will be such that one doesn't have that total artistic freedom to embellish something the way you would if you were writing some little feature story."

Steele feels, nevertheless, that the investigative reporter has all kinds of flexibility to illustrate his points—metaphorically, for example. The following story shows a writer who employs a metaphorical style in his story:

WASHINGTON—In George Orwell's ominous novel, "1984," the government is Big Brother and no life is private. And now, 10 years ahead of the fictional schedule, a real-life federal agency is independently setting up a massive computer network, which has the potential of getting a personal readout on people all across America.

Known as FEDNET, the network is to be controlled entirely by the General Services Administration (GSA), which plans to have it under way by next year. The plan calls for other federal agency computers to hook into the network, which would create a potential for the GSA to gather information from the files of many government departments.

Some communications specialists express concern that FEDNET will develop into an intricate system that eventually could snoop into individual lives, despite federal protections set up to insure the right to privacy.

For instance, Rep. John E. Moss, D-Calif., said he is deeply troubled by the GSA plan because of "the significant danger" in years ahead when future generations of computers could store cradle-to-grave information on people in a government-run surveillance system.

Moss, who authored the freedom of information act on Capitol Hill, charged this weekend in a letter to GSA Administrator Arthur F. Sampson that "experts tell me cooperation among various federal agencies would allow assembly of dossiers on any individual or institution with expansion of the computer system."

FEDNET also has touched off a power struggle in the upper reaches of the Nixon administration, where White House advisers are concerned over what they see as the GSA's grab for power and the cost-heavy way the agency is going about it. . . .

Estimated construction costs of FEDNET range up to $180 million. . . .

Unlike other massive purchases, this one is being made without an appropriation from Congress. Instead, the GSA intends to use a $50 million kitty it controls for government-wide automatic data processing expenditures, as a starter. . . .

[After an extensive description of the system, Kantor quotes Dennis Bracy, a GSA official.]

Bracy admits the agencies "could willingly supply information" to each other through FEDNET in future years, "which is something agencies will have to be very careful about."

Asked if a Big Brother government 10 years from now could use FEDNET to pry into private lives, the GSA official laughed. "Not any more than with a telephone network," he said.

In Orwell's *1984* a time when the fictional government's motto was "Ignorance is Strength," every telephone was tapped.[9]

By SETH KANTOR
Copyright, 1974, *The Detroit News*
News Washington Bureau

In developing the trunk of his story, Dick Lyneis relies on his outline, his list of the high-points, "what goes together and all the documents most important to use and which ones aren't." He says he gets things well-organized, pushes everything else away, and just gets down to writing.

Keep in mind that the main thread of the story should be carried as simply as possible through the single piece. Extra documentation—the development and history of the ABC company, for example—can be written in short sidebars.

You'll note the writers of investigative pieces make statements like the following not usual in straight news stories: "Such is the state of the Philadelphia criminal justice system: all too often, the innocent go to jail, the guilty go free. . ." The investigative reporter is free to offer conclusions because he is going to prove them.

Yet this proof need not be heavy-handed. Stories in the *Wall Street Journal* given as examples on page 146 exhibit touches of wry humour: "What's unusual about Mr. Balentine isn't his lucrative consulting agreement but his candor about it. . . . Just as widespread is the view that such arrangements often aren't what they profess to be and rarely work out well when they are."

Humor does not, however, detract from the serious substantiation of investigative theses. The story continues:

"The trouble is that a retired executive can rarely fill any of these functions satisfactorily at his own company." Mr. Cassell goes on. "Whatever specific knowledge he has tends to quickly become dated, and it's often very difficult for him to be objective about people or suggestions that challenge the way things were done when he was in charge. If a company needs this sort of advice, it's far better off going outside."

Graef S. Crystal, vice president of Towers, Perrin, Foster & Crosby, a New York management-consulting firm, is quite a bit harsher. "In the big majority of cases, calling a former executive a consultant is just a euphemism—window dressing for shareholders," he asserts. "Its real function is to make a top man's retirement easier or help save face for a guy who's been pushed out. I haven't heard of many cases where useful work was actually performed. It gives real consultants a bad name. . . ."

Indeed, in a good many cases, "consulting" agreements are concluded with no real intention that much work will be done. This typically occurs when an executive is asked to resign a post with time still left on his employment contract.[10]

Writing the Series

Most long-term investigations result in a mass of material that, in order to attract and retain readers, must be separated into shorter stories run as a series. Each story in a series often features a different aspect of the investigation but includes, much like a soap opera, an introductory sidebar or statement that briefly describes what happened the day before.

A *Chicago Tribune* series on career schools dealt with the results of a three-month long study of 13 privately owned correspondence and trade schools. The *Tribune* Task Force directed by Pamela Zekman and including reporters William Crawford, William Gaines, and James A. Jackson wrote a series of five stories. They focused on the students themselves, the broken promises made by the schools, the instruction and facilities, the cost, and the sales staffs. In posing as sales trainees and students to document the irregularities the reporters found:

"The State Office of Education spends only $205,000 a year from its $14 million operating budget for six employees to license, inspect, and handle complaints about any of the Illinois-based schools."

The story continues with its other findings: the need for strengthening rules and rewriting vague statutes governing such schools—making the story meaningful to readers.

A *Philadelphia Inquirer* series, "The Farview Findings," by Acel Moore and Wendel Rawls, Jr. ran in five parts: "The State treats patients with drugs, brutality and death," "The pattern of therapy: sedation and brutal neglect," "Hustles, thefts and betting are a way of life inside," and "Close Farview? 40,000 citizens said, 'No' " (The real reason is that Farview remained a sacred cow to politicians, the article said, to provide 500 jobs and pump $7.6 million a year into a local economy.) The final part of the series contained excerpts from tapes made by William J. Thomas at Farview.[11]

Development of a series allows more exhaustive discussion of the subject, and in addition to capturing reader interest, continues to hold it by the promise of more details to come.

Finishing Up

The Farview series contains some strong final paragraphs but investigative stories should close with a punch—a pithy quotation, a summary of the thesis, a surmise about the future, a promise by someone in power that things will change, or that they won't. Some writers finish by lifting their hands from the typewriter; others leave their readers something to remember:

From a Farview story:

"Throughout the social workers' reports of Charles Simon's life at Farview there are frequent notations that the patient 'is resentful.'

" 'I guess I was,' " Simon says. "My life was wasted. But I think I held my bearings pretty well. I didn't cry at all.' "

From the Fednet story:

"The OMB wants Meeker's office to issue separate bid proposals. One would cover the computer hardware. The other would govern communications rules and regulations.

"The net effect would be to delay Meeker's plans so that both Congress and the Nixon administration could draw up a well-planned approach to see that FEDNET could not become a future tool to fold, mutilate or spindle private rights.

From the Nixon jewels story:

"A final decision will have to wait until Catto [Henry Catto, chief of proto-col] returns. Ironically, he will almost certainly have more Arab jewels to worry about when that trip, with its ceremonial exchange of gifts, is concluded."

PRESENTATION

The most common problems in displaying investigative stories are:

- Extremely long text
- Complexity of story structure, making late trims in the composing room difficult and risky
- Inadequate art: too few photos, and these often static and un-imaginative

All of these problems can be anticipated and dealt with if both the re-porter and editor plan for good presentation from the moment base-build-ing begins. Consider these options:

Photographs

- Head shots of principals including series of close-ups taken during interviews; posed medium shots with office, home or outdoor back-ground; informal shots in other settings
- Shots of the action being investigated (for example, a trade-school salesman making his pitch)
- General background pictures, including historical and file photos of the principals and their activities in earlier years
- Reproductions of key documents
- Aerial views (for instance, of land to be rezoned) to which an artist can later add boundary lines, directional arrows, and other identi-fication

Drawings

- Maps showing land holdings, traffic routes, location or flow of ac-tivities, spheres of influence
- Block diagrams or charts showing relationship of the target with other groups or persons

- Simple bar graphs illustrating single points in the text (for example, comparisons of activity or treatment of different subjects against the norms of the target's profession or industry)
- Line graphs demonstrating historic trends
- Mood-setting illustrations or artist's conceptions based on facts reported in the text

Typographic Elements

- Headlines
- Subheads within the text
- Side heads, surrounded by ample white space, running near major points of the text
- Boxes, used in moderation to emphasize short sidebars
- Drop-in or read-out heads spaced through the text to relieve masses of body type
- Reverse or overprinted headlines running into or out of halftone art.

Planning for Art

In base-building and basic research, the reporter should begin to acquire file and background photos setting the scene and illustrating the history of activities being investigated. As he writes his daily memos, he should tell his editor about picture possibilities to which a photographer can be assigned. "Always get the photos as soon as possible," says Pam Zekman. "The situation is never there if you wait and send someone back two weeks later." As his work moves into upper-level interviews and the evaluation before the key interviews, the reporter can suggest additional pictorial assignments, such as the aerials. When he completes his first draft, he should also supply pencil sketches, tables or numbers, and any other information that can possibly be illustrated with graphs and diagrams. As the reporter sits down to start his final rewrite, layout and graphic artists should begin developing the finished art and page dummies. By this stage, it should be possible to estimate the length of finished text within five per cent or so—close enough so that the space can be designed with one or two flexible art elements that can be expanded, reduced, or dropped after the story has been set in type and measured exactly.

The Layout

Ease of reading should be the rule in laying out the story on the page. Just because sixteen kinds of display elements have been listed above, don't try to use all sixteen in one story. Instead, decide on an appropriate amount of display space, then place the elements so that the main text runs in the most compact, uninterrupted form that is reasonably possible. As a guideline, figure that fifty-five to sixty per cent of the available space should be devoted to heads, art, and display elements. If the mix drops to the forty or forty-five per cent range, you are flirting with monotonous grayness.

My own preference is to frame the main story with display elements, leaving the text in squared-off units. If I use art or boxes, I'll try to place them at the top or bottom of a column in order to leave the text modular. I don't want the reader to have to make a decision—or a mistake—in mid-page, trying to find out whether the story reads around a photo or jumps back up into the next column. As in writing, so in the layout should the reader's convenience be the yardstick.

8
Memos
to the Editor

VERY GOOD REPORTERS almost always get offers to become editors, sometimes early in their careers. Some turn them down because they would rather stay in the front lines with their typewriters. This chapter is for the reporter who didn't turn down the offer, or won't turn it down when it comes. It reviews the editor's problems of designing and managing investigative reporting. It also should help the beginning investigative reporter understand the problems of the man he's working for.

THE PLAN

To develop an investigative program, the newspaper editor should consider adopting the following plan. It consists of nine steps:

1. Decide that you want an investigative tone in the local news report and that you are willing to accept the pressures this decision implies.
2. Carefully marshal the reasons for your decision and discuss them with the publisher, telling him you won't raise the budget or hire new people just yet.

3. Convey your investigative attitude to subeditors and reporters. Reinforce it by asking challenging questions and assigning reporters to make aggressive follow-ups on stories that have been treated superficially. Make it concrete by asking reporters and editors for lists of investigative ideas. Study, screen, and merge these ideas into a few attractive, feasible story ideas, then settle on one.

4. Pick the staff member who shows the best combination of investigative attributes. Give him at least a week to study the feasibility of the story before reporting back directly to you.

5. If the reporter's study confirms the feasibility of the project, clear him of other duties so he can begin basic research. Set up a schedule of meetings, at least one a week, to review progress and discuss problems.

6. When the reporter believes he is ready for the key interview, evaluate his research and discuss the key interview plan with him.

7. After the interview, block out the time to do a "feet up" editing job, the kind Neale Copple describes in *Depth Reporting.*[1] This editing entails a single, clear-cut sentence of your purpose and thesis, a background to help the reader understand the circumstances surrounding the story, and interpretation. Interpretation is used here as a superdefinition of the why of the investigation, and the details of the investigation, the facts beneath the surface, and fitting the story into the reader's world. Make your hypothesis work or knock it down.

8. After you are sure the story is solid, let the publisher know it is coming. Be prepared to argue for it but don't try to slip by him if he is not used to high-risk, hard-nosed reporting. If he is not prepared for strong public reaction, it could cost you and the reporter your jobs.

9. A week after the story has run, get the staff together and discuss the story's impact. The way in which individuals respond will help identify other investigative reporting prospects on the staff. The meeting will also help reinforce in staff members' minds your own commitment to quality journalism. Such commitment is a sine qua non for further development.

Of course, the whole project may blow up in your face at any point from Step 2 to Step 9. If it does, you will have to decide what to do about it. You have to make things happen. You can't be half-hearted. If, for example, you run a story about shady retailing practices but delete the names of offending stores, the word will spread quickly. "If there's obvious lack of feeling for a subject by an editor," says Al Delugach, "it's going to be communicated by an attitude, even unspoken, to a reporter. The guidance is negative."

Conversely, your direct expression of interest, motivation, support and counsel for good and feasible projects will stimulate at first a nervous trickle, then a steady stream of ideas—too many, in fact. Readers will be phoning in tips or walking in with inconclusive documents and fascinating but unprovable theories and ideas. Reporters will be baying for scalps. That's when your editing judgment will be put to its severest test. You have to keep on top.

PICKING THE PLAYERS

The first rule to honor in keeping on top is to pick good people. My first piece of advice is simple: don't hire an investigative reporter from out of town. Why?

- Established, responsible investigative reporters are very expensive. Until your paper has a track record—at least a couple of years of persistent performance against tough opposition—you will have a hard time hiring the seasoned investigator. The experienced ones are wise, indeed cynical, about pioneering their craft for a paper whose editor and publisher have not proved their commitment.
- Some self-styled investigative reporters float from city to city, looking for chances to collect scalps and prizes without accepting responsibility. One of these may blow your way and knock over the police chief in six weeks. But he may also skimp on research, hang it all on "confidential sources"—and leave you holding a court summons.
- Even if you find a diamond in the rough, he'll take several months to get the feel of your town, its local power structure and political scene. Unless you and the publisher are prepared to wait, you may be disappointed. My second piece of advice, therefore, is equally simple: pick people on your own staff. Either that or size up new recruits who seem to have investigative potential. Here are the qualities to look for in a reporter who has investigative possibilities:

Self-discipline. Whether he works on a team or alone, the best reporter keeps himself under control. He does not act hastily. He thinks constantly and analytically.

Mental toughness. He has the ability to stand up under fire, to outstare, outtalk, and outthink people who try to foil him. It is the quality of being decisive. It is the kind of determination that produces results. It is difficult to assess this quality in an interview; performance is the best measure.

Persistence. Similar to mental toughness, persistence implies a sort of Oriental patience. When direct tactics cannot be applied, persistence will pay off. When the front door is closed, the investigator walks around the block and finds the landlord, the deliveryman, or a telephone repairman to help him get to the people inside.

Deferred gratification. The investigative reporter does not live for tomorrow's by-line. He enjoys the business of dogged pursuit, of careful deduction, of patient construction of a framework of facts. He doesn't expect a by-line until he has a story that he can stand behind, word for word. Then, of course, he wants it very much.

Single-mindedness. As Ben Bradlee says, "It was no accident that both Bob Woodward and Carl Bernstein were young and divorced . . . nobody clutching them at home, nobody saying, 'Let's slip away for a long weekend.' " Bradlee was talking about the willingness "to put in the time, to invest a sheer godawful number of hours" once an investigation gets under way.

Personal integrity. This quality connotes a devotion to truth. It also implies an integration of self, a wholeness of personality that enables the reporter to withstand personal abuse, uncertainty, frustration, jealousy, backbiting, loneliness.

A broad and open mind. Two traits are paramount in the investigative reporter: he avoids rigidity of ideology or investigative theory, and he looks far and wide for patterns. He sees both the forest *and* the trees, and he then picks out which trees have been planted in rows and which have sprung up from windblown seeds. The true professional also talks openly about his work. He is willing to defend it against criticism, is not afraid to take a problem to his editor, is not crushed when the editor makes a considered and well-articulated no-go decision.

Independence of thought. This quality comes as standard equipment with any model of investigative reporter, new or used. It is his most valuable tool. He is not awed by the folklore of journalism. He does not believe "you can't touch that story." He does not believe the best way to do something is "the way we've always done it." He examines subjects and institutions with fresh vigor.

A sense of outrage. This term is Les Whitten's and it means about the same thing as Bill Lambert's "low threshold of indignation." It is an essentially humanist orientation, most often manifested as a desire to defend the little guy against the big guy. Only a shade or a degree away from obsession or cant, this attribute can easily turn into a pursuit of devil theories, blinding its advocate to plausible explanations. But to some degree, it is present in virtually every investigator. It is the vision that enables him to see that the king is naked.

Competency in writing. The nature of investigative writing sometimes makes it less exciting than a dramatic rescue story. But you must look for a clear writer, one who puts together a well-structured story. Read samples of his writing and check with his last editor to see if the work was his own or needed extensive rewriting. Find out whether he writes easily and automatically, or slowly and laboriously. Is he able to accept criticism? Does an experienced editor on the staff have time to work over his writing?

Evaluate all these factors. Then pick a person who averages four on a five-point scale on all traits.

COACHING THE INDIVIDUAL

Training your own investigative people entails headaches, false starts, and frustrations. A new reporter needs lots of testing before he can be turned loose. He needs to develop judgment and poise. If he can spell and write declarative sentences—and shows a lot of ambition—hire him and send him to the police station. Dave Nimmer, ex-investigator turned managing editor of the *Minneapolis Star,* put it this way: "If a guy hasn't covered cops, then I don't believe he's had his ass kicked around enough to develop the toughmindedness for investigative reporting."

The police station and the editor can't carry the burden of training alone. Fledgling investigators can benefit as well from seminars and academic training, though these should not substitute for practical experience. The American Press Institute in Reston, Va., schedules two-week seminars for investigative reporters. These are intensive experiences with lecturers recruited not only from the top ranks of the Washington and New York press corps, but also from among editors and reporters on newspapers of all sizes.

Most major schools of journalism offer courses that immerse advanced students in investigative concepts and techniques. Some of the best programs are at American University, Ohio State, Northwestern, and Stanford.

COACHING THE TEAM

The outstanding journalist seems to get himself trained—and to get stories by flashes of genius. He often substitutes intuition about a source's reliability for some of the drudgery of building a massive documentary case. But for most mortals—reporters and editors alike—tackling a large institutional or system story in pairs or teams is more practical and efficient. Teaming helps encourage the flow of ideas; teammates check each other and increase the effectiveness of key interviews. A team following a good plan can be far more productive than two journeymen working separately on day-to-day assignments from a city editor.

Jim Steele and his partner Donald Barlett are Exhibit A in support of the team idea. In six years they won fourteen national reporting awards. Such a success rate is reason enough to consider the advantages of team reporting.

The Permanent Team

Permanent teams have been highly successful not only for the *Philadelphia Inquirer,* but also for *Newsday* (the modern pioneer in teaming), the *Chicago Tribune,* and the *Boston Globe.* Their teams range from two to six persons, occasionally supplemented by others for specific projects. The goal of each team is to conceive and develop original investigative stories. Team members look for stories no one else has done, ideally for the story no one else has even thought of. Although some teams—notably those of *Newsday* and the *Tribune*—aim for slow, planned turnover, all lean toward synergistic personal relationships with a high degree of permanence. The advantages of the permanent team are worth analyzing:

Volume. Team members become familiar with a wide variety of reference works, basic and special sources of documents, and bureaucracies. They can move on several lines of inquiry simultaneously rather than sequentially, a fact that can be crucial in probing a changing, developing situation. The lone reporter may be simply outpaced by events. Changes in policy, elections, personnel turnover, death or transfer of key persons, loss of sources—these may cloud or negate the meaning of facts gathered nine or ten months (or two years) earlier. Most teams plan their projects to last no more than two or three months from conception to publication.

Success rates. Largely because they are more thorough, team projects generally produce greater public impact—changes in laws or policies, rises or falls of businesses or government agencies.

Breadth of contacts. Members of permanent teams usually have had experience on two to half a dozen beats, and they are assiduous about keeping up those contacts. On a given project, a team may split tasks on the basis of members' backgrounds. Or, as Bill Lambert points out, a team can merge information from individual members' sources and effectively conceal the origin of key leads. Thus a team rarely has to generate and develop as many new sources on a project as does an individual reporter.

Synergism. The effect of three or four minds analyzing a problem is more than the sum of the parts. At times, the effect seems most exponential.

It can produce unconventional ways of viewing a set of facts, of putting together observations.

Interviewing. When a key interview comes up, the solo reporter must choose between going it alone or briefing another reporter to accompany him. But the team member already has one or more fully briefed veterans working with him. They can concentrate on scripting the interview, on planning roles and tactics, rather than each worrying about whether the other understands the problem. And in the critical phase after key interviews, the team can produce a complete series or story-and-sidebars promptly. This speed of production minimizes the risk of a leak to the opposition or a counterattack by the target.

Continuity and momentum. Perhaps the major advantage of the permanent team is that it permits one project to follow another quickly without cumbersome phases of slowdown and start-up. Sometimes base-building for a long-term project may begin while a current project is being wrapped up. The *Tribune's* great vote-fraud effort of 1972, for instance, called for nearly a year of inside work by task-force member William Mullen in the election commissioner's office. While Mullen was occupied there, task-force leader George Bliss and others were carrying out a highly successful nursing-home investigation.

Self-checking. The best reporter, trying to write a five-part series from 200 pages of notes, a 50-page chronology, 165 index cards and two congressional committee reports, must worry about errors of memory and understanding. If team members check each other's daily notes and story drafts, the risk of error is sharply reduced.

Self-regulation. At the end of a long, hard job, even good reporters can fall into devil theories or impute evil motives to characters who may only be incompetent or stupid. The presence of one to three colleagues, each presumably a strong and independent thinker, reduces this risk of lost perspective.

Simpler management. An experienced team can be easier to supervise than a number of individuals. The wise editor holds the team leader accountable. He spends a good deal of time with the leader but finds this much easier than having to resolve the individual problems and conflicting needs of three or four persons.

Training. About once a year, a new member is taken aboard the *Chicago Tribune* Task Force, while one veteran returns to general assignments or a beat. This rotation reduces jealousy among other staff members. It also helps to test and train.

Team Problems

But team operation, like any other, is not without costs and problems. Because the team works with more direction and fewer burdens than most reporters, as Barlett notes, its salaries may be more efficiently spent, but all investigative work costs money. Further, security is harder to achieve when five people (including the line editor) know something than when a single reporter knows it.

To be able to carry on several lines of inquiry at once is an advantage— but not if gaps are being left or if the same trail is being crossed several times. These errors and omissions sometimes occur in a team effort. The team leader must ensure that every member of the team knows, day by day, what others have found out. Each team member must not only write his own daily memo, but also read the notes of his colleagues. Bob Greene is wont to bring in a pot of coffee laced with Scotch and pass it around at the end of a day. Says Greene: "We talk about what we have found out. One says, 'I think the next person I should go to is this'. . . . We work it out that night, approximately what we're going to do the next day." Then, as described in Chapter 2, Greene reads all the memos and "breaks" them for duplicating and distribution the next day.

The ego and the navel are also matters to reckon with in team efforts. The stereotypical investigative reporter has a strong ego. He may refuse to let others share his prized sources. He may complain that "nobody else does any work." If a person with an excessive ego turns up on a team, he will upset his colleagues and will himself operate at less than maximum capacity. The risk of lapsing into a contemplation of the navel is greatest in a two-person team hidden away in a private office. If two successive projects fall short of expectations, the publisher starts asking what return is coming from that $50,000 line in the budget, and the team may indulge in excessive caution, restudy of procedures, reorganization of files, self-criticism—anything other than tackling a new project aggressively. David Nimmer remarks: "They had better report to somebody [an editor] every day, just for their own benefit. If they're out chasing butterflies, it's very easy to get down on themselves. They've got to feel part of a newsroom."

If, on the other hand, the team starts winning prizes—especially if it achieves results against great odds—an aura of mysticism may arise around its members. The very good ones can handle it. But some are never the same. Some become sticklers. Because methodology paid off, they become infatuated with it. They spend time drawing plans and writing daily memos to themselves and as a result fall behind in the real work. Others get snooty. The victims of snootiness spend much time lecturing about journalism; they may even write books. They don't want to move on a story unless the work plan has been screened by the Pulitzer Prize advisory committee. Such cases are sometimes cured by incanting the classic definition of a courageous managing editor: he's the one who fired a Pulitzer winner.

And reporters not on the team can, of course, become jealous. They can refuse to pass along tips and ignore tips given them by team members. They complain about their own workloads and resent the time investigators spend reading books, encyclopedias, and magazines.

The good editor—the coach—has to manage things to minimize the problems and maintain the advantages of the team.

The Ad Hoc Team

The temporary team put together for a specific story is even more work for the editor than a permanent team. It can, nonetheless, produce spectacular results. After the project is finished, team members return to their beats. The ad hoc team might include one expert and a few specialists picked to supplement his skills and knowledge. Or it might include several experts who don't need the help of specialists. Chapter 9 describes how the ad hoc approach worked on one project for the *Sun Newspapers* of Omaha. One reason it worked so well is that we had used ad hoc teams on at least five major stories in the three previous years (two won national awards).

With a couple of notable exceptions, the strengths of an ad hoc team are the same as those of a permanent one. They can handle about the same research volume, bring in a breadth of contacts, react synergistically, train the newer members, and check each other. If anything, ad hoc teams are more conservative than permanent ones—more inclined to discuss difficult questions at length and less inclined to take chances. Elitism is also less of a problem because team members know they are going back to other tasks when the project is done. The cost per project is about the same as for a permanent team; however, rather than four or five major projects a year, the ad hoc concept envisages only one or two, so the annual cost for this type of teaming is usually lower.

But three strengths of the permanent team—simpler management because of a strong team leader, standard writing procedures for keeping daily reports and producing final drafts, and especially continuity and momentum—are lost with an ad hoc team. The permanent team practically runs on its own. The editor has to intervene more with the ad hoc team. With little operating continuity, he must take special pains to see that the team is protected from other assignments, that the schedule is followed, that the daily reports are written, that the project files are maintained. The editor has to assign writing duties to the team, explain the general approach, then mediate disagreements between reporters, such as an argument about turning a sidebar into a major story. Instead of having reporters continually defining new ideas and exploring feasibility, the editor finds the burden now falls on him. When he assigns feasibility studies, he finds they must be sandwiched into other routines. When a report comes back, the editor may have to make an undesirably quick judgment on a half-developed idea. And when he does decide to form a new team, he must shuffle beats, brief team members, set up a schedule of progress conferences, and arrange new file facilities.

There is also the greater danger of leaks. Especially if the effort drags on for months and several people pop into and out of it, word of the project will get on the grapevine. Less experienced reporters tend to be less scrupulous about keeping their files—and their mouths—locked. So security is also a problem with the ad hoc team.

What is less of a danger, however, are ego trips. They are less of a problem than on a permanent team. The editor, though, must make sure the work is properly apportioned and that people who do the routine records work and peripheral interviews get appropriate credit.

The ad hoc team, then, represents the editor's conscious trade-off of continuity and momentum for a more tightly controlled budget. It is an effective check, certainly, on "head hunting" or make-work by irresponsible persons, but it can also become a damper on reporters' motivation.

THE SINGLE ACE

When you have a Seymour Hersh, a Nick Gage, a Gene Cunningham—or a staff of Stanley Penns and Jonathan Kwitnys—you are better off to leave them alone, asking only that they talk once or twice a week with a senior editor. Such persons develop their own working styles, their own solid sources. Though they may appear to operate instinctively, they work efficiently. They keep their own files. They know most of the standard hustles and games people play, so they know where to look for the chinks in the system. They combine indignation, logical judgment, personal strength, and physical stamina. They have the peculiar self-motivation that management can rarely improve on and can indeed stifle with too many restrictions. Their most common problem is an occasional fit of cynicism or gloom.

Although his salary and expenses may seem high, the solo performer can be very cost-efficient. The editor must develop, with his business manager, a pay policy that permits him to work the hours he feels necessary. Putting the reporter on fixed salary—adjusted for expected extra effort—is one practical approach. If he produces as many as three or four major stories or series a year—stories that build the paper's credibility and cause other good things to happen—he is a bargain. He will also spin off scores of tips and ideas for other staff members and will usually motivate them to do better day-to-day reporting. He may arouse jealousy among the time-servers, but the editor has an easy response to those people: "You get the same results, friend, and you can have the same deal."

The strongest reason for finding your own ace is to avoid the danger of playing safe. An editor has plenty of controls tilting him toward the status quo: his publisher, his elite friends, his conservative staff members, the law, the traditions and codes of professional associations. If he wants his newspaper to do its public duty, he should always find room for one or two iconoclasts on the staff.

EDITING THE PLAYERS

If there ever was a time for feet-up editing, it is when the investigative reporter's first draft arrives. Investigative editing calls for the same kind of sleuthing as investigative reporting. The editor should take the draft into his office, shut off his phone calls and read it through several times. He not only has thousands of his budget dollars in the piece, he has the newspaper's reputation for accuracy, honesty, and fairness on the line. Although the reporter is willing to stand behind every word, the editor is the one who willj be called to account for whatever recriminations ensue. Therefore, the editor should read that story through not once or twice, but six times. Six times? Yes. And each of those times, he examines the story from a different point of view, as we shall see.

First reading. Is the thesis proved? Is is clearly stated and is there enough documented, attributable evidence so that a reasonable reader may understand the conclusions? If not, make notes about what is missing and go on to the next reading.

Second reading. Is the thesis important? Will a significant number of readers see it as important? In short, who will give a damn?

Third reading. Does the story flow? Does it move in a continuous, logical line? Or does it pause frequently to branch off into detailed explanation of some legal point or translation of bureaucratic or technical jargon?

Fourth reading. How can it be trimmed? A story in which the reporter has invested weeks or months will probably be laden with detail, excessive restatement, tedious qualification, and unnecessary attribution. It may help to pencil an outline of the story as written, identifying the essential points, so you can decide how much support each point needs. If one sharp quote captures a key thought, are three reinforcing quotes needed? If three sets of records support a contention, is it necessary to detail all three, or will a single sentence ("City purchase records confirmed the transaction") be enough? Draw a line or put a light X beside each possible cut or compaction. Try to arrive at a balance between enlightenment and boredom. You want to get the story told quickly with strong, clear words. This is the time, for example, to strip out quotes that simply make an interviewee look silly without contributing information about his motives.

Fifth reading. After the cuts and adjustments, will the story read? Will making a sidebar out of the fifth and sixth paragraphs make mysterious gibberish out of everything after the sixteenth paragraph? This is simply standard editing "to conform," but it calls for special care in a long, complex piece.

Sixth reading. Now it is time to test the reporter. If he is a pro, he can stand it. If he cannot, you would rather know now than after the story is printed. Put yourself in the position of the subject of the key interview—or his attorney. Write down in blunt words every question you can think of that challenges the accuracy of the reporter's arithmetic, the credibility of his quoted sources, the logic of his assertions.

By now you have spent at least a couple of hours with the story, and have made marks all over the copy, plus a list of pertinent and impertinent questions. It is time to call the reporter in and go through the list.

Discussions, Revisions

The ensuing discussion can become a morass. Your job is to keep things moving briskly toward reasonable solution of the problem: how to get the piece in print. A good reporter appreciates it. "I'd hate to sell a story to a person who didn't think of asking the right questions," says Dick Lyneis. "I want them to be real tough. I want them to set incredibly high standards. I want him to pin me up against the wall. I want them to make me defend everything I've got."

If your questions from the first and last readings are substantive, it is wise to tackle them first. You may have at least a temporary no-go situation, and you need to determine if it is worthwhile to send the reporter back for more work.

If you can establish that the story has a sound thesis, proved by evidence, the next step is to deal with the hard questions that came up in the last reading. These are questions you, the editor, may have to answer in a phone call or visit from the aggrieved person or his attorney. The reporter should have answers to every one of them. If he does not—if he appears confused or claims "confidential source" too often—you must articulate your reservations now. This can be a delicate problem in human relations—as well as one of the most crucial aspects of editing. Presumably, the reporter has been pouring heart and soul into the project, day and night for weeks on end. Whenever possible, suggest that further checking is in order, that perhaps some other source or record can be found to fill whatever gap has shown up. But if the reporter has simply failed to talk to an obvious person because "he wouldn't tell us anything anyway," then draw a hard line. Such a reporter is making unwarranted assumptions.

If you have a competent reporter at work, there is no serious confrontation on 99 stories out of 100. But you are making a terrible mistake if you avoid the challenging questions. This kind of self-evasion leads to decisions such as, "We've put so much work into it, I suppose we have to run something." That attitude is a disservice to your readers.

Once the critical questions from the sixth reading are answered, the rest of the conference should be a breeze.

The important tasks now are to strip the main piece to greyhound shape, to pull out and rework the sidebars, and to set up the accompanying graphics with the layout specialist while the reporter rewrites. If the main story involves penetrating some corporate labyrinth, you may decide on a simple chart—boxes and connecting lines—to clarify the relationships. If the story is heavy with statistics, simple line or bar graphs can help clear up major points.

Call the company lawyer and tell him there will be a piece for him to go over tomorrow. Stop in the publisher's office and, as bravely as possible, assure him that the "big piece" is in hand and, so far, all looks well.

THE FINAL HUDDLE

During the time between your acceptance of the reporter's story and its publication, you as an editor have hard and critical work to do. You must allow ample time to do it well.

The first step is to seek out a trusted colleague—city editor, editorial writer, veteran reporter—who has not been involved in the story and show him the rewrite. Don't ask for a detailed editing but a fresh viewpoint and a candid evaluation of the thesis, approach, and structure.

Next visit the lawyer. Lawyers think in terms of evidence and proof. That's not a bad viewpoint to have just before you publish. Have the lawyer read everything—sidebars, charts and graphs, headlines, cutlines. Unwitting libel in heads or cutlines is common. Occasionally, the lawyer will also react like a typical reader and tell you he doesn't understand some compressed thought that the copy editor tried to squeeze into a fourteen-count headline. The lawyer's lay judgment, as well as his professional, can be helpful.

After the page is made up, read it again. This may disrupt normal shop procedure, but it should be done in the interest of accuracy. Have the reporter read the page, too.

If time allows, have yet one more new person look at the page. The sports editor, the life-style editor, the wire editor, or some other trusted but uninvolved staffer may spot an error everyone else has missed. Even a simple complaint—"I don't quite follow what this paragraph means"— may suggest a change that adds the final polish to the story.

The final huddle complete, stop and congratulate the reporter for persistence and professional performance. And make sure that he or the city editor is geared for follow-up—not just the next day but two weeks from now or a month from now.

9

The Boys Town Story

LET'S STEP BACK in time a bit and visit Omaha, Nebraska, in 1971. The city is often a surprise to newcomers who have visions of flat, far-stretching Great Plains. Omaha undulates over a series of small hills west of the Missouri River, and all but its newest subdivisions are shaded with full-leaved trees. The city contains some 350,000 people. It is the core of a metropolitan area of 550,000. It has three commercial television channels, two educational channels, ten radio stations, and a morning-evening newspaper known as the *World-Herald*. In more recent years the *World-Herald* has become a formidable, assertive paper whose news columns reflect concern over urban social problems. (though the bulk of its 225,000 daily circulation is in outstate Nebraska and western Iowa).

THE *SUN* STAFF

Its only general-circulation competition in Omaha is a group of week-lies, the *Sun Newspapers*, with 50,000 subscribers. The *Sun* has seven editions, all dated Thursday, each averaging about eighty tabloid pages a week. About half the content of any edition is local for a given neighbor-hood or suburb; the rest is common to all of the editions. I am managing editor, Stamford Lipsey is president and publisher, and Warren Buffett is chairman of the board.

The editorial staff adds up to a full-time equivalent of twenty persons. About thirteen cover the neighborhoods, process photos and copy, write regular features and columns, coordinate communication and production among the seven editions. This leaves seven (including me and my assistant managing editor) available for metropolitan and investigative reporting. Each of the others has some broad subject area of regular weekly coverage: local government, business, health-education-welfare, sports, arts, enter-tainments, and such.

We also have a commitment, which goes back to 1960, to come up every week with at least one but preferably two or three original pieces that will be fresh in concept, thorough in research, highly readable—and a sur-prise not only to our readers but to our competition. We have developed a certain *esprit de corps*. We hold weekly staff meetings at which story ideas are tossed out and a few investigative stories launched. And we have a board chairman and a publisher who believe the only way for the *Sun* to survive in a tough advertising market is to be different, original, and public-service minded.

Every January, just after we've finished the financial budgeting, I make up a list of a dozen or more "untold stories" about Omaha and how things work around here. We discuss the kind of manpower and special resources that will be needed to bring several of them to fruition during the year. Two, three, four times a year, we get together at Buffett's home and spend an evening drinking Pepsi while we discuss progress on these projects and consider new ones.

CONCEPTION

It was at such a meeting in mid-summer of 1971 that we decided to try the Boys Town story. The idea was simply to report how Boys Town raised its money and how it spent the money.

Boys Town had been founded by Father Edward J. Flanagan in an old mansion near the center of Omaha in 1918. About 1921, it moved to a farm ten miles west of the city. It had many financial problems until M-G-M made its famous movie in 1938 with Spencer Tracy and Mickey Rooney. After that, Boys Town's national image grew rapidly, and immediately after World War II, Father Flanagan started a major building project that in-cluded some $10 million worth of new dormitories, a stadium, industrial-training shops, and administrative buildings. He died in 1947, less than a year before the project was completed. For all practical purposes, that was the last big capital expenditure made by Boys Town.

We knew that every spring and every Christmas season, Boys Town sent out a lot of letters asking people all over the nation for money. In the 1960s, we had made a couple of tentative passes at the Boys Town story. We went to the public-relations people, the assistant director, and the director (Msgr. Nicholas Wegner) asking, among other things, how much money they took in and how they used it. We were turned down cold every time. "We just don't discuss our fund-raising program" was the general nature of the replies. "It takes a lot of money to care for a thousand boys."

But it was obvious that Boys Town was not going broke. Its physical appearance (a huge green campus dotted with brick and stone buildings, a large farming operation using boys as low-priced hired hands) and the size of the payroll (some 600 employees) were enough to set aside that possibility. But we felt that the public, both locally and nationally, had a right to know a little more specifically how its donated dollars were being spent. And we were in the best position to find out.

PLANNING AND BASE-BUILDING

It was clear that we would have to start working around the edges, building the best framework for an investigative story that we could, before going back to the leadership with hard questions. We therefore analyzed the possibilities for tackling the story, and they broke down this way—in accordance with what we already knew to be facts:

First, Boys Town was an image. We wanted to find out what made that image and how Boys Town sustained it.

Second, Boys Town was incorporated as a village under the laws of Nebraska. Thus it was required to file a condensed annual municipal budget and brief report of operations.

Third, Boys Town was a U.S. post office. It had acquired this standing, apparently for publicity purposes, early in its life. This meant that it had to file certain minimal public reports with the U.S. Postmaster General.

Fourth, Boys Town operated a school system, accredited by the State of Nebraska and the North Central Association. Again, it would have to make reports of attendance, curriculum, staffing levels, and compliance with health and safety rules.

Fifth, Boys Town was a nonprofit corporation (Father Flanagan's Boys Home, Inc.) chartered under Nebraska law. This meant it had to file brief reports, lists of officers, and copies of its articles of incorporation in the statehouse. It also meant that donations to Boys Town were deductible from income taxes.

Sixth, as a licensed child-care operation, Boys Town had to file other routine reports with the State Welfare Department.

Seventh, Boys Town owned land; there would be records of deeds and mortgages, taxes, and prices.

To measure the Boys Town image, we chose Doug Smith, 24, who was reporting on county government and writing our arts page. We picked him because his rather innocent and youthful appearance masked a sharp, tough mind. I told him to go to the public-relations director of Boys Town, and anywhere else his nose led him, and explain that he was going to do a general historical piece. He was to pick up all of the printed literature he could find, historical and current publicity pictures, and a general account of how the place operated. He was also to try the post office to get an idea of how much mail passed through it each year. But he was, at this stage, to tread softly.

He did just exactly that. He got no figures on the postal volume, but he did get a quote from the assistant postmaster: "People will get everything misconstrued. They'd say, 'Jeez, with that volume of mail, you must be bringing in tons of money.' " Smith also picked up a number of printed handouts that bore the statement: "Boys Town receives no funds from any church, state or federal government." Equally important, he established a working relationship with the unsuspecting public-relations director that would enable him, over a period of several months, to pick up other tidbits and check other information.

ORIGINAL RESEARCH

Mick Rood and Smith made a trip to the statehouse in Lincoln to look at various records. Rood, 27, was our city-hall man with the heaviest record in investigative work. They quickly picked up some discrepancies. Boys Town did receive both federal (school aid) funds and state (welfare and gasoline tax) funds. These funds amounted to relatively small change, as it later turned out, but the fact that they existed was a chink in Boys Town's publicity armor. The opening gave us some reason to question other claims the institution made.

Smith and Rood also got the articles of incorporation and found a set of old bylaws that described how the Boys Town board of directors operated. The Rev. Daniel Sheehan, archbishop of Omaha, was the president of the board and appointed the majority of its members. Monsignor Wegner, who became administrator after Father Flanagan's death, ran the day-to-day operation, but the archbishop appointed him and had ultimate control and responsibility at Boys Town.

Rood checked the state educational records, which indicated that Boys Town's child population was around 665, rather than the 1,000 for which the place was designed. Smith checked land records, which indicated that at the very least, Boys Town's property in Douglas County was worth $8.4 million dollars, virtually all of it tax-exempt.

Rood and Smith also began to develop contacts among members of the educational and welfare staff at Boys Town—some priests and some laymen. These sources described a state of mind among Boys Town management that struck us as conservative, perhaps a bit frightened, and very interested in preserving a tight budget. Nobody would talk to us on the record. Several complained that the management underpaid the staff and refused innovative suggestions. They told of a few capricious firings of people who tried to make changes. There was consensus among junior staff members that Boys Town, though benevolent toward its residents, gave youngsters little encouragement to seek higher education. Rather, the boys were given narrow horizons—vocational training as bakers, metalworkers, or barbers, for example.

Letters and Child Care

I called the administrative aide to our congressman and asked for the report from Washington on the Boys Town post office. A few days later, she called back and read me the figures:

In 1971, there had been 34 million letters mailed from the Boys Town post office.

In 1970, there had been some 36 million letters. As recently as 1965, the total was 50 million pieces of mail a year.

These were staggering figures. There was no way that 700 boys could be spending that much on letters home or to their girlfriends.

I then did a little exploring with people in the private fund-raising business. Essentially, I asked them: If you send out 34 million fund-raising letters a year, how much money do you expect to raise? What kind of dollar return would justify the expense?

Their answers were full of caveats, but the essence was that you couldn't justify it if you didn't net at least $10 million in return. "I know who you are talking about," one of the men said. "Most of the people in our field figure they take in about $15 million a year."

Rood, meanwhile, gave himself a general backgrounding in the field of child care. He wrote and then talked by telephone to officials of the Child Welfare League of America and other associations. He interviewed several local and regional experts in child development and child delinquency. Most of these expert sources regarded Boys Town's large, single-institution approach as inadequate for the kinds of problems children face today.

Rood also learned of a history of strained relations between Boys Town management and the state welfare department, and of Monsignor Wegner's refusal (despite the advice of staff members) to participate in any of several suggested program reviews offered by outside agencies. These points proved useful when we formulated our key interviews.

I also talked by telephone and exchanged letters with the late D. Paul Reed in New York City, executive director of the National Information Bureau, a confidential advisory service for large donors. Reed had little on Boys Town, but sent along copies of fruitless inquiry letters concerning it that he and others had written.

EVALUATION AND GO DECISION

We now had a lot of pieces of a jigsaw puzzle, and we sat down and began to shuffle them. We penciled in some figures. From the school and welfare reports, and from conversation with experts, we figured Boys Town could not possibly spend more than $5 million a year on the operation of the home, school, and village. The management hadn't made a major capital outlay for nearly twenty-five years. It ran a very tight ship. A lot of money was coming in. Assuming the very best—that management had invested it and had drawn interest or dividends ever since the 1947-1948 expansion—Boys Town had to have $100 million or more piled up in endowment. We also knew it had received occasional major bequests, though we couldn't pin many of these down. They were scattered in probate records in hundreds of courthouses in other states.

Late in October, Buffett, Lipsey, and I reviewed the figures and a stack of memos and reports compiled by Smith and Rood. I knew that our framework of information was good as far as it went, but it had gaps. Was it strong enough for us to confront Sheehan and Wegner and bluff them out of more information?

I proposed that we go ahead, that we challenge the archbishop first and try to embarrass him into making a full disclosure and accounting. But Buffett had one more suggestion. Like many wealthy people, he had established a family foundation to donate to worthy causes. He explained that under the Tax Reform Act of 1969—which first took effect with the calendar year of 1970—most nonprofit institutions were required to file Form 990 with the IRS.

"I know that certain church-related institutions are permitted to merge their reports with those of superior church bodies," he explained. "I wouldn't be surprised if that were the case with Boys Town, but we ought to see if they happened to file a separate report."

The Key Record

I had never heard of Form 990, and I don't believe Lipsey had either. The next day I called Melinda Upp, a young woman in Washington whom I had once tried to hire. She was working in a government office. Would she mind going to the front counter of the main IRS office in Washington and asking for the Form 990 for Boys Town? She would be glad to. A couple of days later she called back to say: "They tell me there is such a report, but it's stored in Philadelphia. It will take them several days, but they'll call me when they dig it up."

Well, hoo-ray. We didn't know exactly what we were getting, but it would be more than we had. We knew that the instructions for filing the form called for a list of officers and directors, their remuneration and their interests in the operation if any. It also called for a balance sheet—assets and liabilities—and for an operating report, a list of sources of income and places it was spent during the calendar year 1970. All we could do was wait.

The "several days" stretched into a week. Upp called to say she had rechecked but the form still wasn't in. A week later, I called her, but still no luck. Finally—a full twenty days after she had made the original request—she telephoned: "I'm at the IRS office. They've got the report. It's 94 pages long, and they charge a dollar a page for Xeroxing. Do you want me to get the whole thing?"

"Have you got the money?" I asked. Yes, she could write a check if I'd reimburse her. Okay.

Two days later, the package arrived in Omaha. I opened it and looked at the cover page. After a couple of minutes, I turned to the next page, then the next and the next. I finally walked over to Lipsey's office and said: "Sit down. I want to write out a figure for you." And I did it upside down and backwards, just to give some suspense. The figure was $191,401,421. That was the *net worth* of Father Flanagan's Boy's Home, Inc., at the end of 1970.

There was a good deal more. The report also showed a balance sheet for the beginning of 1970, which gave us two points on a graph. We could extend that line and estimate reasonably that Boys Town's net worth was about $209 million by the end of 1971, and was rising at the rate of about $17 million a year after all expenses. We had a secret weapon in Buffett, whose specialty is analyzing businesses and investments.

We now had a full deck of cards. But it was early December, our busiest time of the year, with our biggest newsholes and with both Rood and Smith tied up on other projects they had taken during our three-week wait. Besides, there was still a lot of checking and interviewing to do. We decided, therefore, to run the story in January—after we were through with year-end reports and fiscal budgeting.

Final Work Plan

I did take the time, during the week after Christmas, to begin developing a final work plan, which I discussed with Rood and Smith. There were many tasks yet to be done, and one of them required that they bring up to date some of the information they had acquired and notes they had made back in September and October.

We still had a few bridges to cross. For one thing, I got sick in mid-January. For another, my assistant left to take another job. It wasn't until the first week in March that seven of us got together in a small meeting room in a midtown hotel: Buffett and Lipsey; Rood and Smith; Wes Iversen, our business writer; Randy Brown, our new assistant managing editor; and myself. Those who had done research reported on what they had and what they needed to do. Brown and Iversen, newcomers to the task force, got their first full briefing. In six hours of talk, we worked up a list of more than 175 specific tasks to be done: further records to be checked, photos to be taken, first drafts of stories to be written and edited—and rewritten, space requirements to be determined, story section to be designed, and an expert evaluation obtained of the Boys Town investment list. We also decided to spot-check other states besides Nebraska and Iowa that might be paying tax funds to support Boys Town.

I made a day-by-day calendar covering eighteen days listing the order in which all of these tasks were to be accomplished, and by whom. We decided, for reasons of security, to move the whole project out of the office and into the basement of my home. We rented four desks, installed three phones and some typewriters and filing cabinets, and we told the rest of the staff we were working on "Project B." I went down to the office every day for an hour or two, but basically the rest of the staff just operated on its own.

We now went into a phase of upper-level interviews, and shortly thereafter the officials of Boys Town began to suspect that we were up to something more than a routine historical piece. Iversen interviewed several alumni of Boys Town. Brown talked with the Boys Town attorneys and obtained a revised set of corporate bylaws. Smith had noticed in the telephone directory that there was a separate downtown fund-raising office for Boys Town, so he and photographer Len Cook visited the place. The sign outside said "Wells Fargo" (that firm had a branch in the same building) but on the upper floors Smith found rows of women typing "personal" solicitation letters and thank-you notes to Boys Town donors. Smith got some revealing quotes from the manager, such as: "Please don't mention this place in your article. You two are the only two who know about it." Rood interviewed the manager of the Boys Town farm. Wes began comparing Boys Town's wealth with that of other large endowed institutions.

THE KEY INTERVIEWS

Our last big job was to interview Archbishop Sheehan and Monsignor Wegner, and then the other fifteen members of the board of directors. Sheehan and Wegner were the key people. We wanted to do them in separate interviews, simultaneously if possible, so that we might check discrepancies in their responses. That turned out to be impossible, so Rood interviewed Wegner on the last Wednesday of our schedule and I interviewed the archbishop on the next morning. We planned these interviews carefully. We actually scripted and rehearsed them, because we wanted to get on tape their "standard" responses to people who asked about Boys Town finances. Rood first led the monsignor through about half an hour of friendly rambling.

Rood asked Wegner why Boys Town continued to ask for money and got a long and discursive answer, including the statement that some day Boys Town might quit asking for money, a procedure that he described as "kind of cumbersome." He went on to say that the purpose was "just to build up an endowment fund. . . . I'd think that some day it would be large enough so that we don't have to worry about it, sending mail out. You get tired of that." But he refused to say how large he thought the endowment should be. At one point he said, "We're so deep in debt all the time." When Rood suggested that Boys Town had rather substantial investments, Wegner replied: "Well, it has some investments, how substantial they are depends on what you mean by substantial. . . . So that word is relative. . . ." The priest became aware that Rood was not just guessing when Rood finally said we had a copy of the Form 990. Wegner flared up: "That's confidential information!" Mick responded gently: "It's public record." The monsignor shot back: "I know that, but it's still confidential!" Repeatedly he expressed concern that public knowledge of Boys Town's finances would cause people to stop sending in money.

My interview with the archbishop was anticlimactic. He would answer "yes" to anything we already knew but would volunteer nothing and would fill no gaps.

I also asked Sheehan why the institution continued to ask for money. Said he:

"We are not sure what the cost will be in operating an institutional type of home in the future." He spoke of increasing salaries demanded by professionals such as guidance counselors, and the general "uncertainties involved in our operation."

He commented: "Across the country, you can see the closing of things like orphanages, you don't see this type of institutional care. You don't see the homeless boys. These boys are picked up in juvenile court. They're not waifs on the street. . . . I think the need is a little different."

As soon as I finished the interview, I called the other reporters and told them they could go ahead with interviewing the other directors, most of whom were rather senior citizens of Omaha's power structure. Their reactions ranged from dismay to innocence or downright ignorance. Two were too old and ill to be interviewed. Only three said anything to indicate they thought Boys Town should be doing anything different than it was doing.

WRITING AND PRODUCTION

Meantime, with most of our first-draft stories in hand, we had designed an eight-page broadsheet section in which to display our fifteen stories and thirty-four photos, plus maps and graphs. We thought it was important to have an interesting display, but not step over the fine line into sensationalism. We set the tone with a photo of the statue that stands near Boys Town's entrance. It shows a boy ragamuffin carrying a sleepy tot on his back. The legend at the statue's base reads: "He ain't heavy, Father . . . He's m' brother." The photo was printed in light blue. Over it, in black, ran a large headline:

BOYS TOWN:
AMERICA'S WEALTHIEST CITY?

On pages 2 and 3, to which the lead piece would jump, we ran a pair of documents facing each other. One was a reproduction of a Boys Town Christmas solicitation letter, which began glumly: "There will be no joyous Christmas season this year . . ." and went on to tug at the heartstrings of its recipients. Opposite it, we reproduced the first page of the Form 990, solemnly sworn to by Monsignor Wegner, showing Boys Town's net worth and its $25.9 million in annual income. I had the job of writing the main piece and then an editorial (to run on our regular editorial page, not in the special section).

We wanted the lead piece to be hard-hitting but not to convey any tone of anti-Catholicism or inference that anybody was misappropriating funds. Thus we chose to avoid any sweeping statements in the lead. We chose a Biblical quote ("Give an account of thy stewardship") to set a mood, then outlined a "tree trunk" story. Working from drafts developed by the other reporters, I wrote an article nearly 4,000 words long. The central theme was Boys Town's dilemma: more money than it knows what to do with and a child population that is dwindling because of the institution's policies. The story moved from the "dash" structure listing highlights of the financial picture to a summary paragraph describing the declining population of the home, then into a series of selected anecdotes from the other stories and extensive quotations from the Wegner and Sheehan interviews. My chief guideline in writing was that a reader should be able, after reading it, to know the salient points supporting the theme and decide whether he wanted to read the other stories. They included:

The Sidebars

1. A somewhat sympathetic story about Father Flanagan and the years in which he founded and built the home.

2. A wry piece by Smith about the fund-raising operation, including its beginnings in 1939 after a professional money-raiser named Ted Miller saw the movie *Boys Town.*

3. A description of the tightly closed legal structure.

4. An account of Boys Town's commercial ventures (particularly farming and the sale of souvenirs to tourists) which raised some $200,000 a year.

5. The history of a short-lived effort in the 1960s to launch a Boys Town School for Exceptional Children.

6. Interviews by Iversen with alumni, including two of the first four boys with whom Father Flanagan began his home.

7. A complete listing of Boys Town's assets. This took nearly half a page in agate type, and was wrapped around a sidebar analyzing the holdings. Buffett was a major source of this piece, which pointed out that Boys Town earned relatively low return on its investments, and that its intangible assets might be worth much more than the "carrying value" at which they were listed. A selected list of stocks, for instance, was carried on the books at $7.8 million. At the time our story was printed, their market value was $35.5 million.

8. A description of Boys Town's land holdings, also carried at quite conservative values.

9. Rood's report on national changes and trends in child-care program philosophy.

10. Estimates of the amount of tax money Boys Town was receiving. This required Rood to call a number of states and, in a few cases, individual county welfare offices and courts. He got the figure well past $200,000 a year, then had to quit for lack of time.

11. Graphs and a story by Iversen comparing Boys Town's wealth with other indices (Boys Town's endowment was about three times that of Notre Dame University; Boys Town's net worth would have ranked it 230th on Fortune magazine's list of the "Top 500" industrial firms).

12. A story compiled by Brown from all of our interviews with directors of Boys Town, listing their reactions to our reporting.

13. A closing piece consisting of interviews with several current Boys Town residents of varying ages and interests.

As to when, if ever, Boys Town would have as much money as it needed, no one would say. What was it doing with all that money? Bergan's policy was to build the investment portfolio high enough to provide guaranteed income against any financial disaster. The place was wedded to an almost frighteningly successful money-raising program without a plan for spending the money.

This was a lot of type, and it took a lot of checking. We could have omitted some of it, but we felt it was important to lend texture and depth. I woefully underestimated the amount of time it would take to cross-check and revise these blocked-out pieces after we had finished the final interviews; it amounted, in the end, to all five of us working hard for a long extra day.

Thus, with this extra checking, with legal reading, and with last-minute cutting and fitting, it was late Monday before the copy was ready. We kept one special compositor on to set most of it overnight and reduce risk of the story's leaking.

Finally, Wednesday noon, after the presses began to roll, I had the pleasure of sending early copies of the *Sun* to the *World-Herald,* the AP, UPI, and the television stations, each copy accompanied by a friendly little note pointing out that the whole thing was copyrighted, and, gee, we would appreciate attribution to the *Sun* whenever they quoted from the story. This was pretty heady stuff for a publication that some folks used to classify as "secondary media."

Both wire services moved long pieces, quoting us liberally. The *World-Herald,* through gritted teeth, also quoted us for several days while scrambling for an angle of its own. *Time* and *Newsweek* both sent staffers to Omaha to do major pieces. Over a period of more than a year, we saw ever-widening ripples of replay in special-interest media (for example, fund-raising publications), general magazines, and books.

The directors of Boys Town held an emergency meeting on the Saturday after our story broke. They decided (as we had suggested in our editorial) to cancel all fund-raising, including the spring mailing, which had been printed and partly stuffed in envelopes. Two months later, Boys Town promised to establish a $30 million endowment for a center for the study and treatment of speech and hearing defects in children. In November, the board promised $40 million more for a national center for the study of child development.

The Follow-ups

During the rest of 1972, we carried three major follow-ups. The last one, in late December, summarized the changes in Boys Town during 1972. Monsignor Wegner was retired in October, 1973, and replaced by the Rev.

Robert Hupp, pastor of the city's richest parish. He was charged with implementing changes recommended after a seven-month study by Booz-Allen and Hamilton, a management-consulting firm. Hupp cut Boys Town's population to less than 500 to conform to contemporary child-care trends and eliminated such practices as reading the boys' incoming mail, regulating their schedules by bells, and feeding them in a giant mess hall. He began using Boys Town's funds to help those who wanted to go to college or take other post-high-school training. And he developed the first formal annual budget in the 57-year history of Boys Town. Unlike his predecessor, he willingly declared that the *Sun* stories "really activated the whole operation into the idea of doing something more."

It must be added that, in 1975, Boys Town again began sending out fund-raising letters. The rationale, Hupp said, was that the original endowment was built up solely for the concept of operating an orphanage for boys. To meet its promises for new programs outside that concept, the board felt it had to raise new money, he explained.

People still asked me about the story. "Did you stop to think about whether to break the story that way?" some would ask. "Certainly you knew it would disrupt morale at Boys Town, would cause some people to lose their jobs, and thousands to lose faith in a respected institution." Yes, we thought about that very carefully. If there were morale problems, they were Boys Town's. We weighed these against what we saw as the public's right to know about the use of its charitable resources. In our view of where a newspaper's duty lies, there was only one answer: publish.

"Have these stories produced long-lasting change?" others ask. Yes— no doubt about it. The change was slower and less fundamental than I personally would have liked. But I also have faith in the basic concept that good reporting aids public understanding, which I believe has produced tempered but implacable pressure for reform.

By 1976, Boys Town's net worth had expanded to $242 million and its boy population had dropped to 398. And several other things had happened:

- For the third consecutive year, Boys Town had made a report to the public on where it acquired its money and how it was spending it.
- Several new members had been added to the board of directors, including representatives from across the nation.
- The basic child-care program had been updated and improved.
- Work had begun on the new centers for the study of children and the study of hearing and speech defects.

I believe the project still stands scrutiny as a "how things work" story. We did not allege any criminal acts. We were not writing about crime, but about institutional inertia. The people who ran Boys Town had been follow-ing an ancient institutional rule: if something is making money, leave it alone.

I hope we did something else. I hope we encouraged newspapers and reporters of the future to meet their obligation to report on the institutions of their society.

III

IDEAS
AND ISSUES

10

The Institutions
of Our Society

MUCH OF latter-day investigative journalism has concentrated on individuals, their peccadilloes and their piracy. Such stuff is often highly readable. The play it gets usually reflects conventional editorial wisdom about what people will read, watch, listen to, and talk about. But it also reflects, in my mind, undue concern by editors with traditional definitions of news: single spectacular incidents, events, conferences, court actions, and political fire and counter-fire.

A reporter and his audience become bored and frustrated chewing over and over the standard fare of political chicanery, misfeasance and malfeasance, influence peddling, business embezzlement and stock swindles, sloppy or corrupt professional practice. If they remain preoccupied with these single-case stories, they may miss the main point: the nature of the system itself. The thoughtful reporter, then, is led to contemplate the institutions that condone, fail to control, or even foster corruption. Behind the story of the individual gone wrong or the individual done wrong is often the story of an institution incapable of performing its duties. It is from stories about our institutions, when they are well executed, that meaningful change in the system is most likely to come. Most institutional problems are complex and rooted back in time. They transcend administrations and transcend politics, Clark Mollenhoff says.

The powers of government are limited. Americans, therefore, have created a host of institutions to serve the specific interests of different publics. They have also created institutions to serve the interests of the public at large—"the people," as it were. These institutions may be governmental, quasi-governmental, public in purpose but nongovernmental in origin, or strictly limited to technical functions.

These institutions may be governmental (bureau of employment services, public utilities commission, economic and community development office, consumer affairs bureau), quasi-governmental (water development district, council on aging, program for the mentally retarded, state rural electric cooperative), public in purpose but nongovernmental in origin (state pharmaceutical association, state restaurant association, cancer association), or strictly limited to technical functions (state geological survey, state building authority, state construction trades council, canners and food processors association).

All these institutions should interest the investigative journalist. I have often said (and the thought is not exclusively mine) that a basic duty of the newspaper is to examine all of the institutions of its society and to report how they work—now how they were designed to work or how their leaders claim they work, but how they *really* work. As Marcia McQuern of the *Riverside* (California) *Press-Enterprise* has put it:

"The stuff that gets investigated is the crooks. But that's the easy stuff. . . . Institutions that don't work the way they ought to are not as dramatic, but if you put the skills of investigative reporting there, you can do some real good."

That's what this chapter and the next three are about. We will look at several levels and types of institutions, public and private; at the relationships between them and their clients, and at ways in which to research stories about them.

DEFINITIONS

Dictionary definitions of the noun "institution" speak of "an organization, establishment, foundation ... devoted to the promotion of a particular object" and of such things existing "within society." The sociological definition speaks of an institution more in terms of an idea: "a well-established and structured pattern of behavior or relationship that is accepted as a fundamental part of the culture, as marriage. . . ."

For our purposes here, an institution is defined as a body of persons working through mechanisms they have designed and control in order to serve common interests which they have defined. What is important is that institutions are created by people and make their own rules. Most are created and supported by such large numbers of persons that they have a power and inertia (both at rest and in motion) of their own. Their formal decisions are usually collective ones. The decisions may be formulated and promoted by relatively few persons, but they are ratified by much larger populations. These populations agree on their goals and define the rules (subject only to principles of law) for achieving them.

A simple analogy: In some respects, an institution is like a dinosaur. It has a large body and a small, slow brain. Innately, it is neither imaginative nor aggressive, but once its power has been activated and directed, results are inexorable. It leaves big tracks wherever it goes. It is designed for the long haul rather than the short sprint. Once it has grown to adulthood, it usually protects itself and its territory fiercely.

Society tends to create its institutions along dinosaurian lines for obvious reasons. It wants institutional actions to be deliberate. It wants institutions to have sufficient power for limited purposes, but not enough to destroy the delicate natural order. It wants institutions to be durable, to carry on long-term purposes and causes.

Well and good. But our metaphorical dinosaur also has inherent weaknesses. It can be fooled by cunning people. It can be hypnotized by a skilled sorcerer, making its gestures meaningless. It can be knocked kicking by a well-directed blow to a vital point. When this happens, the wild thrashing of its extremities can harm others nearby. And when it dies, the stink and the mess can be awful.

ANALYTICAL QUESTIONS

The conscientious reporter considers these attributes when he contemplates an institution. He tries to discover its meaning and purposes and to determine whether those purposes are worthwhile and, indeed, are even being pursued in the given case. If the institution is in pursuit of its purposes, he merely relays this information to his audience without much interpretation. But if he finds the institution has gone astray and is impinging on the rights of innocent people, the reporter retreats to a safe distance, develops a plan for analyzing the institution, and then examines it from top to bottom, inside and out. While he is performing this investigative task, he must remember the personal and professional risks he is taking in working over the powerful pet of a large number of people.

What should a reporter think about when he looks at an institution?

Is there a public interest in its activities? If the institutional interest diverges from the general public interest, what are its impacts on my public? How significant are they? Does the public know what the institution's goals are? Are these goals being met?

When David Burnham undertook his examination of police corruption in New York City, he was guided by the question: "What are the barriers to achieving the stated goals of the system?" After he completed that project, he applied the same approach to his new assignment in Washington, reporting on the policies and operations of the federal regulatory agencies.

The public interest in an institution may be direct, obvious, immediate, as in, say, threats to health and safety. Or it may be less tangible, measurable only in influences such as that exerted by a lobbying organization. Or it may be arcane, as in the case of a group of nuclear physicists seeking to influence public power policy.

As an institution, corporate business, for example—along with its internal operations—historically has been a fourth force or element of the governmental system of the United States. These internal operations of corporate business are as fit a subject for rational public interest and discussion as are the operations of other institutions. Although anti-trust laws, safety laws, interstate commerce laws, and the Federal Communications Commission control the corporation, there are tax laws, subsidy systems, trade tariff policies, and special legal status to protect and preserve the corporation, particularly the large publicly held one.

Public benefits befall less obvious institutions far removed from the governmental-corporate realm. A group of recreation-minded outdoorsmen, for example, may incorporate as a club or association ostensibly for educational purposes. Using the guise of education, the group seeks tax-exempt status while providing few if any educational programs for its members or for the public. Funds earned are deposited in the treasury and spent for social or recreational—rather than educational—purposes. The group grows and later stages a public entertainment event, billing it as a charity performance and soliciting the support services of a charitable organization. In reality, the event becomes a money-making venture benefiting the club when proceeds are divided, with the bulk of the funds going to the club and the charity receiving only a scanty allowance. Since the corporation only—not its members or officers—may be held accountable, the members enjoy the further public privilege of limited legal liability. Unless intercepted by an alert reporter, the organization continues to con the public into attending a "charity" performance benefiting not charity but the sponsoring organization itself.

How accountable is the institution to the public? If the organization is legally incorporated, it has agreed to some degree of public accountability. It is receiving public benefits. It may be tax-exempt. It has official public standing and privilege (for example, limited legal liability) granted theoretically in exchange for a corporate charter. If it is soliciting money from the public, it has agreed to follow certain rules for the collection and disbursement of that money. It may receive tax funds. Even though its purposes are stated as nonpolitical and its activities are entirely legal, it is likely to have some influence on public thought.

Now a caution: it is easy and foolish to extend this kind of questioning into a meaningless quest for insignificant stories about useless information. You can dissect almost any operating institution and find all sorts of mechanical flaws and human failings. You probably don't have to go any farther than your own circulation department, newsroom, or business office to do so, and you'll probably get some public attention in doing it. But you will not be doing responsible institutional investigation. You will be wasting time, boring your audience, and exposing your medium to a lot of unnecessary flak.

In a speech to the Associated Press Managing Editors, Wes Gallagher, president and general manager, gave some examples of what he called "nit-picking wastes of manpower and space." They included "three-fourths of a column on the FBI going to Disneyland to learn how to conduct tours; that the FBI refused to make its internal telephone directory available to the press; that a state supreme court justice keeps a large limousine and is a luxury-loving, cigar-smoking bon vivant. Nothing illegal in any of these, nor significant either."[1]

DISCOVERING WEAKNESSES

Discovering corruption of individuals often leads to discovery of institutional weaknesses, as Al Knight and Richard O'Reilly of the *Rocky Mountain News* can testify. At the end of a 1971 series on bribery of a Small Business Administration official, they discovered that the briber had been outmaneuvering governmental agencies for at least ten years. The reporters wrote:

> Are state and federal regulations against stock manipulation effective?
>
> Is the public provided with sufficient information to protect itself from fraud and misrepresentation?
>
> These are just two of the questions raised by the three-month Rocky Mountain News investigation into the complex dealings of Denver stock manipulator Dalton Carl Smith. ...
>
> The Dalton Smith story, with its nationwide stock and business transactions, offers evidence that a reasonably clever and mobile man can outsmart most of the agencies regulating stocks and business—at least for a while. For instance:
>
> • Smith defaulted on a $75,000 Small Business Administration loan in 1961, but the $60,000 still due hasn't been collected.
>
> • Tax liens of about $100,000 were placed against Smith and his California company, Mojave Electric, but the money hasn't been collected.

- Tax liens of $66,000 were placed against a New Orleans construction company managed by Smith, but the money hasn't been collected.
- Smith hasn't filed tax returns from either Denver or New Orleans in the last seven years, according to the Internal Revenue Service. Yet there is evidence he's had income during that period.
- The loose corporate information requirements of Colorado allowed Smith to hide his central role in the resurrection of Telstar Inc. ...

The story went on to detail the failure of the Securities and Exchange Commission, federal and state bank examiners, the Small Business Administration, the IRS, and the Colorado secretary of state to deal with information that the man was engaging in fraud, the crime for which he was indicted only after the *News* broke its stories.[2] He was convicted in 1973 and finally went to jail in 1974, thirteen years after he had first come to the attention of federal authorities.

Questions to Yourself

The first question a reporter must ask himself is whether suspected weaknesses in an institution are organic. Are the weaknesses, in other words, built into the concept, methods, and goals of the institution? In Boys Town (Chapter 9), for example, they certainly appeared to be. The corporate board was essentially controlled by one person, the archbishop, and several of its members (attorney, architect, banker, merchant) did business with the institution, a situation hardly conducive to critical self-examination. The decision on whether a given attribute is a weakness or a strength depends largely, of course, on one's viewpoint, and the reporter most often takes the viewpoint of his reading public. An engineering society, for instance, may state "public service" as a goal in its corporate charter and bylaws, but most of your public may disagree with the engineers' dogma that competitive bidding for design services is not in the public interest.

The reporter, then, must arrive in his own mind at a clear definition of the reasons he has for investigating an institution. And he and his editor must be reasonably sure that their audience will care about the expected results. Once this has been decided, the reporter faces other questions:

- Where does the institution influence my public? How do I measure that influence?
- What kinds of records does the institution keep? How do I get those records?
- What other institutions have access to information about my target?

These are tactical and operational questions. They help the reporter develop his work plan. Especially if he expects resistance from the target institution, he will do most of his base-building and about half of his basic research before he asks any substantive questions of important persons within the institutions.

Getting Answers

Suppose—just for a moment—that you plan to investigate a major newspaper: how it operates, who has the power, how much money it makes, whether it is unduly influenced by advertisers, whether it exerts behind-the-scenes influence on governmental figures, whether it receives special treatment from taxing and law-enforcement agencies.

This would seem to be a tough assignment. Most local newspapers are closely held businesses, and the industry itself is protected by the constitution from direct government regulation. Hence, most of its records are "private."

But consider some of the other institutional relationships the newspaper and its people have. Think of ways in which to find records and persons who can answer your questions.

Within the newspaper are representatives of several institutions, formal and informal. It may recognize a chapter of the American Newspaper Guild; in most cases, it operates with mechanical unions; there is a management group; overseeing its policies is a board of directors, some of whose members do not always share the views of the editor. Within these institutions, there are often informal factions. In the guild, for example, a group of "old boys" may have fought the original collective-bargaining battle. Their views and insights may be radically different from those of more recent members, some of whom joined the guild only in order to get jobs.

Then there are professional and industrial institutions. These include the American Newspaper Publishers Association, which is largely concerned with legislation affecting newspapers, postal rates, union contracts, advertising-rate structures, and similar issues; the American Society of Newspaper Editors, whose interests may partly parallel but not totally overlap those of ANPA; the Society of Professional Journalists, Sigma Delta Chi. There are also national associations of circulation managers, production managers, travel editors, religion editors, even a struggling young group called Investigative Reporters and Editors. Each of these institutions keeps records, issues reports, holds meetings, makes public statements, publishes newsletters or magazines. Each has officers and staff members who may know the editor, publisher, or other executives of the newspaper, or who may refer you to former employees or executives.

Of course, the trade press, including *Editor & Publisher*, *Quill*, and the journalism reviews, should also be checked. These publications may have printed personnel news, earnings reports, content analyses, lineage reports, or other technical information about your target. The academic press (AEJ Monographs, for example) and university libraries may contain critical or historical studies.

And, despite the First Amendment, state and national laws exist that require some public reporting of the newspaper's activities. Postal regulations require that, early in October, the paper publish a statement of its ownership and circulation. The Occupational Safety and Health Act requires reports of problems and corrective action. The newspaper corporation's legal history is at least sketched in statehouse records. Its directors have access to the minute book. Its land holdings are in the county recorder's office. Its major debts for equipment purchases may be recorded in the Uniform Commercial Code section in the statehouse. Its tax assessment history is public record. And so on.

I belabor the point to emphasize the value of using other institutional records and sources before the investigative reporter starts asking hard questions and exposing his hand to the leadership of the target institution. The reporter must consider not only the tactical value of maintaining secrecy, but more importantly the value of getting information in order to ask intelligent, relevant questions when the time arrives for direct interviews.

Let's consider other types of institutions, their general characteristics and what kinds of stories they may yield.

GOVERNMENTAL INSTITUTIONS

In your own community, there are several major government institutions. In addition to classifying them functionally, as the civic books do, let's slice them vertically in order to expose some of their internal, complementary, and peripheral institutions.

Rather than look at the usual organization chart which places the chief executive at the top and shows lines leading to the people who report to him, we'll observe how these administrators have less obvious alliances.

Executive functions may be divided immediately into elected officialdom and appointed bureaucracy, civil service or noncivil service. Elected officials have special influence and power that derives from their direct connection with the public at large. Most have support from existing political organizations; some also have personal organizations. As long as they are in office, they have access to and some backing from the local establishment, the power structure. This power structure (see Chapter 11) is not exclusively business-oriented. It may include, through various institutional connections and obligations, labor and professional organizations and such influential voter blocs as public-school teachers and public employees. The support is not always solid, but it provides diverse lines of communication through which the elected official team can counterattack the probing reporter. Not everybody reads the newspaper these days, and certainly not all readers believe everything the newspaper tells them. Moreover, they may get conflicting accounts through television news, through a union newspaper, or through the political organization grapevine.

The fact that an institution may be able to influence readers through its own news channels shouldn't cause undue worry to the honest, conscientious reporter. It should simply guide his feasibility study and help him estimate how much of the public will really give a damn about the story idea. It will probably discourage the reporter from treating a single story about favoritism in a zoning case as a major expose. But it may force him to study 60, 80, or 100 zoning cases to prove that favoritism for one developer is part of a truly corrupt conspiracy against the fundamental interests of his readers. So much the better.

The types of stories most likely to develop—and most likely to interest your public—from scrutiny of elected officials relate to misuse of public funds, conflict of interest, personal profiteering, and abuse of power. The types that are most likely to bore your readers and damage your credibility are those of petty privilege and questionable judgment. If the mayor wants to redecorate his office, so what? The facts should be reported, but neutrally. Most of your readers believe rank has its privileges. Most will agree that a public official has to make a lot of difficult judgments, and should be allowed some mistakes. As long as the public is aware of the facts, that is enough.

But if the mayor moves into a new house, and if you can prove that the land was given to him (or sold to him at a nominal price) and that the house was built by a contractor who also got a nonbid (or rigged-bid) deal to build the new jail, which turns out to have a leaky roof—that is something else. The point here, of course, is that you must be able to prove systematic, quid pro quo trading of favors, and prove that it was done with intent to abuse the public trust. You may then have an indictable offense, well worth your investigative effort.

Although many journalists decry a listing of indictments as a measure of journalistic success, setting some such goal in your own mind during the feasibility study is worthwhile. A story geared toward this criterion will demand thorough research and tough final evaluation.

The Bureaucracy

The bureaucracy of local government presents a different set of problems. Its members are not directly accountable to the voters; rather, they are under pressure from the elected officers and from several ancillary institutions. Fairly or unfairly, the public expects more personal and professional integrity from its clerks, lawyers, engineers, planners, purchasing specialists, social workers, and other technicians in government than from the elected executives who direct them. The bureaucrats are the bone and muscle of governmental institutions that the public has created to deliver services. They are expected to resist bribery and favors and to perform their duties even handedly despite the intrusion of mayors, council members, and ward heelers.

The reporter who suspects corruption or systematic maladministration will do well to trace accountability as far up the official ladder as possible. If he finds that a bureaucrat was corrupted by political pressure from an elected official, then he has an investigative project worthy of his efforts, one with institutional overtones. If he can prove that the corruption was widespread but originated within the bureaucracy, he still has a significant story. But if he can prove only that an individual got away with an isolated deal—or a few deals—he has a routine crime story.

An important test of whether or not the story should be pursued is whether the institution proves itself capable of handling the misdeed. If the corrupt individual is fingered by the government and perhaps fired or sent to jail, the investigative reporter turns his attention elsewhere. But if the bureaucrat is shuffled laterally, then emerges a few months later in a position of power, still doing questionable things, the investigative reporter starts to look for bigger, more significant influences.

Bureaucrats have many opportunities to play games in their official positions. In February, 1973, Jeff Morgan and Gene Ayres of the *Oakland Tribune* uncovered one such game in a series entitled "The Claim Jumpers." They discovered that an appraiser working in the Mendocino County assessor's office had been systematically acquiring title to tax-delinquent land by finding persons with names similar to the owners' names, getting them to sign quitclaims, and then arranging to have the land title transferred to one of his cousins until it could be sold. The ingenious appraiser, John R. Feliz, had worked his scam in at least six northern California counties.[3] Only after the *Tribune* series did the district attorneys of the counties involved get together to develop a criminal case against him on charges of fraud.

Working with Bureaucrats. To become really good, an investigative reporter in government soon becomes aware of the bureaucratic grapevine. He will learn how the interests of bureaucrats in Agency A on the third floor may differ from those of bureaucrats in Agency B on the fourth floor. If something fishy is going on in Agency B, he can pick up rumors from sources in Agency A. Even better, the file clerk in Agency A may be able to give him a copy of a memo from Agency B. He will also learn to look for certain key points (the city clerk's office or the auditor's office, for example) where information or duplicate copies of Agency B's records accumulate and can be examined quietly.

A warning about bureaucracy: it can have surprising power of its own. There is a certain camaraderie among public employees. There are also public employees' unions and professional associations, and there are employee's lobbies whose support is important to elected officials. Hence, your suspicions of a payroll scandal in the public-works department may not get the indignant reaction you expect from the mayor. He may be counting on the support of the clerk's and accountant's unions in the next election.

THE LEGAL ESTABLISHMENT

Some judges in your state may be elected, some may be appointed. Their staffs represent a mixture of long-term civil-service bureaucrats, political appointees, and short-term, upward-mobile technicians or would-be professionals. And the attorneys—officers of the court, all of them—are members of several kinds of ancillary institutions. The prosecutors are members of the governmental-political establishment, as are the public defenders. The private lawyers may be members of specialized associations (trial lawyers, forensic lawyers, compensation claims lawyers) as well as city, county, and state bar associations. Together, they add up to something called the legal institution, itself an interesting subject for investigation. Within it run many threads of association, some almost invisible against the gray fabric of the larger institution.

The special interests of lawyers and judges are numerous and their manifestations unpredictable. It was fascinating to me, for instance, to read that the leaders of the bar association in Philadelphia in 1975 voted against the decriminalization of private possession of marijuana—not, it seemed, because they believed pot-smoking to be inherently wrong, but because veteran lawyers were afraid of the effect on their legal business. A senior member of a large firm explained in an open meeting that young lawyers needed courtroom practice, and that defending marijuana cases was a good way for them to get it.[4] Similarly, the great argument about no-fault insurance in the 1960s and '70s has been fought largely on the ground that such plans would deprive claims attorneys of lucrative business.

Any veteran reporter knows a dozen or more prestigious lawyers who were, in their late twenties or early thirties, devastating prosecutors of

professional criminals for two to five years, then went into private practice
to collect large fees for defending the same kind of criminals. And the
veteran knows several judges who, while perhaps excellent technicians,
got their judicial appointments (or party support in elections) primarily
because they had labored long at organizational work or fund-raising in
political organizations.

Examining the System

None of these statements is intended to imply that the legal institution
is innately rotten. They are to suggest some of the background interests
that operate within the institution, and to warn the reporter to keep his
eyes open and remember that justice is not always blind.

The legal system is probably as thorough and accurate in record
keeping as any in American life. Any court of original jurisdiction is dedicated to keeping a complete record of evidence, testimony, arguments,
motions, orders, appeals, and opinions. Its files are a mine of information—not only of the relatively straightforward decisions and orders, but of
the mass of depositions, affidavits, exhibits, and documents that lead to
those decisions.

In examining legal institutions, remember:

- There should be a record of every action, and the record should show
  why the action was taken. If the record is missing or incomplete,
  something may be awry.

- The duties and powers of the courts are usually clearly defined. The
  base-building phase of any investigation, then, is relatively easy,
  though it may be tedious. The broad rules of justice are almost
  literally engraved in stone, but the details in practice are infinitely
  varied.

- Hardly any one in the legal establishment exists in a pure state as a
  "criminal lawyer," "public prosecutor," or "general practitioner."
  In law school, in career changes, in political activities, and in dealing
  with hundreds of clients, most lawyers and judges have developed
  complex *personae,* with varying degrees of alliance or antipathy
  toward others in the profession. This pattern of complex and subtle
  relationships is also the basis of a pervasive and precise grapevine
  within the establishment.

- Bar associations should not be viewed primarily as stalwart guard-
  ians against corruption of the canons of ethics. Most bar associations are highly political, not so much in Democratic or Republican
  terms as in the brokering of more subtle interests, including the civic

and economic interests of clients. Like most associations, they are run by relatively few members. Senior leaders are reluctant to expose problems or to take strong public positions on controversial matters. The goal is often private compromise rather than decisive public action (a trait common to many professional associations other than the bar).

The opportunities for lawyers to get into illegal or questionable activities are limitless. Lawyers handle large amounts of money in behalf of their clients. They set up and dissolve corporations whose true purposes, possibly unknown to the lawyers, may be illegal. They have access to the most confidential personal and corporate information that, if misused, could bring them great financial gain. When they become judges, they are pursued by long-standing business and personal ties that could tempt them into maladministration. It is remarkable indeed that more do not succumb to the temptations.

In viewing the legal system, then, these kinds of story subjects arise:

Conflicts of interest. There is the lawyer who represents more than one party in a complex transaction; the public regulatory official who, shortly after leaving office, begins to represent clients he was formerly supposed to regulate; the judge who hears the case of a former client, or a judge who holds stock in a company that appears before his bench.

Judicial bias. The Barlett and Steele stories of Philadelphia justice could be replicated and perhaps refined in other cities. The *Paddock Newspapers* study referred to in Chapter 6 indicated insignificant differences in the treatment of hometown folks as compared to outsiders.

Off-the-bench impropriety. In November, 1974, the *Boston Globe* reported that a district court judge, Francis J. Larkin, had tried to deliver $1,000 in cash to the campaign fund of Gov. Francis W. Sargent, apparently hoping for appointment to a superior court position. The Massachusetts Supreme Court officially censured the judge for this example of impropriety and ordered him to pay the $15,000 cost of the court's inquiry.[5]

Prosecutorial failure. Sometimes rooted in incompetent police work or in public hysteria over a particularly heinous crime, slipshod work by the prosecutor can lead to innocent persons going to jail or guilty ones being freed.

Corruption of the plea-bargaining process. Any courthouse reporter who studies plea bargaining carefully will be appalled at the potential and actual misuse of the discretionary power involved in plea bargaining. Police informers represented by lawyers usually get a much better shake than the impoverished defendant who has no counsel.

Like many reporters, I spent several of my beginning years being unduly awed by the courts. I still have high regard for the system of American jurisprudence, and view the courage of men such as Judge John Sirica with admiration. But in any given case, I look skeptically at all of the parties involved, watching for hidden connections or patterns of favoritism.

LEGISLATIVE BODIES

Legislators are rarely full-time lawmakers. More often than not, they have private business interests. In city and county government, their duties described in the state constitution or charter may also include administrative or executive powers. Even in large states and in the United States Congress, they may have law practices, corporate directorships or other commitments. In Nebraska and a few other states, legislators are also occasionally registered lobbyists.

And because of the nature of their official duties—balancing the interests of all kinds of persons, associations, political parties, ethnic groups, business interests, and public employees—few of their individual votes can be successfully questioned. They are elected to make pragmatic judgments and achieve workable compromises on the basis of unmeasurable factors of philosophy, changing morals, and changing social needs.

In virtually all states (Nebraska may be the sole exception) legislators are active party politicians, subject to party discipline in exchange for party funds and organizational support at election time. Because their salaries are rarely above those of skilled blue-collar workers, they are subject to temptation and leverage from well-funded lobbyists and their corporate, professional, or union backers. A financially hard-pressed legislator may suddenly find credit easy to get when banking bills are before his committee; if he is on the health and welfare committee, he may find his doctor making house calls and then staying to talk about medical-insurance legislation; or members of the house painters' union may want to show their gratitude by redoing his house free of charge, with paint donated by a major wholesaler. In examining the legislative process, your major problem is one of tracing subtle or ephemeral relationships that are kept secret. The use of public records to build personal profiles is a key.

David Nimmer and Stephen Hartgen used public records in 1970 for their series on influence in the Minnesota legislature. They used the compare and contrast of records methods described in Chapter 3—to trace connections legislators had with various interests, then wrote ten stories that documented the fact that:

- Some legislators who were lawyers practiced before courts or public agencies whose budgets they controlled.

- One legislator obtained loans of $25,000 through men connected with three major lobbies.
- One senator bought land for $5,000 then sold it within a few years for $150,000. The firm that sold him the land was interested in legislation that went through the senator's committee. The senator also got quick rezoning of the land from Minneapolis City Commission, which had a package of bills pending before the legislature.
- One legislator was hired (and continued to practice) as a lobbyist by the state restaurant association after he supported legislation the association wanted.[6]

The Nimmer-Hartgen series illustrates the importance of building a case on patterns. The reporters could have offered a sensational individual story out of any one case, but they achieved far more impact by taking the time to document the pattern of special interest influence on legislators.

QUASI-GOVERNMENTAL GROUPS

Since the 1920s, there has been a proliferation of extraconstitutional authorities, agencies, commissions, and nonprofit corporations established to accomplish the proprietary functions of government. Usually they are at least one step removed from the control of voters; they are governed by commissioners or trustees appointed by a mayor or governor, subject to varying degrees of legislative consent.

On the basis of models created in the 1920s and '30s by, among others, Robert Moses in New York, these authorities build and operate such things as parks, bridges, airports, docks, stadiums, auditoriums, and convention centers. They operate housing projects, issue bonds, manage warehouses, lease property to private business, form holding companies and nonprofit corporations to execute functions in behalf of government. To structural reformers of government, they are creative instruments performing vital activities that would be legally impossible under existing state constitutions and city charters. Often they are exempt from laws requiring public access to records, bidding for purchases, advertised public meetings, and general public accountability. Because they are isolated from the elective process, these institutions are subject to manipulation. The reporter, therefore, would do well to check their activities periodically and to maintain files on the construction firms, architects and engineers, lawyers, bond counselors and underwriters who seem to do the most business with them.

In a different category of quasi-governmental units is the special type of governmental district that develops new suburban areas. It may be called a water district, sanitary-improvement district, development district or some other innocuous name. But typically it is a legal institution of government that has the power to levy taxes and sell bonds to finance streets, sewers, water systems, parks, street lighting, and other amenities. In some states, each platted lot in a subdivision is entitled to one vote in any district election. This means that until 51 per cent of the lots are sold, the developer and his backers control completely the spending of public money within the special district; practically, they control public decisions until most all of the land has been sold, whereupon they depart with their fortunes. Often, near the maturity of the bonds that financed the amenities, they leave the homeowners to face "balloon" payments on the principal.

Investigation of the worst of these districts typically reveals that the developer, his wife, his attorney and perhaps their banker make up the district board of trustees, which for several years has been meeting when and where it pleased with little or no public notice, keeping minutes that meet the bare minimum legal requirements and are locked in the lawyer's office safe. Dogged pursuit of the minute book may also reveal that the district contracted for its public works with a contractor friendly to if not owned by the developer; handled its high-interest bond sales through a bank of which the developer was a director (and to which the district paid arguably high fees); perhaps got its insurance and surety bonds through a company or general agency in which the developing group was interested— and so on.

Although one must stretch the imagination slightly to include educational institutions in the quasi-governmental category, one must recognize that public educational institutions are controlled by boards of trustees or regents, often political appointees. Budgets of the schools are governed by legislators. Public and privately endowed universities receive major portions of their income in grants from government agencies, particularly in health fields. State and federal agencies also provide financial help for students—abuse of these loans has been a fertile source of stories.

A privately owned institution may claim business privacy, but it is also required to file various summary records, licensing applications, and other state and federal government reports, and it also produces catalogs, bulletins, memoranda, and public-relations material that are relatively easy to obtain.

Both public and privately financed or endowed universities fall into patterns of institutional inertia or sometimes outright deceit. The *Riverside Press-Enterprise* encountered such a situation in 1973 when it set out to report on the growth of Riverside University, a onetime business school that, under new ownership, suddenly began claiming large enrollments as a result of a broad range of new academic offerings. The school turned out to be using a variation of the trade-school scam: an institution whose main purpose was enrolling students whose tuition was paid by Uncle Sam, and teaching them with faculty members whose credentials were either faked or somewhat inflated.[7]

In most states, the public universities have grown so large that they are almost unmanageable. They are spread out on multiple campuses, support competing departments and colleges, and are run by administrators squeezed between political pressures from trustees or regents and parochial pressures from tenured faculty members who have their own fish to fry. With what I would call almost undue restraint, a team of student reporters at the University of Minnesota in 1973 did a series on actual and possible conflicts of interests involving faculty members, several of whom were officers of major stockholders in firms doing business with the university. In one case, a professor used university facilities, research funds, and graduate assistants to develop concepts for a "speech compression" machine that he then patented and sold to the university, among others.[8]

In general, investigation of such government-related institutions is a little more time-comsuming than investigation of regular government agencies. The people in these institutions are not as used to dealing with reporters and they sometimes tend to avoid or obfuscate the policy of keeping public records available. They keep extensive records, however, and most of them are clearly public.

PUBLIC NONGOVERNMENTAL INSTITUTIONS

The ways in which to classify institutions as public but not governmental are endless. However, certain classifications are of special interest, such as business corporations, lobbies, labor unions, and charities. What follows is a brief discussion of some aspects of these institutions:

Business Corporations

Consider the political and social aspects of the business corporation that offers its stock and debentures for public sale, and hence is called a "public" company. Chapter 13 deals in some detail with the problems of covering their operations and policy decisions. Their additional interest to the reporter lies in these aspects:

- Millions of individuals hold investments in them; the personal fortunes of readers are affected by the ups and downs of corporations.
- Many corporations are the major suppliers of goods for the government. They are spurred by profit motives to obtain and increase their business, which sometimes leads to questionable sales and promotion practices.

- Through special depreciation allowances, research grants, industrial-development bonds backed by public credit, local tax forgiveness or deferral, and direct subsidies, these companies are often beneficiaries of government funds. Taxpayers have a direct interest in how this money is used.
- Most publicly held companies are big enough to have marked political influence in their factory cities, their home states, and in Washington, D.C. They actively seek special treatment by the government, and they have lobbies working on any legislation that tends to regulate them or affects their markets and their taxes.
- Despite their efforts, most large corporations are supervised to some degree by state or federal regulatory agencies, or both. Whenever a target industry realizes that regulation is inevitable, it plays a principal role in writing the regulatory legislation. And once the regulatory agency is set up, the industry naturally tries to influence it and limit its powers. There is a legitimate public interest in these relationships. Morton Mintz of the *Washington Post* has almost made a career out of reporting on the drug industry and its relations with the FDA.

The investigative reporter must be aggressive in examining the impacts of publicly held companies. He must arm himself with basic knowledge of the corporation's public effects, and he must be prepared to argue hard to overcome the traditional defense of "business privacy."

Critical Businesses

Publicly held or not, certain businesses whose goods and services are important to everyday life deserve special attention. These include providers of food, transportation, shelter, heat and light, health care, and communications. All have special laws pertaining to them, all are regulated in some way, all receive direct or indirect subsidies—and, with few exceptions, all have some protection for their mistakes. The radio and television industries, for example, undergo considerable regulation, but in exchange get renewable monopolies on their broadcasting channels. The newspaper business escapes most direct governmental regulation, but benefits from special legislation, such as the Failing Newspaper Act (a limited exemption from antitrust law), and, in most states, from some legally guaranteed and highly profitable governmental advertising. It also escapes much of the public scrutiny to which other critical businesses are subjected. I personally think it deserves more scrutiny and questioning—not only in the journalism reviews, but in the public print and broadcast media.

The *Minneapolis Star* took a bold step in 1975, for instance, when it published a series of articles reporting not only on its own management, financial position, and policies, but also on the opposition *Tribune,* the St. Paul newspapers, and the radio and television stations in the Twin Cities.[9] Arnold Ismach, a professor of journalism at the University of Minnesota, described it as "a landmark piece of journalism . . . the *Star* [became] perhaps the first newspaper to tear down the paper curtain surrounding the business."[10] Legislative reporter Peter Ackerberg, business editor Richard Gibson, and business reporter Jim Jones used standard investigative technique, including multilevel interviewing in all of the subject organizations, to put the series together.

The series ran in six parts each of which was a profile of a segment of the media. The premiere piece, a profile of the management, ran two full pages. The series probed into the finances of the corporations, their acquisitions and mistakes in acquisitions, and into such subjects as a management style change from the entrepreneurial to the more cautious, management-by-objectives manner.

Because of the entanglements most critical businesses have with government, masses of data are available on them as industries and as individual companies. To get at some of them, you may have to invoke the federal Freedom of Information Act and whatever state "public records" laws are available—simply because most regulatory agencies become quite protective of "their" industries. If you are targeting a company within a critical industry, therefore, you will want to find other sources of information in addition to the agency. Congressional committee staffs and files are among the best repositories of facts, analyses, and expert opinions. The trade press of the industry is also an excellent source of information. Base-building in these ways will help you prepare for informed questioning of regulatory agencies' staffs, and for reasoned argument for more public access to the agencies and their records. You should compile, compare and contrast information from all of them (and others cited in Chapter 13) before you start direct interviewing in a regulated critical industry. The corporate public-relations, legal, and executive staffs, you will find, know exactly what they are required by law to disclose. Your best hope for obtaining more information is through informed questioning which forces them to respond and to resolve discrepancies.

In general, it is bootless to start investigating a critical corporation or industry without an unimpeachable tip *and* solid documentation of the salient points of that tip. Reporters researching vague rumors and hunches have been known to disappear under mountains of meaningless data before ever getting to their first interviews. The best work has been done by reporters who were willing to invest years in studying a specific industry from all angles—social, economic, political—and then moving ahead on a specific story only when they have obtained expert sources either inside a given company or familiar with the industry.

Labor Unions

Regardless of what you think of their social value and the wording of their constitutions, labor unions are as susceptible to corruption as any other kind of institution. They usually have large memberships led by small, expert cliques. Many unions have accumulated pension funds and investments that give them enormous economic leverage. In more than a few cases, trustees of these funds have shown all-too-human tendencies to invest in companies owned by their relatives and confidants, to form their own insurance companies, and to commit other forms of hanky-panky.

As a result, labor unions are now required to file several federal reports of activity and sometimes even more detailed records in states that are not traditionally oriented to labor interests. United States Department of Labor Forms LM-2 and LM-30, for instance, show political expenditures by union locals and by individual officers. Records of lawsuits filed over union money, records of action by the National Labor Relations Board, and union publications often yield clues of irregular activity. And the patient development of inside contacts will eventually unveil, as in any institution, persons repelled by the organization's dirty politics and money-grabbing. The public and the investigative reporters of today owe much to the pioneering—and sometimes dangerous—efforts of reporters like Victor Riesel, Wallace Turner, and Clark Mollenhoff in the 1950s and Jonathan Kwitny and Seymour Hersh in the 1970s for the exposures that led to stricter laws of accountability for union officials. Hersh's 1976 series in the *New York Times* on Sidney Korshak, veteran labor lawyer, broke new ground in describing the often gray and obscure relationships among labor leaders, corporation officials, mobsters, and lawyers who avoid "labor trouble" by arranging sudden contract settlements, often without the knowledge or consent of rank-and-file members.[11]

Unions, of course, have become major political forces. The traditionally liberal-thinking reporter must be especially careful to avoid stereotyping labor-union leadership actions as unswervingly altruistic, just as he must avoid stereotyping every business executive's actions as venal. Unions have many public impacts more profound than just the effect of their contracts on the cost of living. Most national unions support active communications networks that influence the social and political ideology of millions of people. Some unions maintain expert technical staffs in fields like public health, industrial safety, consumer protection, and economic forecasting.

Lobbies

Lobbies are so numerous and so diverse that they defy classification. Some of the big ones—the unions, the utility companies, the United States Chamber of Commerce, the National Association of Manufacturers, the American Medical Association, the National Rifle Association—are widely known. But there are thousands of small lobbies in every state capital and in Washington. There are even lobbies for lobbyists—such as the associations of national executive secretaries and chamber of commerce managers. Lobbies are important to the smooth functioning of government because they are factories of technical information and well-organized avenues of access to government.

Lobbyists can also be sources of information for the investigative reporter. The reporter must remember, however, to check their self-interested statements. Lobbyists know a great deal about other people: legislators, public executives, lawyers, other lobbyists, and potential antagonists, which makes them valuable but sometimes risky sources. Lobbyists as a group cannot be expected to love inquiring reporters (though many of them began as journalists). They are risky because the lobbyists' grapevine is efficient and pervasive; they may provide you with information, but they will also provide information about you to your target.

And of course lobbyists are worthy targets of investigations. In the Tallahassee (state capital) bureau of the *Miami Herald*, Bill Mansfield and Bruce Giles have refined to a science the challenge of card-indexing the contributions of lobbies, lobbyists and leaders of industries to individual legislators. They then compare these figures with the legislators' votes on key issues.

Nonprofit Charitable Corporations

Many kinds of organizations, including lobbies, are incorporated "not for profit." But the category of nonprofit institution that gets probably the least attention is the one allowed special tax status under Section 501 (c) 3 of the Internal Revenue Code. This section of federal law covers virtually every organization that solicits money from the public for humanitarian purposes.

Many of these organizations go unwatched because, in every community in which they operate, they select directors or trustees who are prominent, influential, and widely respected by the public. How misplaced this respect can be was illustrated anew in 1975 when Larry Brinton of the *Nashville Banner* was assigned to investigate United Cerebral Palsy of Middle Tennessee. Within two weeks, he had compiled information so damning that it eventually resulted in the resignation of all sixteen of its directors, the firing of the executive director and her secretary (who was also her niece), and the suspension of the assistant executive director (mother of the executive director and grandmother of the secretary). Larceny charges were later filed against the secretary and against the president of the UCP chapter, who was also an executive of South Central Bell Telephone Co.

The *Banner*'s reporter (and the Tennessee attorney general, in a follow-up investigation) found that despite annual telethons proclaimed as big successes, less than a third of the dollars pledged found their way into local UCP programs. The organization was so short of money that several directors had to sign personal notes totaling some $34,000 to meet the payrolls. A car bought with UCP funds (from one of 32 different bank accounts) had been titled in the name of the executive director. Donors' money had been spent on gifts for board members, office workers, UCP officials and others apparently not connected with UCP.[12]

Within the context of institutional investigation, two aspects of the UCP story are of particular interest:

Brinton discovered and reported that at least six persons in the Nashville newspaper and television businesses had received regular payments from UCP. They included Robert Battle, executive editor of the *Banner*, who received some $4,300 in unrecorded payments over a nine-year period as a publicity consultant to the charity. He repaid the money after the stories broke.

Brinton had most of his information in his hand in February, but his publisher decided not to print it until after the annual March telethon. (Other circumstances did force a decision, however, to break the story two days before the scheduled telethon. See Chapter 11.)[13]

These factors hint of the "power structure" kind of pressures reporters often encounter when they report on local charities. Brinton's tactical problems were considerable, but he used good compare-and-contrast technique to solve them. In addition to obtaining the IRS Form 990, he held early interviews (with witnesses) of the woman in the middle of the mess, then checked and refuted several of her claims about the number and salaries of persons on the payroll. By cross-examining the auditors who had certified the association's financial statements, he proved that the books were inaccurate and misleading by normal accounting standards.

PRIVATE INSTITUTIONS

Can an institution be truly private? With the changing trends of judicial opinion, especially in civil-rights decisions about public privilege for discriminatory organizations, the question is becoming tougher and tougher. Nevertheless, many institutions purport to be, and are generally accepted as, private. Churches and social and fraternal organizations are the most numerous of these. Churches, of course, have the protection of the First Amendment as well as the tradition of centuries to support their arguments for privacy. Their clergymen deal in the most private kind of human problems, and my own view is that just about anything that church members want to do or say about their spiritual lives, thoughts, doctrines, and problems should be their own business.

I differ with many churchly types, however, when they argue "privacy" about the conduct of secular institutional business. Any institution, religious or otherwise, which accepts tax exemption or other special treatment from the body politic implicitly accepts public accountability as well. Churches as institutions have large resources of money and political connections. When they apply their power, it is a public matter. Every church should make a public accounting of any money it accepts from the public at large—that is, from other than its own members. And when churches actively lobby for public money, as in periodic attempts to influence legislation providing support for church schools, the accountability should be absolute. As a general policy, the media have a responsibility to report on any political activity—any attempt to influence elections or legislation—by the institutionalized church.

The record is replete with examples of the misuse of publicly donated funds and of outright hustles by some ministers. An example came to light in Denver when the weekly *Rocky Mountain Journal* (successor to the old *Cervi's Journal*) began examining three corporations set up by the Rev. Charles E. Blair: Calvary Temple, Life Center, Inc., and the Charles E. Blair Foundation.

Because the *Journal* had just two full-time reporters covering the entire business and political scene, the investigation was not a classic according to our Chapter 2 model. Len Ackland, tipped by a business source, interviewed several elderly persons who had failed to receive promised interest payments on investments they had made in the Blair Foundation. His story ran on January 30, 1974. Over the next six weeks, he developed three additional stories on the temple's operating deficit, on its attempts to sell some real estate, and on its commingling assets with the other two corporations. The combining of funds was a clear violation of law. By April, the state securities division, which had previously said the church's sale of securities was not subject to law, changed its mind and charged the pastor, the three corporations, and three other corporate officers with defrauding investors.

In May, Ackland's colleague Gordon Yale reported that two of the three supervisors appointed by the securities commissioner to salvage the operation had clear conflicts of interest. His story and later stories by Yale and Ackland helped expose a compromise that Blair and his associates had made with the securities commissioner. Through more than a year of investigation sandwiched among other duties, Ackland and Yale developed sources among disappointed investors (most of them elderly), among court aides and supervisors who were gathering documents, and among persons in official agencies who knew there were strong pressures to settle the case without criminal action. By early 1976, however, the pastor's No. 2 man, Wendell Nance, had been convicted of securities fraud and fined. Blair was found guilty on seventeen counts of securities fraud and fined. Both were given suspended sentences.

Neither of the reporters claim their work was solely responsible for the official action (Denver's two dailies generally followed up on the *Journal's* reports rather than generating their own). Without much question, however, their stories forced the understandably reluctant securities commissioner and district attorney to haul a church and its officers into court. If they had not, several hundred investors could have been wiped out. As it turned out, most of the investors got their money back.

I would follow similar policies about reporting on fraternal and social organizations. Only when their institutional actions impinge on public policy—or when they hide illegal activity behind a false fraternal front—do their meetings, motions, and membership rolls interest me. The fact that many fraternal organizations also operate insurance companies should intrigue any investigative reporter.

There are, of course, dangers in simplifying the categories and characteristics of institutions. Few exist only to serve a single, simple purpose. Most fulfill other functions—sometimes coincidentally, sometimes purposefully, sometimes covertly.

Churches certainly do. They are community and social centers. People form friendships there; people find spouses and in-laws there. A bible-study club may spin off a couples club or an investment club. Membership in a given church may denote a certain social status or political coloration. Because ministers receive a few perquisites (free golf at the country club, free lunches at business clubs) they may become carriers of messages from one civic faction to another, knowingly or unknowingly, gladly or grudgingly. The mayor's pastor carries extra weight in meetings of the ministerial alliance, at diocesan headquarters, or among the rabbinate. Nothing sinister about it. Just natural. That's the way things work.

Similar generalizations may be made about the ranking of social and professional clubs of men and women in any given city, or about the business institution that is the town's principal employer. The company does more than just business; it becomes a center of power. Its executives, through their work with the community chest, the symphony, or museum board, or in other institutional roles, dominate the choosing of civic priorities and the setting of community values.

The wise investigative reporter is sensitive to these pervasive influences. He reads the papers every day, including the business and women's news sections. He visits now and then with the religion editor, the suburban and district reporters—and, yes, the sports editor. Perhaps only in his head, but more likely in file cards and a notebook of organizational tables, he is keeping constant check on his community's power structure, on those who run its institutions.

11

Webs and Shadows

AS THE BEGINNING reporter progresses through coverage of politics, business, labor, government, crime, community organization and virtually any other real-world subject, he becomes aware of the existence of power structures. Formally or informally, he begins to define and chart these webs of influence, to identify the interests of their members, and hence to understand better why and how things happen.

HOW POWER STRUCTURES WORK

A power structure exists within every institution. Where the interests of institutions overlap, additional power structures develop to compromise the areas of conflict. Certain persons—call them movers and shakers—emerge as the brokers of power. They figure out how to balance, to merge the interests of blocs, groups, and individuals. They work out policies, sell their ideas to (or impose them on) others, and get a consensus to move in a given direction. Their success breeds success. Others accept their judgments and respect—or fear—their power. Persons who want to move up in the ranks curry their favor. These persons run errands, gather information, keep track of the dissidents, and use their own influence and leverage to advance the policies of the leaders. The leaders reward them with business, money, prestige, public recognition, or whatever it takes to motivate them. By ostracism, firing, withholding favors or at times even employing physical methods, the leaders punish those who do not go along with the agreed goals.

That's the way power structures work. The techniques are the same in a labor union, a political party, a business organization, or a women's caucus. And when the leaders of several power structures come together, the result is a community power structure, always a worthwhile subject for journalism, which seeks to tell how things work.

WILLIAMS'S PROPOSITION

Compressing and reinterpreting a great deal of American urban history, I will offer Williams's Proposition: today's community-power structures are a pragmatic, legal replacement for the old political-boss system.

The boss system arose in the nineteenth century as a result of the unprecedented, unplanned growth of the cities. Public roads had to be built; police and fire departments had to be established. Rudimentary water and sanitary systems became functions of local government. The bases for free public education were laid, and demands arose for massive new public works; city halls, jails, poorhouses, hospitals, schools, parks, courthouses, streets, tramways, lighting systems. First scores, then hundreds, then thousands of immigrants poured into major ports daily. For the purpose of meeting these demands, a new class of professional politicians emerged. It consisted of men who were willing to cope with the raw power of universal male suffrage and who could do business with the merchant, the financier, and the industrialist. They became known as political bosses, and they dominated the urban scene for more than a century. Perhaps best symbolized in mass memory by William Marcy Tweed of New York City, the boss operated from these major premises:

Political professionalism: He defined and organized the mechanisms to manage urban life. He built a base of popular power by providing the urban immigrant (boys and girls from the farm as well as craftsmen and laborers from abroad) with jobs, housing, a degree of access to government, and the crudest kind of social services.

Laissez-faire economics: He attracted cheap labor. He promoted transportation and communication to expand markets. He provided a friendly governmental atmosphere, and he encouraged high profits and minimal governmental regulation as incentives for business growth.

Social mediation: He conceptualized, perhaps even before Karl Marx, the existence of a class struggle and accepted the role of mediator. He solicited the votes of the masses in order to gain power; he obtained the acquiescence or active support of the wealthy in order to conduct the grubby business of government. He controlled public budgets.

The boss and his lieutenants sold building and service contracts to the businessman. They sold social services and offered relatively low taxes to the masses in exchange for votes. All they wanted in exchange was a percentage of every deal.

NEWSPAPERS VS. BOSSES

For generations, the system worked. Then, beginning in the latter part of the nineteenth century, the bosses' power began to wane. Historians continue to argue about what started bossism's long, slow decline—a process that covered more than half a century—but unquestionably the media were involved. Some credit the *New York Times* with instigating the reform and progressive movements in its investigative reporting of Tweed's Tammany Hall in the 1870s. The muckraking magazines of the early 1900s exposed "the shame of the cities," the power of the trusts, and the corruption of state and national legislatures. Newspapers—among them the *Toledo Blade,* the *St. Louis Post-Dispatch* and the *Kansas City Star*—not only exposed local corruption but also became active participants in the reform movements that followed the overthrow of the bosses. That the executives of other newspapers later followed their lead has come, as we shall see, to complicate life for the investigative reporter today.

Most historians agree on the emergence, from about 1900 to 1930, of two major schools of governmental reform—the social and the structural. Each closely resembled reforms urged by newspaper editorialists. The social reformers helped install officeholders who came to be viewed as "popular" bosses. They espoused a more active social role for local government, aimed at providing lower-priced public utilities (water, gas, electricity, and tram systems), free public baths, schools, parks, work-relief programs, libraries, and public hospitals. Their theory was that an enlightened mass electorate could be trusted to define public needs and provide financing through increased, progressive taxes. The structural reformers, on the other hand, strove to limit the powers and budgets of elected government. They sought stronger legal controls, limitations on officials' power, auditing procedures, at-large elections, professionally trained officials like city managers, and smaller bureaucracies. Their goals were defined largely by business values, and they wanted government operated by businesslike standards, including cost-effectiveness. As the twentieth century wore on, they tended to favor the establishment of nonelected quasi-governmental corporations, commissions, and authorities. As a general proposition, they distrusted pure, vote-oriented democracy.

Neither view won clear supremacy, and probably neither will. At their extremes, both concepts have their flaws. The result has been an uneasy balancing of concepts, usually through the mechanism of a community power structure. It is today's community power structure that seeks to handle the complexity of urban life, the fragmentation of functions, and the general distrust of pure democracy. The power structure has arisen because of the relatively limited power of elected officials, the growing sophistication of experts in using mass media to marshal public opinion, and general revulsion toward past excesses of unchecked reform movements, both structural and social. It is the power structure of movers and shakers that tries to ameliorate community tensions.

For our purposes, a community power structure may be defined as an informal coalition of persons of influence who share general values and can work effectively to achieve common goals. The particularly operative words here are "informal," "influence" and "general." They emphasize the fluidity that makes it difficult to trace exactly the workings of a power structure.

MESSAGES FOR THE REPORTER

For the reporter, this capsulized view of community history and sociology carries two messages. One: the media—and particularly local newspapers—found and fulfilled a crucial role in rooting out institutional ills in the old system. Two: the leaders of local media became key participants in the new system. In most cities, the publisher and senior editor of the newspaper (and nowadays the general managers of the leading television stations) have become central if sometimes diffident figures in the community power structure. In communicological jargon, they provide informational input and output for the decision-making process.

Today, the publisher, as a businessman, is expected to participate in decisions affecting the interests of business. The editor, as a newsman, is under pressure, sometimes direct but often unconscious and subtle, to pursue the goals set by the community leadership. It is true peer pressure. The editor sees and socializes with the power people; they assume that he shares their values and goals. Sometimes he values their friendship and patronage so much that his editorial judgment is marred. The dilemma is a real one for the conscientious editor. Kenneth MacDonald, retired editor of the *Des Moines Register and Tribune,* puts it this way:

"You ought to be sure that your reporting is not distorted in any way by the fact that the top officers of your company may be involved [in a community project]. It would be easy to say, 'Well, you shouldn't be involved in anything because it produces a conflict of interest.' But when you think of the newspaper in a city this size [300,000] there aren't too many institutions that are really going to take an interest in the long-term life of the city. If the newspaper as a business holds itself completely aloof, you are taking a fairly sizable chunk of the community out of the planning process."

In giving a specific instance of the editor's dilemma, MacDonald cites the efforts to build a new civic center in downtown Des Moines:

"This newspaper's officers—the president particularly—are taking a very active role. He's helping solicit money, on the theory that a city can't go on existing as a cultural and sociological entity if it isn't anything but a collection of shopping centers. . . . So we are trying to divide ourselves down the middle. We're trying to allow the people who do not have an editorial connection to participate in the planning and fund-raising—but in the meantime we're encouraging our news staff to cover this just precisely as they would any other project. I wouldn't solicit a dime for it because I'm primarily identified with the editorial side. That isn't any easy answer, it's just an illustration of how difficult the problem is."

Let it be stressed right here that the community power structure is not, *per se,* a creature of the devil. Conceptually, it is reasonable. It is not always monolithic; indeed, in communities of more than a few hundred thousand people, it is usually in flux and tension as coalitions evolve and dissolve around specific issues. But like any institution, it is susceptible to manipulation and corruption, just as the old boss system was. And just as under the old boss system, when one set of interests captures the machinery and imposes its own oligarchy, the effects on the dissenting minority can be quite abusive.

POWER STRUCTURE GOALS

In all too many cases, I suggest, this abuse of power and of minority interests has happened in medium-size to large American cities. Those in the power structure select and elect the politicians under this proviso: "As long as you serve our interests, we will keep you in office."

In such situations, these principles tend to dominate:

• Government powers must be limited. There must be tax incentives and freedom from regulation for business.

- Physical growth of the city is a major goal. Growth attracts labor and provides demands for goods and services.
- The popular vote on issues should be avoided. To whatever degree possible, the machinery for raising money, organizing public opinion, and establishing community priorities should operate outside the written structures of state constitution or city charter.
- If there is a potential profit in any program or project, let business—especially local business—do it. This is a blunter translation of the dicta by Abraham Lincoln and others about government's doing for the people only what they cannot do for themselves. A great deal depends, of course, on one's definition of "the people."
- If a need cannot be met through profit-motivated business, then let the government handle it—but contract the work as much as possible to business.

In operation, the system has certain self-fulfilling characteristics. The dominant interests define the goals, establish the ways and means of meeting them, declare the results to be socially desirable. They arrange the contracts on terms that meet the private, professional, or corporate goals and needs of power-structure members.

If cornering profits were the only controversial aspect of the system, life would be fairly easy for the reporter. For without questioning priorities—or the means by which they were decided and met—he could simply report on the visible division of the proceeds. But the conscientious reporter knows that public interest goes far deeper than curiosity about profits and possible payoffs. Agreements reached privately among members of the power structure mean that public policy is being set without the participation of the mass of people who will be directly affected. If, for instance, the power structure directs its efforts toward attracting new residents to the city, it means public resources may be diverted from improvements in the older part of town. If a new public art museum is built, it means the annual cost of operation must be built into future budgets. If 90 per cent of available transportation money is put into new freeways, it means 10 per cent or less is available for exploration of alternative systems.

If these decisions are reached by a truly public process, fine. But they rarely are. More typically, the decisions are reached by a relatively few persons with special interest in the outcome, and then relayed to the masses through a publicity campaign. People without access to the power system—people whose homes, families, and jobs will be affected—have little chance to influence the decision.

In a small community, word of mouth may suffice to tell everyone that a key decision is in the making. But in larger communities, the decision-making process becomes less and less accessible to the ordinary citizen.

By the time the community grows to a hundred thousand or so, the workings of society have become too complex and the power network far less visible. The bonds of friendship and membership in relatively homogenous groups have been strengthened by more calculated transactional relationships. People may be denied access to the system simply because they cannot know how the system works. Once more, the reporter's challenge becomes one of telling how things work. Once more, his goal is not to discover criminal activity, though he is always on the alert for signs of it.

I recommend general, descriptive stories about local power structures as good starting points for reporters who want to develop investigative skills. In executing this kind of story, the reporter is also building valuable background. There are several ways in which to undertake stories on the power structure. Here are four: identify the influential, describe the case of a particular leader, draw profiles of the real leaders, examine the local charities.

IDENTIFYING INFLUENTIALS

Perhaps the simplest and clearest story on the local power structure for the average reader to grasp is to point the finger at those with influence. I did an identification story for the *Sun Newspapers of Omaha* in 1966— and ten years later I was still getting occasional requests for copies. To do the piece, I read a good deal and talked to a sociologist friend, then did a small-scale feasibility study to decide which were the most prestigious banks, businesses, and civic boards in Omaha. I then talked to about fifteen men—former mayors, business board chairmen, and old-family heads—to build a list of thirty to thirty-five institutions they regarded as most important. Then I obtained current and recent lists of the directors, trustees, and officers of these organizations and started making file cards on each individual. I listed his political party affiliation, his primary business, his directorships in other businesses, his civic trusteeships, his in-law relationships, his major customers and clients, and miscellaneous notes about his interests and expertise.

I wish I had had a computer. I wound up with more than 250 individual file cards, which I laboriously and somewhat arbitrarily sorted into three major groupings:

1. The twenty most influential men in town. Each was a member of three or more of the thirteen dominant business, cultural, and civic boards in addition to his own business.

2. About 100 near-influentials, generally men in their thirties and forties. Most were active vicars—senior executives, consultants, or close associates—of the top twenty. Some, however, were chosen because they

represented special interests such as labor, blacks, educational institutions, religious or ethnic groups.

3. About fifty professionals and technicians—lawyers, architects, economic specialists—who not only did business with and for the influentials but had gained enough stature to sit on two or three boards.

The rest of my cards were unclassifiable. On them were the names of those of old families, a few harmless alcoholics, perhaps a score of seventy-five- to ninety-year-olds who had become inactive, and a few middle-age types who had shown promise but somehow failed to penetrate the inner circle.

I talked to about fifty persons in the three significant groups, and I got most of them to discuss fairly freely their own roles. They told me how they made civic decisions, how they sold them to the public, how they selected young prospects for civic advancement. I found that much of the talk centered on a couple of bond-issue proposals that had failed at the polls despite strong power-structure support. Hence, this lead:

> There's a gap about 20 years wide and three elections deep in Omaha's power structure.
> The results:
>
> • The really powerful men—those with money, prestige, time, and a desire to do good works—have largely withdrawn into a circular world in which they serve on each other's boards, raise funds for each other's cultural and welfare projects.
>
> • Some executives, influenced by the experience and advice of superiors, are reluctant to enter the quasi-public work of "civic affairs."
>
> • Political leaders, estranged from the power structure by a series of unhappy experiences, find it hard to muster top-level support for major community improvements. . . .[1]

I learned several things from the project. One was that the classic power structure, the one described in the sociological literature of the 1950s, was undergoing change, much of it resulting from the social and political upheavals of the 1960s. Although the twenty most influential Omahans remained powerful, their strategies had been refuted by the voters and they were having to open their councils to new voices.

I also learned not to rely solely on quantitative data. Although virtually every one of my influentials agreed with my methodology, it wasn't until after the story appeared that several of them asked: "Why did you leave Mo Miller off the list?" He was only the president of the biggest bank in town. Checking back, I discovered he tended to avoid other board memberships, so he failed to meet my numerical test. If I had measured the number of Omaha National Bank officers on the prestige boards in the city, I would have realized that Miller had vicars on almost every one of them.

Another weakness was that I didn't describe very well the network of information that served the men at the top. I concentrated too much on their personalities. In retrospect, I wish I had traced the flow of ideas through this network and showed how they were modified as they went up and down the power structure. Had I done this, I would have pinpointed much better the influence of the board of the United Community Services (it may be the Community Chest or United Way in your community) and its budget committee and professional staff not only on "private" charitable policies but on the policies of hospitals and of city and county health and welfare services. I certainly would have described better the impact on the community's playhouse, symphony orchestra, and art museum of persons interested in promoting fund drives for other causes.

I did obtain some discussion of the trading of favors that goes on among the powerful. Later experience, based on much closer observation, taught me that ego-stroking is a powerful tool in the hands of the influentials. Once a senior leader has determined that his economic interests are going to be helped (or at least not hurt) by supporting a civic program, his acceptance of the general chairmanship can be motivated by nothing more tangible than a bronze plaque worth maybe $50 that he knows he will receive when the campaign is successfully completed. Once he has received the plaque from the hands of another influential, he also knows that he can call on that person to spearhead a drive for him—and that he will have to arrange a testimonial dinner and plaque to balance accounts.

THE CASE STUDY

The single case method is also a good way in which to describe the exercise of civic power. The *Minneapolis Star* used this method effectively in the 1960s to trace influences on a few major public-policy decisions. One series of articles detailed the battle of social and political interests over the appointment of a controversial new member to the city's human-relations board. Another, by David Nimmer in 1969, was labeled "St. Paul Decision Makers" and discussed the failure and eventual success of a six-year effort to rejuvenate the central core of Minnesota's capital city. The series ran some 12,000 words, broken down into ten stories that ran for a period of twelve days. The series took a historic approach, covering the period from 1956 to 1969. Here is a sample from early in the series:

St. Paul's downtown was in trouble that day in 1956 when Philip Nason drove over to Minneapolis to see the Dayton brothers about building a Dayton's store in St. Paul.

And Nason—who at the age of 44 had already served two years as president of St. Paul's First National Bank—knew how serious the trouble was.

"We didn't have a new hotel in the downtown," Nason said, "nor did we have a first rate merchandiser such as Dayton's."

"All we had were three third-grade department stores and the downtown was dead."

Nason was convinced that someone had to do something about the downtown and he wasn't afraid to take the lead.

Nason wasn't a member of the "old-money" class. He was proud of, and often talked about, the days he and his brother spent washing cars for money to go to high school.

During his college days, first at Carleton and later at Harvard, Nason began to develop a "civic" consciousness.

It was an attitude that meant a man involved himself in the activities of his community, helped make the decisions which shaped its future.

This philosophy hadn't been shared by many of the city's older businessmen who were more content to remain aloof from St. Paul politics and development. . . .

So Nason didn't have to push aside any old, family barons to become St. Paul's premier mover and shaker as far as downtown development was concerned. He merely stepped into a void. . . .[2]

In subsequent stories, Nimmer described Nason's overhaul of the St. Paul Chamber of Commerce and running battles with legislators, with an attorney for opponents of the civic center, and with members of the power structure—battles that culminated in a 1969 decision to build the civic center and sports arena. Here are excerpts from the closing portion of Nimmer's final piece:

. . . The Civic Center issue offers other clues about the process of decision-making in St. Paul:

• *St. Paul suffered from a "sugar daddy" complex—Let one of our millionaires do it for us. And there was a limit to what the wealthy men were willing to do.* . . .

• *The new leaders in Civic Center were not scions of wealthy families but part of a new generation of professional managers.* . . .

• *Members of the City Council, with perhaps one exception, never took any key leadership roles.* . . .

• *Personal feelings as well as logical arguments played important roles.* . . .

• *The decision-making group in the Civic Center issue remained fixed. Almost no new faces appeared during its six-year history.*[3]

To write his case-study series, Nimmer took three months, reviewing files, tracing the history of legislation, reading court records, and, finally, interviewing and re-interviewing more than a score of the acknowledged civic leaders. To do a meaningful case study on a contemporary issue, however, a reporter rarely has such chunks of time. He is lucky if he has as much as two weeks to interview in depth fifty, sixty, eighty persons. To do it successfully, he must know intimately the private as well as the visible channels through which power flows. What lawyer would most likely carry messages from Corporate Executive A to Politician B? What assurances will Labor Leader C want before he agrees to support Councilman D?

One way in which to handle breaking case studies is with the ad hoc team of reporters whose members know all the key people. Another is for an investigative reporter to develop the contacts through a thorough "how things work" piece on the influentials, then keep his files and sources current in readiness for a new case.

KEY-MAN PROFILES

The key-man profile is another good method for describing power structures. The *Maine Times* carried an interesting example of the use of profiles in 1974. The *Times'* cover said:

Q. WHO RUNS MAINE?

A. THESE FIVE MEN.

The story inside carried short biographical boxes on each of the men, surrounded by text containing passages such as these:

The men who run Maine do not derive their power from any public office they hold but instead from their influence in the public sector.

A *Maine Times* investigation led to five men who are the core of Maine's power elite. There are others who have great influence, but if you trace the decisions which have affected Maine most in the past twenty years, you keep coming back to these five men.

While the positions the men hold in the business world gave them their potential power, it is equally important that they have chosen to exercise that potential—each in his own way.

The five men are:

William Henry Dunham, chief executive officer of Central Maine Power, whose influence spreads to practically every New England power company; and whose views are listened to by a major paper company, a bank, a private college, and public television.

Robert Nelson Haskell, president of Bangor Hydro-Electric, Maine's second power company, who ruled the Legislature with an iron hand for four years and whose influence is felt on a bank, on a major land-holding company, and on the state university.

Horace A. Hildreth, former Maine governor, former U.S. ambassador, former university president, head of a mini-conglomerate in Maine communications and still a major force in Maine Republican politics.

Edward Spencer Miller, who runs the Central Maine Railroad, supports oil Down East, and who emerges as the tough guy of the group. His influence spreads to other industries, a major paper company, and a couple of banks.

Curtis Marshall Hutchins, founder of Dead River Co., which is into oil distribution, timberlands and lumber. Hutchins is the most ubiquitous of the group. He is one of Maine's leading entrepreneurs, and aside from his links to the traditional auxiliaries of power—banks, a paper company, railroads—he has also served on environmental boards and study groups for planning Maine's educational future. . . .

The exercise of power is seldom so obvious. Nor is it always so predictable. Ex-governor Hildreth, for instance, has thrown his television stations into the battle against oil prospecting on the Maine coast. . . .

In trying to analyze the power of these five men, several factors become clear. First, they form something of a club. Although relations between them are not always ideal, their paths constantly cross.

Each one is significantly involved in Republican politics.

Each one has spread his base beyond the corporation which he heads. The usual method for spreading this base is directorships on other corporations. And, after a while, the directorships begin to overlap.

In Maine, paper companies, banks and railroads have traditionally shared, or interlocked directorates. The reason . . . was a lack of qualified people (according to the businessmen who dominate such Maine boards. . .). . . .

If you ask Hutchins outright if he or his company benefits in any way from his board memberships outside Dead River, he replies with a stern "No!"

But if you turn the question . . . in hypothetical terms, he gives a different kind of response. For example:

"Mr. Hutchins, isn't it possible for a person who serves on directorates of several companies to use information gained to his own company's advantage?"

"I couldn't deny that," Hutchins said. And he leaned back in his chair and smiled. Almost chuckled. . . .[4]

Another excellent piece in the key-man genre was done by Alice Blankfort in the weekly *Chula Vista* (California) *Star-News* in April and May of 1972. The subject was C. Arnholt Smith, who was virtually exempt from critical examination by San Diego's two dailies while controlling scores of corporations with paper values near $1 billion. After *Life*'s investigative team in March reported on Smith's efforts to squelch a Department of Justice investigation of his power and interests, Blankfort compiled a three-part series on the ways in which Smith exercised influence in the operation of local banking, local airlines, local ground transportation, the San Diego Padres, a local hotel, and several other city activities. She went into court records more than thirty years old and delved into library books, newspaper files, confusing corporate reports, election-contribution lists, and similar sources to put together a series on Smith's self-dealings and political contributions at all levels, from local elections to the Nixon presidential campaigns. Despite weeks of effort to talk to Smith and his associates (including long waits in his office lobby and a hand-delivered two-page list of questions) she was never able to get the key interview. Nonetheless, she came up with leads such as this one:

For almost 40 years, people in San Diego County have been gossiping, speculating and whispering about one man—and never so much as at present.

Today, people in Washington and in Sacramento—perhaps even in Podunk are asking the question San Diegans have chewed over for decades:

Who is C. Arnholt Smith?

Through the years, bits and pieces have emerged. The outlines of the vast financial empire he has built dominate not only the luncheon chitchat of local businessmen, brokers and bankers, but also in concrete fashion (Westgate Plaza Hotel, U.S. National Bank Building, Fashion Valley) the landscape of San Diego.

Too, the shadow is reaching into the national political arena, with a Senate committe probing accusations of favoritism by U.S. Attorney Harry Steward to Smith's right-hand man, Frank Thornton. . . .

One measure of the awe, indeed fear, that this question evokes is the reaction of those who are asked it. During the past three weeks, I have asked this question of more than 40 San Diegans—political insiders, bankers, journalists, executives, lawyers, hostesses. Curiously, not a single one wanted to be quoted, not even the several who had nice things to say.

Even when assured that they will not be quoted, many who have good reason to hate and fear C. Arnholt Smith continue to describe him as "charming," "a great benefactor to San Diego," "kind," "a very loyal man" and "a financial genius."

Balancing the picture, understandably, are other descriptions—"ruthless," "greedy," "a man without friends" and "a virus."

The descriptions . . . in many ways reflect the moral conflict that may be inherent in the American System.

On the one hand, there is admiration for the self-made man.

On the other hand, there is growing distaste for the methods and manipulations that may be necessary in order to reach not just the corridors, but the innermost councils of pelf and power reaching right up to the White House itself.

What need a man do to gain personal control of an empire worth almost $1 billion? And at what cost to public and personal morality?[5]

Writing such a lead requires the investigative reporter to present facts supported by records, which Blankfort did each Thursday for three weeks. Her final piece began:

In more than 50 years of dogged labor, C. Arnholt Smith has clawed his way from a grocery store counter to the summit of a financial empire worth almost $1 billion.

He owns four homes, and even claims a personal color—Smith beige.

He has shared intimate occasions with President Nixon and moves easily in the highest circles of Republican politics. He also has contributed generously to many Democratic campaigns.

Now beset by lawsuits, public hearings and press exposés, Smith maintains that his companies have been "badly abused, badly handled, not credited for contributions" by outsiders.

"When the time to check out comes along," the 73-year-old magnate told a stockholders meeting last week, "we will feel a great deal of satisfaction."

But the results of so many years of so much power wielded by one man, raise questions not only of the effect on stockholders in Smith's companies, but on the general public morality, the morality and ethics in our political and business processes, and even on the integrity of law enforcement itself.

Smith financed almost the entire San Diego County campaign of attorney general Evelle Younger, for example, through contributions and loans. Smith, his daughter and Smith's long-time associate Frank Thornton gave or loaned $37,821 out of $40,051 spent on Younger's campaign. . . .

A full Internal Revenue audit of Smith's dealings, according to one expert estimate, would take 10 to 15 agents a full year. . . .

Complicating such an audit is the fact that Westgate-California (of which Smith and family own 53%) has changed its own auditors four times in the past four years.

. . . Smith's long-time house counsel, C. Hugh Friedman, went into "private" practice . . . This means that corporation records which might have been subject to scrutiny are now "privileged," a confidential matter between an attorney and his client, thus not open to subpoena.

The change . . . came some 18 months ago [about when] Smith's long-time protégé and frequent business partner, John Alessio, foundered on the shoals of federal laws against tax evasion.[6]

OF POWER AND CHARITY

The charitable organization study is still another approach for a reporter to take in telling how things work in the community. Larry Brinton's coverage of United Cerebral Palsy in the *Nashville Banner* (see Chapter 10) became just one of a series of studies of local charities. Published over several months, his series was able to give Nashville residents a composite picture of how relatively few local leaders controlled their local institutions and set priorities and agendas for social action. From the standpoint of the investigative reporter, its most disturbing implications were in the pressures Brinton's publisher, Wayne Sargent, and his editor, Ken Morrell, felt in deciding when and how to use the story. When Brinton began uncovering scandal, the directors of UCP refused to talk to him until Sargent and Morrell accompanied him to UCP board meetings. The Gannetteer, house organ of the Gannett Newspapers, which owns the *Banner,* reported:

One of the first major questions was when to break the original story. Because most of Brinton's inquiries had brought no satisfactory answers and some of the responses had turned out to be false, part of the story could have been published in February, well in advance of the scheduled March 15 telethon to raise funds. . . .

Because of the apparent scope of the story and its possible adverse effects on well-managed charities, however, a decision had been made to delay publication until after the telethon.

But one of the UCP sessions . . . on March 10 was also attended by Irving Waugh, president of WSM-TV, which had contributed free air time for the telethon for the past decade. Because of so many unanswered questions ... WSM-TV canceled plans for the 1975 telethon on March 13 and the Banner went to press. ...[7]

Such are the pressures on editors and publishers who become, albeit reluctantly, ex-officio members of the power structure. They have to deal daily with community leaders (who in this case—as in most—included a labor leader, a congressman, a prominent minister, and other nonbusiness persons) who can and will argue that reporting the truth will hurt the community. Brinton was less than happy with the original decision to delay publication, but he was better off than many reporters in similar situations. His editor and publisher did back him when it counted, and did finally make the agonizing decision to tell how things really worked.

12

Buying and Selling Government

"THE GREAT AMERICAN GAME"

"In a rather quiet voice," psychologist Kenneth B. Clark tells us, "a recently retired vice-president of one of the largest corporations in America told the group that one of the persistent problems faced by his office was how to keep the accounting records of the corporation in such a way that they would . . . obscure the fact that regular operating expenses were payoffs to municipal officials to expedite . . . new construction. . . . Casually, this participant cited this as just another example of a prevailing functional immorality with which big business had come to terms."

Clark, a professor of psychology at City University of New York, was writing about a meeting of business executives, college presidents, judges, government officials, managing editors, professors, and theologians discussing ethical and moral problems of American society. He continues:

"I eventually asked why this powerful corporation did not bring this matter to local and federal law-enforcement officials. My colleagues clearly considered my question naïve. They reacted to my persistent questions as if I were an unrealistic child who did not understand the economic and political rules of the great American game."[1]

These are words to think about as you look at the institutions of government wherever you are practicing journalism. They underline the importance of understanding how government really works. You need to open your mind to the possibility that corruption exists in your town and in your state as it does about everywhere in American society. You should not accept the facile axiom that yours is an unusually clean town or an unusually clean state, and that the governmental system invariably roots out the few criminals who try to corrupt local, state—and national—politics.

Clark's words—and those of the experienced journalists quoted throughout this book—are also to be weighed in another connection: are you a pawn in the game? Consider the notion, if you will, that by not doing more critical and analytical reporting on government, you are tacitly condoning or perpetuating a system of misplaced values and illogical "rules of the game" that hurt the majority of your readers. By reporting only the official versions of the news—the occasional indictments and civil lawsuits surrounding the most flagrant corruption of government—you may in effect be validating the system. Conversely, by finding out and reporting on how things really work, you may help to build a base of public understanding that will militate—ever so gradually and sometimes even perversely—toward development of new values, fairer rules. For instance, the reporting in the middle 1970s on the magnitude of money spent by American corporations to bribe foreign officials and finance American political campaigns has had an effect. It has at least laid the base for grudging congressional consideration of new legal definitions of propriety and impropriety.

Assumptions and Values

To be a successful investigative reporter, you need to assume that the institutions of government are under constant and pernicious attack by both external forces seeking special advantage and internal operators who figure that graft is one of the perquisites of office. The assailants are not only corporations but unions, professional associations, and organizations whose stated purposes may sound entirely altruistic.

You need also to assume that within these institutions, most of the people are still either essentially honest, unaware of what's going on, or merely jealous of the grafters and graftees. This majority comprises your best resource, your best hope for doing reporting that will effectively describe our systemic problems.

"When I see someone in a position to take graft," says Lou Rose, "I try to think of all the worst things they could be doing. What are the inherent possibilities here, what is every single advantage that somebody could get out of this? You've got to train your mind not to accept anything at face value. Put down every single thing you can think of, no matter how incredible it may seem, and then gradually go down the list and cut them off: this can be done in this case, this can't be done, this is a possibility, but can I prove it?''

Rose's is a sound approach to examining the workings of government. Clark Mollenhoff, too, stresses the power of money. Mollenhoff, who cut his investigative teeth covering the Polk County Courthouse in Iowa, has suggested in an American Press Institute seminar that the way to start is to ''follow the dollar'' in the county courthouse.

> ''I do not mean the mere superficial tracing of the mechanics of collecting taxes and spending government funds,'' Mollenhoff says. ''I mean a detailed analysis of the loopholes in spending procedures.'' Mollenhoff suggests that the investigative reporter write ''a series of articles dealing in detail with each county or city office and covering these main points:
>
> 1. The law setting up the office, and all of the functions performed by the office.
>
> 2. The detailed information kept in the office and available to the public, and the reason for it.
>
> 3. The personnel of the office, the selection of employees, the handling of leave, and any outside business connections of the office holders.
>
> 4. The financial dealing of the office with an emphasis on the legal safeguards against fraud and how they are administered. This should include a list of those on the outside with whom the office deals and an explanation of whether business is done by bidding or otherwise.
>
> 5. The office holder's own analysis of his personnel, the efficiency of his budget, and the adequacy of laws applying to his office.''[2]

The reporter who follows Mollenhoff's suggestion will be accomplishing several things. He will be learning how to find, use, and interpret records; how to observe what is happening; how to interview thoroughly; how to compare and contrast information from records and interviews, and how to build a research base. He will be covering the lines of inquiry that are most likely to identify blatant corruption. Moreover, he will be preparing himself to go beyond the issue of conventional graft to issues that underlie public morality. He will be developing the beginnings of wisdom about how the system works.

Rules of the Game

Understanding how the system operates is important if the reporter is to retain his readership—and his own sanity. He may be disappointed at the public reaction to some of his early ''exposés.'' He will find out that in what Clark calls ''the great American game'' there are rules—which most of the participants and spectators accept—allowing certain levels of questionable activity. These rules are part of the set of values that define, at present levels of public understanding, the functional American morality. The rules are at times confusing. In a sense, they are analagous to the distinction made in the rules of football between belting your opponent with your taped and splinted forearm (legal) and hitting him in the mouth with your closed fist (illegal).

The investigative reporter's dilemma is in deciding how much "unnecessary roughness" or "personal foul" is in the spirit of the game. He knows that a certain amount goes on all the time, and that the referees overlook or fail to catch much of it. The reporter who applies only the criterion of legality and relies on the officials to catch the infractions has a relatively easy time. The reporter who tries to consider the spirit of the law—or, even more difficult, to question the moral basis of the law—is in danger of being trampled in the eternal progress of the game without ever having gotten the crowd's attention. Only the toughest and smartest survive to report the basic issues and to get the rule makers to consider change.

THE USES OF LAND—AND DOLLARS

"Follow the dollar," Mollenhoff says. I would add: don't limit yourself to internal leakage or to the crass, direct skimming of tax money by a bureaucrat or elected official. Think also of areas in which people outside of government can make big "private" money by influencing the decision-making process.

Land use may be the biggest single area. Bob Greene is fond of pointing out that the second Pulitzer Prize won by *Newsday* was for an investigation of the government of Islip, N.Y., that focused largely on land dealings between politicians and developers. If a local planning body decides to rezone a 160-acre farm to, say, fourth residential, it is enabling several kinds of people to slice up a pie worth at least $12 million over the next several years. The land itself may jump immediately in market value from about $100,000 to $800,000. Depending on who took the risk, the speculator and farmer will have different shares of a paper profit of $650,000 or more. Then come the developer, engineers, architects, lawyers, bankers, mortgage companies, financial consultants, building contractors, and real-estate brokers, all entitled to a share of the pie before the last young couple has plunked down $40,000 for a modest home. And this estimate does not include the potential generated for farmers, speculators, developers, and those whose adjoining land may later turn into shopping centers or apartment complexes.

So far, it's the American dream in action—a gee-whiz story for the real-estate page, as long as everybody has acted according to the law. But there are at least two aspects of the situation that should trouble the investigative reporter:

1. As a matter of long-term public policy, is this land-use decision the right way to go? What hidden and deferred costs does this decision impose on the public treasury and hence on the average working man who will pay the future bills? Is the local government's duty one of encouraging this process, or of considering less expensive alternatives?

2. What if everyone does not follow both the letter and spirit of the law? What if, as Clark has suggested, there are other, extralegal costs? What if a naïve (which is to say, inexperienced) developer follows the law and finds his rezoning applications or building permits hung up in the bureaucracy while his competitors' go sailing through?

Consider the first question. The official encouragement of urban sprawl carries several direct costs that are spread across the whole public-revenue base and hence become unaccounted subsidies to the successful developer. Highways must be built or extended to serve the new development. The school system must expand perhaps, leaving buildings in the older parts of the city underutilized. Property values in the inner city may be gradually eroded, adversely affecting the tax base. Public utilities must make new capital expenditures that become part of the rate base and are eventually added to customers' bills. The supply of productive farmland is directly reduced, and the more intangible values of green spaces are sacrificed to "progress."

And what of the second question, the possible violation of laws governing land use and conflict of interest? The collision between law and special interest has become a fruitful area of investigation for a relatively few newspapers that have chosen to spotlight it. Their editors and reporters recognize that the decisions of the community planning staff and commissioners—finally ratified by the city council—carry so much economic impact that some persons are willing to take legal risks to gain their benefits.

A Hypothetical Case

The reporter's interest may be piqued, for instance, if he hears that the speculator's wife is a sister of the wife of the planning commission chairman. But that's hardly an investigative topic, yet. It's information worth filing, however, because it may fit into a pattern, something the reporter keeps looking for. Does he find that this particular speculator is getting ninety per cent of his rezoning applications approved whereas others are getting only twenty-five per cent approved? Interesting, but still no exposé. Does he find that the same lawyer, banker, and perhaps the same architect or land planner work on all the winning cases? The reporter makes notes and keeps looking. He checks the reports of political-campaign contributions, looking for a line between the successful speculator and his associates to the major political group. He may have lunch with an architect whose clients have not been successful with their planning applications. The reporter makes typed notes, indexes and files them. He isn't ready yet.

Perhaps he decides next to do a thorough personal check on the key individuals involved (see Chapter 3). This research may indicate any of several possible links in the hypothetical chain. He may find that the developer is an officer or incorporator of five different small corporations; he may find that in a recent divorce suit the chairman of the planning commission filed a financial statement that showed he owed $25,000 to a bank whose president is a director of one of the speculator's corporations. Interesting.

At about this point the reporter begins to formulate an investigative assumption. He rereads the law on bribery, conflict of interest, and reporting of political contributions. He reviews recent and current studies on the social-cost trade-offs involved in encouraging the unbridled spread of urban areas in order to pursue the elusive goals of balanced economic growth. He then goes back and rechecks the political-contributions report, looking not only for the names of officers of the speculator's corporation, but also for the names of their wives and corporations of which they may be officers. If he has access to a computer, and if the number of documents he turns up begins to climb into the hundreds (each containing numerous bits of information), he considers designing a set of forms whose contents can be punched into data cards. On several sheets of paper, he pencils a rough chronology: the dates the various corporations were formed, the dates of rezoning actions, the dates of political contributions made by the interested persons. If the dates begin to form a pattern, he is now ready to postulate one or two or three investigative lines:

- That a systematic flow of political contributions or other favors are related to rezoning decisions
- That a speculator, by arranging a personal loan for the planning commission chairman (or a key city council member) acquired political leverage
- That the payoff was made in another way, by issuing stock in a closely held corporation or by deeding to the key politician (or politicians) a few choice lots in the proposed development

A Real Case

Proving a postulate, of course, is difficult. But the reporter can explore and write about institutions short of exposing outright corruption, and provide his readers with insights into what's going on. A small-scale example of this tack was provided in April and May of 1974 by a class of eight University of Minnesota journalism students. Each student averaged about fifteen hours a week for three months gathering information about planning and zoning in five suburban communities west of Minneapolis. They conducted about 125 interviews with politicians, land developers, real-estate dealers, citizens, planners, and legislators. They also ran public-records checks on key individuals involved in major rezoning cases. Including their weekly class conferences and their arduous writing sessions, they invested close to 1,000 student hours.[3] An experienced reporter or team could probably have done it in fifty to sixty per cent of the time.

Their stories were published in the weekly *Minneapolis Sun Newspapers*, a suburban group of papers that circulate in communities in the Twin Cities area. While the students didn't help put anybody in jail—and didn't try to—they did, in some fifteen stories, detail these circumstances:

- In one community (Maple Grove), the mayor and six planning commission members held land (either personally or through a corporation) that the commissioners were considering rezoning.
- In another small town (Minnetonka), a former mayor-councilman had great success in obtaining rezonings for himself and speculators. Another former mayor said of the man: "He's selling a service, the ability to get a rezoning through the council. But you can't blame (him). It takes a willing buyer, a willing seller, and a willing council."
- The enormous increase in land values. They traced the nineteen-year history of a piece of land from the time it was bought for $370 an acre and the bulk of it sold ten years later for $1,450 an acre—a gain of about 290 per cent. Over the next nine years, its value rose to $8,050 an acre, an increase of more than 450 per cent (one three-acre tract sold for $60,000, a gain of nearly 1,230 per cent in eight years). But also illustrative of the stakes involved, the 1971 purchaser, a developer, filed for bankruptcy less than three years later.
- In Minnetonka, the city council overruled the planning staff and commission and granted the rezoning of a parcel (whose title was not clear) to a development company that had collapsed eight months earlier and had been banned by state security officials a month earlier from selling stock.[4]

The Fruits of Favoritism

Local government dealings in real property often reveal not only conflicts of interest but naïvete, vulnerability, or unconcealed admiration by public officials toward the sharp promoter, or con man. The *Boston Globe* reported an example of official gullibility, or worse, in 1971 under this lead:

> A Boston real estate developer pocketed close to $1 million this year by selling downtown property he acquired largely from the city on the unfulfilled promise of constructing a major office building there.
>
> Today—nearly two years after the construction deadline for the promised skyscraper—the city has neither the building nor the prime parcel of Park Square land....
>
> A Globe investigation ... suggests a series of apparent deceptions, municipal slip-ups and official mismanagement, all leading to personal gain and public loss.[5]

The story went on to detail how the developer, Bertram Druker, negotiated purchase of the land from the city for $18 a square foot while Eastern Gas Co. (with which Druker had a resale agreement) had an appraisal indicating $64 a square foot was its true value.

A different kind of favoritism for downtown land owners may lie buried in your state's and city's laws. We discovered it in Omaha in 1969 while investigating the implications of the city's downtown master plan. The city had agreed to create a number of "superblocks" by vacating more than 200 blocks of streets and alleys. Under state law, the vacated streets would then become the property of abutting property owners. The city had already vacated a street for a new hotel, providing what we and planning officials conservatively estimated to be a $500,000 subsidy. Our calculations indicated that the land scheduled to be thus "given" to property owners over the next twenty years would be worth $35 million.[6]

Consultants and Contributors

Think about the consulting business related to land use. Think not of the leverage that a speculator may be trying to acquire, but of the leverage the politician has over people who want to sell services to the government. Think particularly of land planners, engineers and architects. The professional ethics of these groups generally stipulate that there should be no price cutting and no competitive bidding for service contracts. The government should hire firms on the quality of their work and pay them according to schedules agreed upon by the professional society and perhaps officially approved by a state board of examiners.

If this is so, then how can public officials decide which of several consultants to choose for a job? Their rates are at least nominally the same. Their professional qualifications are similar. They are all licensed, all are experienced in the kind of work that is specified, and all assure the public officials that they have the personnel to put on the job right away and to finish it on time.

If you were a public official looking at a list of such applicants, how would you pick one? Let's try Lou Rose's theory. What are the worst things a public official can do to benefit from the situation? Can he ask for money under the table—an outright bribe? He can, and many have done so without getting caught, but there are risks. Some other possibilities are suggested in the lengthy court document that Spiro T. Agnew signed just before he pleaded *nolo contendere* in 1973 to charges of official corruption in connection with awards of engineering contracts during his term as governor of Maryland.

Can a public official use leverage to make money out of the deal in a way that will not expose him to criminal indictment or conviction even if it is discovered and publicized? Yes, he can let it be known that his party or his campaign needs funds for the next election. Once that "voluntary contribution" is in the party coffers, it may find its way to the approving official and, at the least, relieve some of his fund-raising chores during the next campaign. The wise official probably won't make the pitch for money personally; he'll let the county finance chairman know what consultants are being considered for the work, which pays a fee of $100,000. If the campaign chairman visits one of the consultants and comes back with a $5,000 contribution, it won't take very long for other consultants to figure that 5 per cent of the gross fee is about the price of getting a contract. Those people are very good with figures.

That is essentially the sort of system that *Newsday*'s team described in a series that began Sept. 28, 1970. They studied the activities of 134 consulting firms (and 20 subconsulting firms). Together, they had received $36,398,414 in fees—most of it for architectural and engineering work—from Nassau County over a seven-year period. They found that 128 of these firms had contributed $833,330 to the Democratic Party of County Executive Eugene H. Nickerson. The figure, *Newsday* asserted, was "a bare minimum of the actual amount that may have been contributed" because it covered only the publicly visible (or legally reportable) areas of direct contribution, purchase of testimonial dinner tickets, and program ads. To write the story, *Newsday* modestly told its readers, required "541 interviews and the study of more than 13,000 documents, journals, lists, accounts, and construction and design reports." [7]

There are still other possibilities for a reporter who wants to report on land use. One might be a careful analysis (based on a thorough background in public-cost trade-offs) of the long-term cost to taxpayers of a series of zoning decisions. Such a story would begin to define the basic public-policy issues. A second possibility might be to check into the uses of state land. There are wheelers and dealers involved in state land just as there are in local properties.

SHAKEDOWNS AND GRAFT

There are various forms of shakedown by and of government employees, some provable, some not. All forms of shakedown corrupt society and its government, whether the shakedown involves kickbacks for public inspections or kickbacks of government inspectors.

The community's health and safety powers, for example, provide public officials with another opportunity to exercise leverage. These powers—police powers—are at the core of government. They have been extended far beyond the job of arresting thieves and into the regulation of businesses for health and safety reasons. The people who control building permits, elevator permits, sign permits, restaurant permits, and many other kinds of licenses have the power to harass businesses. I have heard many stories from businessmen about abuse of this power, but I have never been able to get attributable statements, documentation, or direct observation of these alleged shakedowns.

The proprietary functions of government—exercises by extraconstitutional agencies or authorities or commissions (see Chapter 10)—represent a rich territory for grafters, graftees, and their pursuers. When investigating the government as proprietor, it is wise not to look just for indictable offenses. Look also for variations from traditional record keeping, auditing, and public-accountability standards of consitutionally created offices. Such variations are stories in themselves. They serve a valuable public-information purpose, and they raise fundamental questions about the excesses of structural "reform" that remove these proprietary activities from public scrutiny.

Newsday in 1972 told, for example, how the Metropolitan Transit Authority (whose basic business is running the subway system and the Long Island Railroad) bought a profitable private airport and turned it into an instant money loser. For *Newsday*, the project was a quickie: five reporters, ten weeks of work. Even though the state "open records" law did not cover MTA, the reporters were able to document how the airport experienced a half-million-dollar drop in operating revenue, how it abandoned a profitable contract with one fixed-base operator to enter into a money-losing one with another who bestowed favors on the MTA manager, and how an experienced administrator was fired by MTA six months after he attempted to clean up the problem.

Particularly pertinent to the subject of buying and selling government through graft are two quotes *Newsday* published from William J. Ronan, chairman of MTA:

> "If anything, the more autonomous the public agency, the more its operations and finances should be an open book."
> —*From a study headed by Willian J. Ronan, 1956*

"The records of this agency, as you know, are not public documents and are made available only to duly authorized government agency units."
—*From a letter by Ronan to Newsday, 1972*[8]

"Flower Funds" and Bagmen

The raising of political funds from public employees—a form of shakedown—is a commonly abused perquisite of elected office. Most courthouses or city halls have their "flower funds" into which employees are expected to pay a percentage of their salaries each month to the departmental bagman. Some of the money may actually be spent to decorate wakes and weddings in the name of the elective official. Little of it, however, can stand comparison with the laws covering kickbacks and political contributions. Reporting on such funds probably will not win either journalistic or popularity contests, but it will enlighten the public and give the reporter insight for more important stories. An example of this type of exposé is contained in a lead from the *Boston Globe:*

> Officers of the Boston Fire Department are pressuring subordinates in the name of Fire Commissioner James Kelly to contribute to Mayor Kevin White's re-election campaign, the Globe Spotlight Team has learned.
>
> The solicitations, which appear to violate at least three campaign fundraising laws, are being made only to men who already have or are seeking the most desirable jobs in the 2,000-man department.
>
> Men who refuse to contribute contend they have had their promotions delayed, while others have been transferred against their wishes. ...
>
> More than $49,000 was raised from at least 91 men during one soliciting blitz shortly before Christmas ... [in March] many of those who had given in December were solicited again but told this time to give $100 in cash or in undated checks. ...[9]

Four months later, the fire commissioner (who had retired after the *Globe* stories) and a deputy fire chief were indicted on nine counts of conspiracy and violation of election laws, and the acting fire commissioner was named as an unindicted co-conspirator. Although the fire commissioner and deputy fire chief were acquitted of conspiracy, charges by the attorney general were still pending on violations of election laws.

When a reporter is faced with documented evidence of law violations, as in the Boston instance, he is compelled to publish it. But in many cases, it is wiser to be patient and develop a careful system or process story, including the whole ambience of public attitude and long-standing practice. This course is preferable to writing a series of unrelated, small-scale stories on low-level individuals. The latter, in the reader's mind, may add up to nitpicking and harassment. An accumulation of cases describing a corrupt system, on the other hand, will command public attention.

THE SELF-DEALERS

Corruption at city hall—on the council, in the mayor's or city manager's office—can assume so many forms that it is impossible to describe the various possibilities. In cities that have never experienced aggressive investigative reporting, some manifestations of corruption may be easy to identify and document. A notable example is the work Rick Friedman's staff did for the *Star-Tribune* publications in the first year (1973-1974) after they established an edition in Tinley Park, Ill. In two adjoining small communities they found entrenched mayors and councils whose self- dealings and conflict of interest almost beggared description. In Orland Park, a town of less than 9,000, they were able to document more than $200,000 of self-dealing in public funds among five officials; shortly afterward, the mayor and three other officials resigned. In Westhaven, a town of 1,500, they found evidence that led to the federal indictment of the mayor on conspiracy and extortion charges. He was convicted on both counts and sent to prison.[10]

As a small-town paper with a small staff and limited budget, three points are worth particular mention about the *Star-Tribune*'s effort:

- Much of the legwork was done by Barbara Hipson, just a year out of the University of Illinois. Nightly, Friedman recalls, he and editor Dennis Wheeler would go over Hipson's findings and brief her for the next day's work. She took such abuse from the officials under investigation that Friedman or Wheeler or both periodically accompanied her to village board meetings.

- Operating on a low budget, Friedman was obliged to use a trusted state legislator (a practicing attorney) as an informal libel lawyer. "He didn't ever charge us for the service," Friedman recounts.

- Although the *Star-Tribune* was boycotted by most advertisers in Westhaven (and was still being boycotted in 1976), Friedman found other rewards. "When I hear someone on the street holler, 'If it wasn't for the *Star-Tribune* we wouldn't know what was going on in this town,' " he says, "I figure we've done something, and nobody ever did it before."

Uncovering city council corruption in a city as large and complex as Chicago is, of course, a different matter. Ed Pound of the *Sun-Times* performed an imaginative study of public records in 1972 when he exposed the secret land dealings of Alderman Thomas Keane, which eventually resulted in Keane receiving a five-year federal prison sentence. Pound figured out how to trace secret trusts through which Keane owned land that was benefited by city council actions he arranged. Although the land titles were recorded in named or numbered trusts that were managed by a bank and that concealed the true owner, Pound examined an apparently unrelated file in the Uniform Commercial Code section of the secretary of state's office (see Chapter 3). He found that banks that lent Keane sizable amounts had recorded the transactions in the UCC office and that listings of Keane's collateral showed some of the trusts as his assets. From there, it was relatively easy.

Justice on the Take

The administration of justice is not always a matter of following the dollar. Remembering Chapters 6 and 10, the reporter should think creatively about methods for measuring the performance of judges, prosecutors, attorneys, and court staffs. Doing so will not only turn up cases of individual misfeasance, malfeasance and nonfeasance, it will also do much to lend perspective to the problems of policemen who are frustrated by what happens in court to some of their good cases.

In investigating how certain kinds of oil are used to turn the wheels of justice, the journalist would do well to be on the lookout for two things: cronyism and fixes. The cronyism is that between judges and attorneys. It was at the heart of the first huge project Keith McKnight and Andrew Alexander did for the *Dayton Journal Herald:* the connections between a federal district judge and a coterie of attorneys who specialized in bankruptcy proceedings. The setup enabled the attorneys not only to collect fat fees, but occasionally to acquire companies that could be stripped of their assets (through intermediaries) or rehabilitated and sold profitably to insiders.[11]

Individually, fixes are virtually impossible to document. The *Minneapolis Tribune* took a different approach in August, 1973, when it studied forty-one criminal cases involving twenty persons linked to a pair of known "fences." The evidence showed that these persons maneuvered to have their cases heard by a specific district judge, and that they then generally got out with fines and probation even though many had extensive criminal records. The judge sentenced them the day they pleaded guilty rather that ordering presentence investigations. He retired shortly afterward under pressure from his peers.

The *Tribune* meanwhile pursued other aspects of the judicial system. Its stories told how defense and prosecuting attorneys "shop for judges whose sentencing patterns and biases are advantageous," and how other judges often ignored the presentence investigation. The series also reported on how heavily the county attorney's office relied on plea bargaining—with the inevitable result that some felons with records went free or got only nominal sentences.[12]

State Government

Hundreds of millions—if not billions—of dollars flow through the machinery of most states every year. Because everything is on a bigger scale than it is in the town, city, or county, life is relatively easier for the investigative reporter. The magnitude of the deals produces detailed masses of documents distributed to more and more offices or left lying unnoticed in places such as UCC files. This means more potential sources for the reporter and reduces the possibility that the principals can wipe out all traces of a corrupt deal. It also means that the kind of quantitative analysis pioneered by Meyer, Steele, Barlett, Harris, and Isaacs is more likely to be useful.

Bill Mansfield and his associates in the Tallahassee bureau of the *Miami Herald* published a sixteen-page tabloid section titled, "The Greening of the Legislature." As noted in Chapter 10, it demonstrated with remarkable clarity correlations between the size of lobbyists' (and their employers') contributions to state legislatures and their votes on key questions affecting the lobbyists' interests.[13] A computer job, obviously.

No. When I asked Mansfield the question, he replied:

"I certainly wish I could tell you that our contribution files were computerized [but] they are not. We have . . . not come up with a satisfactory system we can afford.

"However, we have had fair success in using our card system, which now [early 1974] contains something over 50,000 names . . . all major contributors to the past three gubernatorial races, virtually all contributors to the current six state cabinet members [elected statewide], major contributors to the past two senate races and all contributors to candidates in the 1972 legislative races.

"We program into the files . . . lobbyists, attorneys who practice before the Public Service Commission, officers of firms doing business with the state and the like. This allows for quick checks for daily stories as well as project-type efforts."

I am reminded of Ben Bradlee's remark: "If I were starting all over again and was an investigative reporter, I would dream of the assignment of asking, 'Where are the pressure points in this town? Who's applying pressure on whom and why?' It's lobbying, it's manipulating. . . ."

PUBLIC MONEY AND PUBLIC WORKS

The management of public money is, in my view, too little understood by most reporters. In almost every city, the municipal budget is the biggest cash-flow operation in sight: it is a maze of different sources and routings of money. Yet how many investigative reporters can thread their way through it? Direct local taxation is usually less than half of it. There are federal and state funds. There are funds generated by bond sales. There is income from proprietary functions, and there is income from investments, sinking funds, and pension funds.

Not only should the investigative reporter have a complete understanding of the public budget, he should also be able to think of ways in which money can be made by outsiders handling this money. Money earned by banks that hold public money in demand deposits is one way. So is money made by financial consultants who recommend investments and management of the money flow. So is money paid to bond attorneys and bond underwriters for selling, issuing, and transferring bonds. How does the city select the people who perform these functions? How much does it pay for the services? How do its actions and payments compare with state law, with its charter requirements, with the practices of other cities? How do the fees paid by government compare with those paid by businesses to the same people for the same services? If there is a difference, why does it exist?

A good beginning exercise for the investigative reporter anxious to learn about the management of public money is to find out how much of it is deposited in each local bank and then ask several knowledgeable people why the money is handled that way. Generally, you will find that demand deposits of public money, on which the banks pay no interest, are sometimes highly profitable because the banks may, in turn, lend out sizable chunks of that money for days or weeks at a time, earning themselves short-term interest. Another point to check, whenever bank calls—quarterly reports—are published, is what percentage of a bank's liabilities are in public deposits. Most states have legal restrictions on this percentage, but the law is not always followed. When a small, poorly managed bank is overloaded with such public deposits, the safety of public money may be endangered.

No reporter can become an instant expert in all of these systems and possible profiting from the storage of public funds. He cannot afford the time to audit every transaction of all the divisions of government. He can, however, develop contacts in different offices, read the published budget dockets, and, particularly, know the laws governing the handling of public money. He should build good relations with the official auditors—not only the senior government auditor (who may be elected or politically appointed) but career technicians (ideally, protected under civil-service rules) who perform the detailed audits.

But the problem of understanding money management is not one encountered by only the local reporter. Most statehouse reporters don't have a thorough grasp of the subject either. The majority of them seem to figure they have done enough if they report on the governor's annual budget message and the consequent politicking over the allocation of money and the assessment of taxes. Far more significant and sometimes venal stories may lie buried in the day-to-day procedures for investing state funds or the selection of banks to hold state deposits. Even more fascinating is the handling of little-noticed long-term funds such as pension accounts. When these fall into the hands of politically active trustees or self-serving advisers, watch out.

In 1974, two staff members of the *New Orleans States-Item* took a look at a Louisiana state pension fund. Patricia Gorman in New Orleans and Bill Lynch in Baton Rouge worked together to examine and analyze the investment decisions of the Louisiana State Employees Retirement System. They found that the fund had lent more than $52 million over a period of three years to entrepreneurs to build hotels, motels, shopping centers and similarly speculative real-estate ventures, many of them backed by politically influential persons. The third story in their series contained highlights such as these:

> • The system has already incurred a paper loss of more than $30 million on $73 million in common stock purchases. . . .
> • Only recently [after the *States-Item*'s first story] has the 10-member board which governs the system turned to an investment counseling firm for expert advice.
> • None of the board members nor director Roy B. Shaeffer Jr. has any expertise in the field of investments.
> • Very little, if any, independent investigation has been made by the board or Schaeffer into the financial background of applicants for multi-million dollar loans.
> • The director and the board have relied heavily on appraisals of property about which serious questions may be raised.
> • The director has relied on the recommendations of a mortgage firm which has a vested interest in promoting a loan.[14]

Developing such a story does not require the reporter to prove that a corrupt payoff has been made, though this element may provide icing on the cake. The reporter is fulfilling his function—finding out something the reader needs to know—simply by scheduling occasional audits of annual reports of such agencies which may not surface in the state auditor's or other routinely covered offices.

Rewards for the Faithful

Leasing office space from private entrepreneurs is another way in which state officials can use public funds to reward their faithful. The proliferation of welfare services, special programs for the handicapped, suburban or regional offices of major departments and divisions—all of these produce a demand for space that may not justify the construction of large new central facilities. Developers of shopping centers like to attract such offices because they help increase customer traffic. When the rents are competitive and the facilities suitable, there is little for the reporter to comment on. But when a leasing decision runs counter to common practice, it is usually worthwhile for the reporter to take a second look, watching particularly for one or more of several patterns:

- Negotiated rentals of unoccupied space in old buildings that have been losing commercial tenants.
- Commissioning by the state of small new buildings on a lease-purchasing basis. A private promoter may finance, design, and construct a building, then lease it to a state agency at something akin to a guaranteed profit.
- Behind-the-scenes promotional efforts by architects, developers and bankers to lure state offices into new locations.

Much of these enterprising programs are just normal competitive fun within the rules of the great American game. The investigative reporter observes and perhaps keeps a file of tips, clips, and announcements about such promotional deals. He may become intrigued enough to build a list of the principals involved in each agreement, cross-indexed to his list of politically active persons and organizations. Then, when he has reason to question the logic of a newly announced enterprise, he can probe for a soft spot.

We did that once after the governor of Nebraska announced that the state was going to take over an aging office building in downtown Omaha in order to centralize its various operations and reduce its rents. Because it was illegal for the state to go into debt for such a purchase, a nonprofit corporation had been formed to hold the building in trust, issue revenue bonds, and then turn over the title to the state after the rents had paid off the debt.

The original announcement attracted little attention except for a single, breathless story in the downtown-based *World-Herald*. We read it and asked ourselves: is it logical that the state should buy a 105,000 square-foot building, 63 years old, in a declining central city location? No, not on the face of it. I assigned a summer intern to check each of the scattered state agencies in Omaha to learn how much rent they had been paying, what kind of clientele they served, and whether those clients would be better served in the new downtown Omaha location. Four weeks later the intern, Jim Polson, came up with a story explaining, among other things, that:

- Rather than reducing its rent bill, the state would incur a threefold increase.

- The firm that was selling the building expected also to obtain a nonnegotiated contract to manage the building for the nonprofit corporation. It would also hold the mortgage on the building.
- The attorney for the seller also was the resident corporate agent of the purchaser, the nonprofit corporation.
- The building's occupancy rate had declined from 91 per cent to 71 per cent over the preceding five years.
- The building might need repairs totaling some $250,000 to meet new fire codes for high-rise structures.
- The building was to meet the state's needs in Omaha for "twenty-five to thirty years at least," according to the state director of administrative services. The state, in other words, would wind up with a building 90 or more years old while its seller would walk away with profit on the sale, interest on the mortgage, and a fee for management.
- Although it would be acting in behalf of the state, the nonprofit corporation would be exempt from state laws covering open meetings, open records, public bidding, hiring and purchasing. [15]

The story raised questions of conflicts of interest, evasion of constitutional restrictions, and technical evasion of laws against the state's operating commercial ventures, but there was no discernible effort by state officials to pursue the questions. Several weeks after Polson's story appeared, the state quietly canceled the agreement, making the questions at least temporarily moot.

Patronage. Patronage is a key factor in state politics. It, too, is a way of rewarding the faithful—with public funds. Top-level jobs filled by gubernatorial appointment are legally up for grabs with every change in administration, and changes are usually reported thoroughly by political journalists. But another aspect often escapes attention. The experienced reporter reads with jaded eye the new governor's announcements about "lopping off the deadwood" and "tightening up" the operations of his predecessor. Usually, these statements are just a routine part of the first act—or prologue—of an oft-repeated scenario. The next act calls for rewriting many civil-service job requirements. This practice, of course, flouts the theoretical goals of making jobs open to the best qualified people regardless of race or sex.

There are further possibilities in the study of state-management practices. Too many reporters, I believe, accept the facile conventional wisdom that prison guards, state-hospital orderlies, and certain other classes of employees don't do good work solely because their jobs are patronage jobs, and the public doesn't pay them enough. This may be a contributing factor, but I suspect an equally important one is the kind of management policy established by legislatures or governors and carried out by politically appointed division and department heads. Employees working under Kafkaesque conditions quickly learn not to question the logical bases of public policy.

The Big Deals

Without question, public works is one of the biggest spending items of state government. Highways, prisons, state office buildings, universities, vocational schools, hospitals—even when operating budgets and payrolls may be tight, these construction projects seem to survive. Politicians like them and their constituents like them. They are tangible and visible evidence of state government activity—much more popular than social programs. They are also political plums to be distributed judiciously to cities or areas that voted correctly in the last election. The names of currently reigning officials are engraved on cornerstones or embossed on big lobby plaques. Design and construction of public works provide short-term payrolls and retail business boomlets to deserving towns. And obviously, the award of a major construction contract to a campaign contributor is a highly satisfactory device to ensure future contributions.

The ability to arrange the most self-serving contract—in spite of bidding laws, conflict-of-interest laws, bribery laws, and detailed auditing procedures—is a test of any politician's mettle. In studying the possibilities, the reporter should consider:

- Specifications. Sometimes specifications are written to apply to only one supplier's version of a product (lighting fixtures, guard rails, doors and windows, heating systems).
- Official discretion. The amount of leeway given to officials in applying laws that require acceptance of the "lowest *and best* bid" is often used to justify high prices for goods or services. Exposing a single instance of abusing such discretion means little. Studying its application to thousands of purchases over a period of a year or more may reveal patterns.
- Brokered contracts. A brokered contract is one that involves a political insider who sets up (often through a screen of corporations) a construction company that has little or no staff of its own, but bids low and then subcontracts the work to unreliable or financially shaky companies.
- Change orders. The insider gets the job at a ridiculously low price, then reaps fat profits from changes in specifications after construction has begun.

The people who make these deals are experienced and have good legal advice. In working on multimillion-dollar deals they build almost invisible corporate networks through which to launder records of money flow. The reporter's best hope is to find a conscientious or disgruntled insider who can provide files of correspondence, canceled checks, supporting memos, information about secret meetings—which the reporter must then double-check through hotel and travel records, interviews with other participants, and public documents. Lacking such help, the reporter should not make too much out of a single case. It is too easy for the principals to counterattack with charges of nit-picking or political ax-grinding. Patience, careful file-building, and constant probing along channels of political communication are the best strategy. If careful analysis after a year or two of note-taking indicates a pattern, the reporter and his editor may decide that exposing the existence of a pattern will help readers understand how things work. If the pattern is clear, its publication may help shake conclusive evidence of illegality out of the political network. Even if no further evidence emerges, the reporter has achieved a result under Don Barlett's rule: As long as you are providing information the reader hasn't had before, you are accomplishing something.

Prisons are among the most notable examples. One of the more thoughtful jobs of reporting on the problem was done in the *St. Petersburg Times* in late 1970 and early 1971. Florida statehouse reporter Martin Dyckman spent several months visiting prisons, talking to convicts, guards, wardens, and staff members, and then interviewing judges, attorneys, and penologists. The next session of the legislature adopted six major prison-reform bills. More than five years later, I asked Dyckman to assess the results. He responded:

"I think the series did help create a climate of opinion [that] resulted in several reforms. The parole commission was required to interview prisoners at least once a year . . . The state began building small prisons (300-600 beds) rather than relying on large ones, and work-release has been stepped up. . . . Unfortunately, the trend . . . has been reversed due to the massive overcrowding which results from current [increasing] crime . . . and a sharp rightward turn among sentencing judges.

"Consequently I feel we have after five years achieved no *fundamental* reform of the process. The parole commission is still wickedly arbitrary in the exercise of its power . . . the parole/probation system is still so under-financed that judges cannot be blamed for refusing to entrust doubtful prospects to [it]. . . ."[16]

In the spring of 1976, reporting on issues facing the Florida legislature, Dyckman wrote in the *Times:*

There were 8,811 convicts among 6.7 million Floridians in 1970.

There are more than 16,300 convicts among us now—a gain of 4,900 in the 14 months since the surge began . . . as many in 14 months as there had been in the preceding 14 years. No other large state has so high a ratio of convicts to free citizens.

. . . [Hardly anyone] pretends the system is cost-effective. Not the men who run it. Not the judges who overload it. Not the police who are kept busy by its failures. Not the people who have to find the money to make it run.

"As I've tried to say many times, prisons alone aren't the answer," says Gov. Reubin Askew.

. . . There isn't enough work, schooling, bed space, or supervision for so many people.

"There's a lot of things we don't do that we otherwise should and would be doing," says David Bachman, assistant secretary for operations of the Department of Offender Rehabilitation. "We've been spending the bulk of our time finding bed space and other things go lacking . . . Our primary effort has been to find a place for them to sleep."

Except for a minority of incorrigible criminals, most judges, legislators and corrections officials still believe that well-supervised probation and parole is [the] more effective (and far less costly) way to make law-abiding citizens of people who have broken the law. It costs $15 a day to keep a prisoner; only $1 a day to supervise him on probation. . . .[17]

Dyckman reported that Governor Askew was asking for $65.3 million for new prisons and $93 million for prison operations for a year, compared with $3.5 million for better parole and probation supervision. The raw figures suggest that there is something askew in public policy not only in Florida but in most other states, which follow similar priorities.

THE FEDERAL ESTABLISHMENT

The reporter who nibbles at the edges of the federal establishment is doomed to frustration. If he climbs the ladder of bureaucracy, deals with the official sources, and follows the tracks of the Washington press corps, he may bag an errant congressman, general, or cabinet member now and then, but he will likely be diverted from the task of telling his reader how things work.

In writing about the federal government, an investigative journalist's best course is to concentrate on analyzing the system. He should learn how pressure is applied from within and without to set agendas, establish priorities, and serve special interests. He may begin by looking for specific abuses, but he will eventually turn to reporting on the bureaucracy and the elected administration as a process, as a chain of events shaped by forces and policies several layers removed from the visible structure. The journalists who have been most successful at this approach are those who served their apprenticeships in conventional reporting—police beat, legislature, bureaucracy, Congress—then deliberately broke out of the mold to test theory against reality. These are journalists like Carl Bernstein and Bob Woodward; Don Barlett and Jim Steele; Seymour Hersh; David Kraslow and Stuart Loory; Clark Mollenhoff, George Anthan and Jim Risser; Bill Lambert; David Burnham. There are others, but I list these reporters to emphasize the value of independent, unconventional thinking about coverage of the federal establishment.

Bernstein and Woodward, who worked together so well they became known as "Woodstein," demonstrated anew the importance of going outside official channels for information. They proved a point that is important to any reporter dealing with large and complex institutions: talk to as many people as possible. Do not—repeat not—accept the version of the top official. All along the chain of bureaucracy, bits of knowledge are carried in the minds and files of functionaries, bookkeepers, administrators, technicians, and telephone operators. To some, compartmented in their daily routines, the knowledge may seem insignificant. Others, pressured by prevailing mores and office policy, may know the information is important but are afraid to volunteer it. A few, tortured by guilty knowledge, may seek out a reporter whom they know to be aggressive and willing to take risks. The key operating principle of the "Woodstein" type of reporter is that it is virtually impossible to conceal all traces of any large-scale operation, corrupt or otherwise. Once such a reporter has developed a sound investigative assumption and identified the logical line of inquiry, it is simply a matter of time and patience until he fits the pieces together.

The Need for Expertise

One seldom-recognized role of the Washington reporter, particularly an expert in a given field, is that he becomes an unofficial channel of communication between government agencies. This role puts a burden on the reporter to protect the confidentiality of sources at every terminal of his private network. But if he plays the game straight, it also enhances his credibility and makes it almost necessary for a reclusive bureaucrat to answer his questions. The bureaucrat knows the reporter is an expert, not easily deceived. The bureaucrat cannot afford to ignore a call or brush past the reporter in a corridor; the reporter may be giving him a chance to comment on damaging information.

Members of the *Des Moines Register* and *Tribune* bureau in Washington—Clark Mollenhoff, George Anthan, and James Risser—became experts in the field of agribusiness. Mollenhoff was known popularly for his work in the 1950s and '60s in pursuit of corruption in labor and links between organized crime and governmental officials. Less widely recognized outside Washington and Iowa was the reputation he and the *Register* and *Tribune* built over decades scrutinizing all levels of farm-related business. The investigative reporting of Nick Kotz in the 1960s was significant in shaping federal legislation to regulate small packing plants that had enjoyed mutually uncritical relationships with farm-state departments of agriculture. In the 1970s, Mollenhoff, Anthan, and Risser teamed on a succession of projects to investigate:

- Corruption in the marketing of commodities, with special emphasis on the casual attitude of the Commodities Exchange Administration toward the Chicago Board of Trade and other private marketing agencies that had failed in their promised "self-policing" policies. Some twenty months after this effort began, Congress passed a law instituting new controls on the commodity markets.

- Weaknesses in the structure and failures in the administration of the Packers and Stockyard Act, which was designed to control monopoly trends and protect livestock producers in their dealings with packers. Within months after the series started, there was bipartisan support in Congress for extensive amendments of the 51 year old law.

- Widespread corruption, bribery, and conflict of interest in the inspection and certification of American grain destined for shipment abroad, particularly through the Port of New Orleans. Risser, who had worked on both of the previous series with Mollenhoff and Anthan, did extensive work in the New Orleans area, checking records (see Chapter 6) and interrogating dock workers, grain inspectors and others connected with the scandal, in which more than fifty persons and corporations were eventually found guilty of criminal violations.

The corrective legislation created a new federal grain inspection service with jurisdiction over all shipping ports, tightened the procedures for weighing, and established a more restrictive conflict of interest standard. James Risser was awarded the Pulitzer Prize for National Reporting in 1976 and several other major awards for his work on the grain inspection phase of the four-year project on regulations of grain trading.

In each case, Mollenhoff and his colleagues identified patterns of almost incestuous relationships between commercial interests and the federal agencies that were supposed to regulate them. In the grain-handling scandal, they found records showing that the Department of Agriculture had ignored official reports from its own personnel and had licensed inspectors whose salaries were paid by the private interests they were supposed to be inspecting.

Two key points manifest themselves in an analysis of the *Register* and *Tribune* team's work:

- There is plenty of room for significant investigative work outside the "glamorous" subjects of crime, misdirection of intelligence efforts, and waste in national defense.
- Specialization in a particular field by a reporter or team pays off with the development of personal expertise and solid sourcing.

The Importance of Sources. . .

Sourcing, with all its perils, is still a major component of investigative reporting in Washington, a town of nervous executives and hidebound bureaucrats. It was a key to most of Seymour Hersh's major stories of the 1960s: the secret bombing of Cambodia, Henry Kissinger's wiretapping of his aides, the spying by the Joint Chiefs of Staff on the National Security Agency, the involvement of the CIA in the collapse of the Allende government in Chile. Hersh, wrote Ann Pincus in 1975, "has brought us face to face with more public moral dilemmas in the past six years than any other reporter."[18]

Hersh didn't establish his sources overnight. He began developing them in the early 1960s when he worked on the Associated Press special-projects team. He used some of them to put together his exclusive stories of 1968-1969 about the My Lai massacre in Vietnam. And the general nature if not the names of his sources can be inferred by following his trail of stories about military and diplomatic secrecy; most of them are linked to what is euphemistically known as "the intelligence community." One of his biggest and riskiest stories broke late in 1974 when he revealed—with no documentation and no direct attribution from identifiable officials—that the CIA had spied extensively on domestic political groups.[19] The story took Hersh and the *New York Times* near the outer limits of reader credibility. Indeed, he received criticism from many competing editors and Washington correspondents, and was pointedly bypassed by judges for both the Pulitzer and Sigma Delta Chi awards. But his stories shook both the White House and the Congress into investigating the CIA, and their findings confirmed all of what Hersh had reported, and more. He got little professional recognition, however, until he received the Drew Pearson Award more than sixteen months later.

Hersh always seeks records to confirm his oral information, and he reads extensively (including underground newspapers) to get ideas. His basic approach is to start with interviews. He gets an idea from his reading or a direct tip from a source, and he then goes from one person to another, expanding his information at each step. He is "the best telephone interrogator I ever heard of," said one of his *Times* colleagues. "He can call someone up with just a shred of evidence and get an entire story." A former source of Hersh's put it this way: "Talking to Sy was quite an experience. He's like a threshing machine."[20]

... And Records

At almost the opposite end of the journalistic spectrum are Barlett and Steele, who do not rely on sources. Though they have won awards singly and jointly for reporting on national government, they are based in Philadelphia and go to Washington only occasionally. When they do, it is usually to search records: congressional committee reports, SEC filings, annual departmental budgets. These searches may then lead them to private or public experts whose interpretation or defense of policy documents is essential to their story. This analytical approach led to several of their widely honored original stories such as "Oil, the Created Crisis" (1973), "Foreign Aid: The Flawed Dream" (1974), "Auditing the IRS" (1974) and "The Silent Partner of Howard Hughes" (1974). The last series, which appeared four months before the death of the reclusive billionaire, described the links between Hughes and various branches and departments of the federal government. Because of Hughes's personal invisibility and the ironclad secrecy of his companies, the story had to be built on the discovery, linking, and patterning of records from scores of agencies and departments within the government. To show that Hughes's companies had done more than $6 billion in federal business, Barlett and Steele searched ten-year records from the Army, Navy, Air Force, National Aeronautics and Space Administration, Department of the Interior, Federal Aviation Administration, Department of Health, Education and Welfare, Law Enforcement Assistance Administration, National Science Foundation, General Accounting Office, and the Central Intelligence Agency—among others. They went through congressional committee files and Internal Revenue records to discover how Hughes's charitable foundation had "enjoyed six years of freedom from the laws that thousands of other foundations must abide by." They reported that the IRS, while refusing to release its letter rulings on tax arguments (many involving Hughes's companies), was seeking a change in the tax laws that would, *ex post facto,* validate its position.[21]

In "Auditing the IRS," a project that won the Pulitzer and several other prizes, the *Inquirer* pair worked with documents for months before beginning substantive interviews with IRS officials, tax evaders, tax accountants, and congressmen.

"We deal very, very little in sources," says Steele, but they do consult some knowledgeable people at times. As Barlett explains, "We have built up a substantial survey of sources who are expert in certain areas. If we want to know about foreign tax credits, we've got three people we can call." "One of the ways you find them," Steele adds, "is when you go to a congressional hearing (or hearing record) and see who has testified on various things."

Freedom of Information

Like most experienced reporters covering the federal government, Barlett and Steele know how to use the Freedom of Information Act. As amended in 1974, the law establishes the right of citizens to have access to and receive copies of any document, file, or other record in possession of any federal agency except:

1. Information properly classified under criteria set by order as secret for reasons of national defense or foreign policy
2. Information related solely to the internal personnel roles and practices of an agency
3. Information specifically exempted by statute (such as income tax returns, patent applications, and completed census forms)
4. Trade secrets and commercial or financial information obtained from a person and privileged or confidential
5. Interagency letters or memoranda that would not be available by law to a party other than an agency in litigation with the agency
6. Personnel and medical files whose disclosure would constitute a clearly unwarranted invasion of personal privacy
7. Investigatory records—and even here, the agency must prove that disclosure of the records would produce one or more of six specific harmful effects.

There are two other special-interest exemptions relating to banking and oil-well information that, according to the Freedom of Information Clearinghouse in Washington, "are not relevant to most applications of the act."

Although a reporter's verbal invocation of the act (5 U.S.C. 552) will not always produce an immediate response from a reluctant bureaucrat, the law has tended to open up many agencies to public, and journalistic, scrutiny. And all bureaucrats know that if you write a formal request letter, you are setting in motion a procedure by which, within thirty working days, they must either prove to you that the records are exempted from public inspection or face a court order. If you win the lawsuit, the court may order the federal government to pay your attorney's fees. Advice on the proper form for letters and legal appeals is available through the Freedom of Information Clearinghouse, Box 19367, Washington, D.C. 20036, or the Reporters' Committee for Freedom of the Press, Washington, D.C.

Despite the complexity of our federal government and the problems of covering it, the fact remains that it is also made up of mortals, most of them very sensitive to public pressures. Any reporter who has been schooled in municipal and statehouse bureaucracy, and who has learned how to gain the confidence of honest functionaries, can open at least 95 per cent of the inner doors if he plans wisely and works doggedly and persistently. Our governmental system is still one of the most open in the world, and the journalist who reports on it will help prevent the self-dealers from closing those doors.

13

The Business
of Business

THE CORPORATE GOVERNOR

"A view of the world that finds government standing solidly at the center of the social forces which govern our daily lives is a view badly out of focus with the times. For better or worse, large corporations are now also, and coequally, our governors. Most of us work for them. Most of us have a strong sense of allegiance to them. The economic means by which we sustain our communities comes in large measure from them. Our social lives are shaped in large part by them. The air we breathe, the water we drink, the land we stand on are altered by them. This is true not only for individuals, but also for whole cities, as many an alderman in a one-company town has ruefully learned. . . ."[1]

Paul Gruchow and Paul Berg, free lance writers, made that statement in a special business-labor issue of the *Twin Cities Journalism Review* in mid-1975. In the months that followed its appearance, I happened to ask more than 100 reporters and editors what they personally thought were the undeveloped or underdeveloped areas of news in which investigative reporters could profitably spend more time. Fully seventy-five per cent of

them said, "Business." And of the sixty or so who had not written exten-
sively about business, the rest of the answer was a litany:
"I'd like to do more, but—"
"I don't understand it—"
"It is the toughest kind of reporting—"
"It's so hard to get records and information—"
"Business news doesn't get much space or play."
A good investigative reporter recognizes the existence of all these
factors, but doesn't let them faze him. The more he studies, the more he
realizes the integral and impelling nature of business activity in American
life.

The better a reporter accepts the fact that government and business
interests sometimes meet, the more intelligently he will think about investigating business. To quote John Kenneth Galbraith in a 1975 report of the
Institute of Policy Studies: "To deny the political character of the modern
corporation is not to avoid the reality. It is to deny the reality."

A Special Status

Common law, constitutional law, and statutory law all recognize the
business community as the provider of jobs, the supplier of goods, the taker
of risks, the creator and mover of money. The law bestows a variety of
benefits and privileges on the entrepreneur, the investor, and, particularly,
the corporations, all legal, that are the major structural elements in the
American economic system. From the standpoint of the journalist, these
special benefits also constitute his major reason for reporting on business.
For the fact remains that though a business may be owned by "private"
persons and have "private" rights, its activities and its impacts are essentially public.

Government is a major customer of business, which is one reason
businessmen curry the favor of public officials. Government protects and
stimulates business through subsidies, research programs, and tax incentives. Finally, government is the regulator of business morals and practices.
Legislators, judges, regulatory agents, and elected officials hold life-and-
death power over companies and thus economic power over their executives
and their employees. All of these factors contribute to a natural, almost
hypnotic preoccupation by business (and labor) leaders with politicians and
bureaucrats.

In addition to its government connection, business also has special
status with the public. The concept of "free enterprise" is so fixed a part of
the American dream that most people tend to give special homage and
concessions to people and institutions who take risk, create wealth, move

and control money, explore frontiers—and grow big, rich, and influential. This attitude, though by no means universal, occasionally creates problems for the reporter who asks questions that some might consider impudent. If the questions can be interpreted as threatening the welfare of business, then they stir up people who fear for their jobs or their vision of democracy.

The most consuming and popular reason for more perceptive reporting on business is simply because that is where the power is. Business is money. Business is motive force. Business creates ideas, some good and some bad. Business influences the goals and standards of society. Business has tremendous impact on both the natural and the man-made environment. In my view, much of the "environmental" reporting done in the late 1960s and early '70s missed this last point: the way business decisions impinge upon the physical form of our lives through architecture and urban planning.

The decisions of business leaders affect your readers in many ways:

- As consumers. Your readers need to know about the quality of goods and services being offered them and about the operating rationale of the marketing-pricing system.
- As investors. They want and need to know about how the economic system works, and, more narrowly, about the good guys and the bad guys who sell stock, promote new companies, issue bonds and debentures, and influence the value of investments.
- As plain people. As workers, voters, taxpayers, they want and need to know about public-policy issues such as industrial safety, corporate ethical values, political activity, the management of the environment.

"The paradoxical problem of American society," says Kenneth Clark, "is that it has been too successful; it is affluent and efficient even as it has legitimized and accepted pervasive dishonesties as the price of apparent success. When dishonesty appears to work, it is difficult to argue persuasively for honesty....

"Reality, efficiency and morality are defined as if they were synonymous. That is real and moral which leads to success. If this is...too abstract an approach even for a pragmatic moralist, then outright moral cynicism and hypocrisy are available as alternative approaches....

"Fortunately for the future of a civilized society there exist these human beings who...remain concerned about moral and ethical values and justice in the affairs of men.

"They also seem to have the courage to risk the repeated expressions of their concern and thereby serve as a gnawing and irritating conscience....[3]

Recognition of the American dilemma Clark describes and the "courage to risk repeated expressions" of concern are attributes the reporter needs if he is to undertake an investigation of business.

High-Risk Reporting

Published statements that tend to injure the business reputation of an individual or corporation are one of the more common grounds for findings of libel. Although public-relations considerations may militate against filing suit, the business operator who is willing to ignore his PR advisers will usually have more legal resources than the average plaintiff. And a newspaper that may be one of the best-financed and best-managed businesses in a given city is hardly a match in court for many a multinational corporation.

Not only does pragmatism argue for constraint, but so too does audience receptivity to most stories about business. Unless the reader can see some clear threat to his own job or family security, he tends to resist a full-page story tracing the collapse of a pyramid of a dozen corporations. If the elements of a criminal conspiracy are not clear, a large percentage of readers is willing to give the benefit of doubt to the afflicted businessman who has taken a big risk and lost.

At the level of the individual reader, response to an unpleasant business story may translate into a "kill the messenger" attitude: "If your reporting threatens my job, I don't want to hear what you're saying." This syndrome may emerge, for example, after a long-standing environmental problem is reported, resulting in regulatory legislation, legal action, or administrative pressure on the offending company. The reader is not alone in his resistance. There is support in many editorial and publishing offices for the notion that complete and candid reporting will create a crisis of consumer/investor confidence and may deepen rather than help to cure a problem created by bad business management. On a more mundane level, there is for some editors and publishers the stark fear of losing advertising revenue.

Dealing with businessmen can be rough. By definition, most are tough, decisive, aggressive people. A reporter who tells something about a business that its boss doesn't want known may encounter negative reaction in places he doesn't expect—from friends, attorneys, or employees of the business. Dick Gibson of the *Minneapolis Star* tells of discovering, after his staff had reported aggressively on illegal political contributions by a Twin Cities corporation, that the company had instituted a plan to make relations difficult for *Star* reporters. It included delaying responses to routine inquiries and cross-examining reporters about the purpose of every question. "We didn't mind," Gibson says. "At least we now know what rules we were playing under."

Any experienced reporter has encountered all or some of these back pressures. Many have decided, for just these reasons, to stay away from reporting business policies and affairs. But the best of them have not. The best of them go the other way. They educate themselves, improve their strategy, tactics, planning, and technique, and do truly sophisticated reporting that sets the stage for reasoned discussions of public policy toward business.

LEARNING ABOUT BUSINESS

The student journalist who wants to write about business had better know what he's writing about. He should schedule courses in economics, business administration or management, perhaps introductory accounting, trying all the while to develop an understanding of both the broad forces and parochial concerns that influence business decisions. In his campus newspaper or magazine experience, he may tackle stories about local real-estate operators who set levels of service rendered and rent charged for off-campus housing. Or, he may look carefully at the influence of a large local employer on the community as a whole. *The Medicine Jug* of Mankato State College in Minnesota, for instance, devoted twenty-four of its magazine pages in the spring issue of 1975 to team reporting on the workers, the ownership, and the management of a local foundry, one of the principal employers in the community.[4] At Ohio State, the daily *Lantern* has had its share of complaints from real-estate people for reporting on housing-code violations and questionable maintenance policies of campus-area landlords.

For the working journalist, it's usually on-the-job training in business reporting. "Everybody comes to business reporting with a certain amount of innocence," said Richard Gibson, business editor of the *Minneapolis Star.* "You really need to have a curiosity.... I had a choice of jobs and I said, 'I don't know anything about business, I'll take that job.' " In addition to his daily business reporting, the working journalist watches for short courses or weekend seminars that he can attend (ideally at the company's expense) to learn about economic issues. he may also enroll in night school or in a master's-degree program to gain a more complete and formal understanding. He subscribes to the *Wall Street Journal* not only to acquire its insights into business issues, but also to study the superb journalistic technique of its writers and editors. He reads issue-oriented books about politics and business, learning the patterns and themes of the government-business relationship. And if he is working on a story about a specific industry or company, he haunts the university or public library, reading the trade magazines and newspapers of that industry.

This kind of conscientious reporter also talks with and learns from the business journalists in his own organization. He accepts assignments to cover luncheons of Rotary, Kiwanis, the Chamber of Commerce, not so much to report on the turgid speeches as to become aquainted with businessmen. These luncheon chats eventually ripen into sources that can enrich his base-building and improve his research into specific stories. he makes friends with those in the business offices of his own newspaper. There he will find auditors, tax specialists, business and advertising managers, all of whom are versed in both general business issues and specific local business concerns. Finally, he visits with his publisher whenever he can, knowing the boss is as well-informed as any person in town on current trends and problems. The business reporter, like any other, is careful to maintain his journalistic independence, but he recognizes that all these people can become valuable sources.

The first problem that confronts the budding investigative reporter doing a major business story is the secrecy of most business operations. He learns that if he starts asking questions without knowing his target, he will run into a stone wall. So he backs off and develops a checklist of possible sources to explore *before* he undertakes interviews with managers and owners. From the feasibility study and base-building to the key interview, these sources are of two kinds: they are either people or documents.

PEOPLE AS SOURCES

There are any number of people who, in their occupational capacity, can be helpful to the business reporter. What follows is a list of some twenty categories of people whom the reporter should consider good sources:

Local inspectors: City and state technicians have access to plants and offices as part of their public duty. They not only make factual reports, they know many persons in supervisory and middle-level management. Health, building, and industrial safety inspectors make frequent checks on virtually any business larger than the "mom and pop" grocery store. Some are required by law and agency rules to protect business confidentiality, but they also compile detailed records that are open to the public.

Brokers: There are two important kinds of brokers—the specialist and the stockbroker-investment counselor. The counselor has wide acquaintance in business circles; he also has independent sources of financial analysis, either through his national office or through contracted business-reporting services. Almost every industry also has its specialized brokers who arrange sales and mergers of companies. The specialist knows who is doing well and who is doing poorly, who is having labor trouble, cash-flow embarrassment, or capital problems. Often you will find brokers informed and informative about a situation you are investigating.

Former employees: Particularly at the second and third levels of management, persons who have recently retired, quit, or been fired can help you build a picture of the personalities and issues within a target company. Obviously, their judgments or information may be biased. Top-notch reporters of business make it a practice to have lunch or a farewell drink with any executive who has been replaced. There may not be an immediate payoff from such a contact, but the person may become an excellent source.

Independent experts: Just as every industry has its brokers, it also has its academic and technical experts, many of them working for universities. They gather and analyze data, define issues, propose solutions, and share their expertise with congressional committees, legislatures, and the public. Many of these experts also sell consulting services to industry and are on a first-name basis with industrial leaders; hence, in a given case, their loyalties may be divided. But in most instances, the expert can tell you where a target company may stand within the industry, what its general tactics and policies are, and how its owners and managers are viewed. In a similar category is the business census expert who, in most states, is attached to the leading university. He compiles and publishes data on such matters as business activity, employment, the money supply, capital-spending plans, and consumer demand. Though he is usually scrupulous about protecting specific information concerning individual companies, he can usually provide sound guidance in response to general questions.

Competitors: "The kind of thing you find very often in business stories," says Len Ackland, "is other businessmen who are really upset and irritated at the crooks. . . . You have to walk a fine line with good guys to get them to talk, to come out against one of their own: 'I know not all of you are crooks. If you want to make people realize there are good businessmen, one way is to have the bad ones weeded out. . . .' " To survive in a competitive market, any businessman keeps track of what his competitors are doing. Through conversation with customers and with former employees of his competitors, he gleans information about their operational weaknesses. The journalist routinely visits with all the leaders in a particular type of business to pick up information from competitors. He knows that here, too, he runs the risk of getting bad or biased information, so he looks for ways in which to corroborate or refute what a competitor tells him.

Politicians: Legislators and executives collect a lot of intelligence about the strengths, resources, weaknesses, and temperament of businessmen. They regard businessmen either as contributors of money and suppliers of goods and services (friends) or as noncontributors and unsuccessful bidders (enemies).

Lobbyists: Not only the overall industry, but your specific target company may have representation at several governmental levels. The industry-wide lobbyist will be a relatively accurate if guarded source; the company lobbyist is likely to be somewhat less open unless you can pin him down on specific questions that he is legally required to answer. In addition, look for countervailing lobbies: public-interest (consumer) agencies as well as supporters of opposing interests (the association of independent telephone companies as opposed to AT&T, for example).

Bankers: To most reporters, bankers are from another planet. They are taciturn, formal, and precise. They make multimillion-dollar decisions that appear to be based on one-sentence or one-paragraph letters from creditors or other bankers. Outwardly, they seem to think solely in terms of dollars, and are rarely swayed by appeals to emotion or philosophy. To understand and make friends with a banker, a reporter must realize that what really is on the banker's mind is the character and reliability of the person or persons involved in a transaction: will the person, whether he is an individual borrowing for his child's education or a corporate finance officer borrowing operating funds, stand behind his promise to repay? Most bankers—not all, but most—are concerned with stability, prudence, scrupulous adherence to legal or contractual responsibility—and to utter confidentiality. Within the breast of such a banker beats a heart that is chilled by the very notion of deception or abuse of the law. The challenge to the investigative reporter is to find such a banker, to build over a period of years a relationship that eventually enables him to ask direct questions about specific cases with the explicit understanding that the information thus obtained is never to be linked to the banker. Once you have proved yourself in this relationship, you have a key to one of the gates to knowledge of the business community. Your banking friend can help you decipher fuzzed-up annual reports; read the statements on the condition of other banks; watch for out-of-balance situations in the local or regional money flow. If you want a reading on the reputation of an out-of-town speculator, your banker friend can provide it in detail. Bankers who will establish and maintain solid relationships with reporters are often found at the senior vice-president level, personally secure and appropriately concerned with the ethics of business.

Suppliers and customers: The building-supply dealer knows a lot about the financial status and operating methods of a home builder or residential developer. The buyers of homes in a subdivision established by the developer may have experienced tax problems, maintenance problems, or other surprises discovered after the sale. Or they may contradict your theory that these problems exist.

Industrial or professional self-regulators: The real-estate industry, the broadcast industry, the securities industry, the architectural and engineering professions—among others—have codes or canons of ethics and good practice, some of which are monitored by professional staffs, committees or commissions, or both. Though they are often self-protective or self-serving, the people involved in these activities can help you form a picture of the norms and standards of the industry or profession.

Legislative staffs: Lawyers and research technicians for congressional and state legislative committees acquire and analyze large amounts of information about businesses, not all of which appears in their formal reports. For journalists they respect, they are usually helpful and relatively unbiased sources.

Consultants: Virtually every business firm deals with a variety of consultants: advertising and public-relations agents, management men, architects, engineers, lawyers. Because most are pledged to confidentiality for their clients, their value is more likely to be as check points and touchstones than as inside sources. But former consultants (for example, the agency that just lost the ad account) should not be overlooked as sources of hard information. University-based consultants often reserve the right to publish their findings for scholarly purposes—or, in the case of public universities, may be required to report through public channels.

Innocents: Workers and functionaries in the target company may be willing to talk freely about what they do, how they execute company policy, what they understand to be the goals and concerns of the institution. They may also, once you have established mutual confidence, be able to obtain specific information about internal operations and politics. "Always be kind to secretaries" can be extended and generalized to: "Always listen to the little guy." The obvious peril is that the private in the ranks doesn't have "the big picture" and indeed may be getting a distorted view. Yet, his information must be evaluated carefully and cross-checked as you piece together the puzzle. But well-developed contacts within the rank and file—usually made away from the innocent's office or plant—can be invaluable.

Law enforcers: As distinct from the regulators (who sometimes become overly sensitive to industry interests) the district attorney, the fraud-division investigator, the securities-division lawyer, are often willing to trade information with the well-informed reporter. The reporter, of course, must maintain his confidences, but he can often gain from such a relationship. Gene S. Anderson, chief deputy in charge of the fraud division of the prosecutor's office in King County, Washington, spent several years with the Department of Justice in Washington, D.C. He told me how stories in the *Washington Post* about consumer frauds in the late 1960s activated the U.S. Attorney General's office to establish a fraud division. "It was like walking through a ripe apple orchard," says Anderson. "The cases hung down ready for the picking. As expected, the press responded enthusias-

tically. . . . The value of such media attention became quickly a lesson in law enforcement. In the fraud area, publicity deters, brings in leads, and emphasizes for the public and the criminal-justice system that . . . it's not just the mugger who is a threat to society, but the banker who abuses his trust as well.''

Anderson eventually was recruited to Seattle to establish a similar function with respect to consumer frauds for the prosecuting attorney there. Of his relationship with the Seattle media, Anderson has written:

> "An investigative reporter's story obviously is important if a public agency such as the prosecutor acts on the disclosure and effects of public remedy. The prosecutor's case, on the other hand, is important if the reporter and the newspaper report it as such. . . . Where the chemistry of mutual trust exists such an agency and reporter can work together in a symbiotic relationship like the rhino and the bird—and pass the horn back and forth depending on whose turn it is to do the goring. In some instances an investigative reporter is tipped in advance that a fraud scheme is a subject of investigation . . . [Using his] skills and his own resources and judgment, the reporter does his work and files his story giving a picture to the public that even a creative legal pleading cannot hope to match. A short time later the fraud division files a . . . case and the paper gives it good coverage and relates it to its earlier story. The quid pro quo? The reporter may well bring in his next hot lead to the prosecutor. Further, in this era of guilty pleas (close to 90 per cent of our dispositions) it is difficult to get the story out any other way. . . . Investigative reporting is a public service, prosecuting fraud cases is a public necessity. If on occasion they work together behind the scenes to strengthen their respective roles and their ties to one another, I feel the results are worthwhile.''[5]

One need not debate the symbolic quality of Anderson's metaphor to grasp its rhetoric: if the public prosecutor's work is not publicized, its deterrent effect is lost. It is to his and the public's advantage for him to have a close relationship with the reporter. In addition to helping the reporter with information about local scams, the active prosecutor may provide leads to documentary sources in other jurisdictions, such as news of a lawsuit filed against a local business in another state.

Noncompetitive reporters: Following up such an out-of-state tip may connect you with a reporter several hundred miles away who can check files for you and who—if he senses a possible story for himself—may work cooperatively, agreeing to hold publication of his story until you are ready to break yours.

Public-relations people: You will want to talk to the PR team at some point, but you should avoid substantive conversations until you are well prepared. In any sizable corporation, public-relations people know exactly what the law requires them to make public, and they usually brief themselves thoroughly on whatever topic you are interested in. Most of those in public relations will try to tell the truth as far as company policy and

company interests allow. Many have a newspaper background. "They are human beings who know a hell of a lot about what is going on," says Dick Gibson. And, Gibson adds, they can be particularly helpful when asked about a company other than their own.

Top managers: The higher the reporter goes in management, the more likely he is to get specific answers. But until he is prepared to ask hard, specific questions and to follow through on openings, it is best to keep questions to senior managers soft and general. Most top management people are articulate and logical arguers. If your questions expose ignorance of basic issues, you may be cut short and lose your entrée for further interviews. Think of any interview with top management as a key interview, which means that it calls for very careful preparation.

Owners: Single proprietors or corporate chairmen, of course, are the ultimate sources. They also have the most at stake (personal investment, reputation, continuation of the business) in the answers they give to your questions. They are likely to shut off your sources and perhaps seek retribution directly against you if they sense you are going to be critical. These factors suggest staying away from the owners until the elements of a strong story are clearly in sight.

Obviously, not all of the sources cited above will be helpful all of the time. Still, it is a good idea to explore each area of expertise represented on this list. And at each stop, remember, you will be looking for documents to corroborate what you have learned through interviews. The documents, in turn, will help you take the next step up the ladder.

DOCUMENTS AS SOURCES

Businesses generate and keep records. The ideal situation would be to have access to internal records but rarely is the ideal attained. Your documentation, therefore, must be built from external records. Listed below are more than a dozen places where records relating to businesses are available:

Inspection offices: Specific references to the subject you are investigating (for example, a pattern of short-weighting packages by a supermarket chain) may be on hand at your local inspection office. These offices can lead you to individual inspectors who have access to the business. They can sometimes fill in, confirm, or refute key dates, names of company personnel, and other details that are unobtainable from the company itself.

Courthouses: Deeds and mortgages are filed in the county recorder's office, for example. "Land is involved in so many transactions," observes Jonathan Kwitny of the *Wall Street Journal.* These records tell you what

property the company, its owners, and managers hold, as well as the names of their attorneys, agents, and bankers. Further, they give you clues about holding companies and subsidiaries operated by the company.

Secretary of state offices: Incorporation papers, charters, reports of dissolution, payment of taxes—these records are among the routine files in state secretaries' offices. From their files you can obtain the names of incorporators, sometimes major stockholders, attorneys, and always the statutory or resident agent, the person designated to accept service of legal papers. Company records filed with the secretary under the Uniform Commercial Code Section list major chattel mortgages or secured loans (on the order of $100,000 or more).

Public companies: Annual reports, press releases, speeches by managers, company newspapers, presentations to legislative bodies, stock prospectuses, rate filings, and tariff laws are worthwhile sources if read diligently and compared closely. Most of these official statements, available in the offices of public companies, are carefully thought out to say only what is to serve immediate company interests. Some, however, take on added meaning when read against other company statements made to other audiences at about the same time. Barlett and Steele, for example, used stories from the Hughes Tool Company employee newspaper as a supplemental source in their 1975 report on the Howard Hughes empire. Ponder this excerpt of theirs regarding the Howard Hughes Medical Institute, the foundation that owned 100 per cent of Hughes Aircraft Company stock while enjoying technical exemption from the Tax Reform Act of 1969:

> On the 1964 information return it submitted to the Internal Revenue Service, the medical institute estimated the fair market value of the aircraft company stock at $150 million.
>
> Eight years later, at the beginning of 1973, the medical institute placed the book value . . . at $154 million . . . an increase of less than 3 percent during a period in which the company's sales went up more than 100 percent. . . .
>
> The Hughesnews, the company's employee publication, carried a story in its June 4, 1971, issue assessing the company's performance. . . .
>
> Reporting a speech by Allen A. Puckett, executive vice president and assistant general manager, the Hughesnews story stated:
>
> "Through wise capital expenditures, Hughes had emerged with one of the most modern and efficient plants . . . In 1970, the company invested $27 million in new facilities and equipment. . . ."
>
> And in its May 25, 1973, issue, the Hughesnews again reported on another Puckett speech:
>
> "Hughes Aircraft . . . will have expended $192 million for new buildings and equipment in the decade through 1974."[6]

The reporters went on to explain that by keeping the book value of its stock low, the institute and the aircraft company were avoiding millions of dollars of charitable payouts that might be required under laws regulating private foundations. Because the stock was not sold publicly, Hughes Aircraft was not required to report to the Securities and Exchange Commission, though more than 10,000 other companies did report.

Under 1976 rules of the SEC, any company with more than 500 stockholders and more than $1 million in assets is required to make a public annual report to its stockholders. It is a basic document for the business journalist. "Read it backward," a wise business writer once said, and his advice is sound. First read the auditor's opinion, a brief letter normally saying that a certified public accountant has examined the books of the corporation, made the tests he considers necessary to check the bookkeeping, and has found that they reflect the company's condition according to "generally accepted accounting standards." Alexander Auerbach of the *Los Angeles Times* says that if the letter is more than two paragraphs long, "you start paying attention [particularly] if you start seeing things where the accountant says we can't be certain that this company should be valued as a continuing operation, then you know it's got a big problem." Auerbach cautions that the only audited (sworn) portions of the annual report are usually the pages carrying such headings as "balance sheet," "changes in financial condition," "income statement," and "shareholders' equity."[7] Each table usually carries footnotes, and to an expert they are the most informative parts of the report. They may indicate changes in the company's accounting method from year to year, or they may reveal bookkeeping devices intended to gloss over the company's weakness, for example, in cash position or other significant areas. A full treatment of a public company's annual report is not within the scope of this book; any serious journalist studying one, however, should sit down with his own company's accountant and discuss its meaning.

Regulatory agencies: Agencies that regulate businesses come in several flavors. Federal agencies like the Federal Communications Commission, the Interstate Commerce Commission, the Nuclear Regulatory Commission, and the Food and Drug Administration require extensive reports from companies doing interstate business. Some of the regulatory connections are obvious, but others are not. If you are in Washington and uncertain of all the agencies that may affect your target business, a good place to start is the Office of Management and Budget, which maintains an index of every type of report form required by federal agencies from more than ten sources. Most of the agencies listed above gather their reports under the general theory of protecting the public health and safety.

Viewing business from a different angle is the Securities and Exchange Commission. Its general mission is to protect the integrity of the system of financing business—buying and selling stocks, issuing debentures—which has been interpreted with increasing breadth to mean giving the public all "material information" concerning the safety of their investments. Especially in the post-Watergate era—after the discovery of illegal corporate political contributions, executive slush funds, and bribes to foreign governments—the SEC has strengthened its regulations and their enforcement in order to give the public greater knowledge about the use of corporate funds. Some of the SEC's most important reports, available in Washington or in any of several regional offices, are:

- Form 3, the insider report, requires any officer, director or holder of more than ten per cent of the stock of a public company to show his full "beneficial ownership" of stock.
- Form 4, an amendment to Form 3, must be filed within ten days after the end of a month in which an "insider" changes his stock position by sale, purchase, gift, or in any other manner.
- Form S-1 is the registration form for companies first coming under SEC jurisdiction. It gives extensive detail about the formation of the company, the personal and business history of its officers, the capital structure, lines of credit, and similar facts.
- Form S-8 is required whenever the company proposes to offer new securities to the public.
- Form 10-K, in the words of Auerbach, is "the annual report without all that rubbish."[8] The 10-K must be filed with the SEC not later than ninety days after the company's annual audit. If you can't get a copy from the company itself, try your stockbroker.
- Form 10-Q is a quarterly version of the 10-K, issued within forty-five days of the close of a business quarter. It is not usually certified by an independent auditor.
- Form 8-K records "material corporate events." It must be filed within ten days after the month in which "events" like a change of ownership occur—or changes in assets, lawsuits in which the company is involved, defaults on senior securities, changes of accountants, changes in conditions of debentures, and offerings of options on five per cent or more of outstanding stock.
- Form 13-D is filed by any individual acquiring five per cent or more of a company's stock.

The SEC has several publications that keep reporters and persons in the financial community abreast of its reports and actions. There is a daily *Digest,* a weekly *Docket* and a monthly *Summary of Transactions and Holdings.* Full-time business reporters get themselves on one or more of these mailing lists and read them with all the eagerness of a soldier getting mail from home. For the general reporter seeking information on a single corporation, the more efficient method is to go to an SEC regional office and search the public file. There are also commercial services in Wall Street that will ship you copies (at twenty cents or so a page) of whatever information on public companies you need—and you will get them faster than by writing letters to the SEC bureaucracy. A special note on banks. They must file information very similar to that shown in SEC 10-K reports, but where the information is filed depends on the type of bank. It may be with the Controller of the Currency, the Federal Reserve Board, the Federal Deposit Insurance Corporation, or your state banking agency.

Not all federal agencies are as aggressively public as the SEC. Their interpretations of the public right to access vary, but the reporter should always explore fully whatever files these agencies have, and should, when the stakes justify the expense, test the agencies' resistance through use of the Freedom of Information Act.

Would that all state regulatory agencies were uniformly thorough and reliable in their records, but they are not. Except in a few states—New York and California, for instance—state insurance departments are viewed with suspicion by experienced reporters. The quality of state banking departments, industrial-safety departments, utility commissions, and other state regulatory agencies varies wildly from state to state.

Prospectuses and proxy statements: Depending on the jurisdiction involved, prospectuses are required by the SEC, your state securities division, or both whenever promoters issue stock or bonds. Prospectuses are among the most complete public records telling how things work within a company at a given moment (the time of offering the stock), what factors may affect its future earnings, what persons hold notes from the company, what persons have peripheral interests in it, and so forth. Proxy statements, sent to stockholders before the annual meeting, give details of proposed changes in corporate direction and policy as well as information on such matters as efforts by outsiders to take over the company.

Investment services: Working for pay, investment-service companies gather information not only from 10-Ks, prospectuses, and other public reports, but from their own business-intelligence sources. Their evaluation of a company's management and policies is likely to be clearer and more pointed than the carefully guarded statements of the company itself.

Trade press: Every industry is served by one or more special-interest media, some of which are quite sophisticated and aggressive. Many public libraries and most large university libraries keep collections or can help you find back copies of media that cover your target business. Check the annual indexes of publications like *Iron Age, Chemical Week,* and *Architectural Record* for the names of your target company and its managers and owners. In addition to this independent trade press, there are numerous "captive" media (house organs) of business, particularly those published by the big oil companies—*Marathon World,* for example—that are less penetrating but often contain little nuggets of information in their flattering profiles of companies and management people.

Courts: Business and businessmen are used to litigation. They sue to collect bills; they are sued by suppliers, customers, and creditors; they sue over trade secrets and contracts with former executives and consultants; they sue or are sued over taxes; they may go through bankruptcy proceedings. As a result, our courts are a real fount of facts about business corporations. The owners of companies and their managers go through divorces and property settlements; company founders leave wills that must be filed for probate. All these legal actions leave a solid record of changes, transactions, crises, and policy shifts. Says Dick Gibson: "Every reporter on our (business) staff [goes] down to the courts at least once a week. We get the daily summaries printed in the legal newspapers of both of the Twin Cities. We read them very carefully, and it pays off."

All these legal factors emphasize how important it is for the investigative reporter to check court docket indexes for the names of a target company and its owners and managers. When he finds a trail, he pulls the case files, which contain trial transcripts, court orders, executions of judgment, and similar documents. And he learns to look, if a case has not yet been tried, for depositions in which parties have in effect given testimony under oath. Depending on the status of the case, the deposition may be in an attorney's office, on the judge's desk, or in a file in the clerk's office. In any event, it is as public and official as if you had heard it given from the witness stand while court was in session.

One of the most useful courts for business reportage is the United States Tax Court in Washington, D.C. A business or person who has protested an Internal Revenue Service claim for taxes must file voluminous records in this court, which makes them part of the public record. Since 1975, the system has been expanded to include a number of "small claims" tax courts around the country. Similar tax courts operate in some states. Also well worth checking are the dockets and records of the National Labor Relations Board.

Legislative committees: Congress and your state legislature consider many proposals affecting business. Every time they do, they take testimony in committee, circulate questionnaires, make studies of their own, and compile a record of arguments. What the business executive or lobbyist says during this process is frozen in a record, and it may be different from what he says in more public statements or what he may tell you in an interview. Committee reports often contain tables and analyses that help sort out conflicting statistics and expert opinions.

Bureau of the Census: The Census Bureau compiles data not only on the population but on several kinds of business activity. While virtually none of these facts can be traced to individual companies, together they constitute probably the most accurate information available on industry-wide trends. Occasionally, by careful deduction, census data compiled on a state or metropolitan-area basis, or both, will yield clues to the activity of a single dominant company.

Credit agencies: Documentary information from credit companies is very sensitive and harder to come by than it used to be, particularly since the upsurge of consumer-oriented privacy legislation. Nonetheless, most experienced investigative reporters develop contacts that can provide such information—if the reporter uses utmost discretion about what to publish and how to attribute it. Your own newspaper's business department may subscribe to one or more credit-reporting agencies. If you are not the confidant of a senior bank officer, one of your editors may be. Only in the most critical cases—those in which some sort of criminal activity is suspected—can the reporter call on his source for actual documents, and then he and his editor have a serious ethical decision to make about publishing information they contain.

Who's who publications: There are scores of who's who publications— national, regional, and state—and they are also categorized by the activity of the whos in them. Probably ninety per cent of their biographical sketches are self-written, self-serving, and not carefully checked by the editors. But good reporters use these books as leads in searching for patterns of marriage, bloodlines, or corporate, school, and other ties that may help clarify the motivations and operations of a target company.

Trade and professional directories: Subject to most of the limitations of biographical directories, trade and professional publications may still be useful when you are looking for sources in distant cities or regions. They cover about every field: medicine, undertaking, architecture, law, petroleum marketing, and so on.

National newspaper and periodical indexes: Magazine and newspaper indexes of business stories are available in your major state and university libraries. If they don't have the actual newspaper or a microfilm of it, they will probably have a computer or mail relationship with a regional or national library network that can help trace the activity of your subject in other states.

What I have outlined above is close to a score of documentary sources of business information. The reporter who carefully blends information garnered from documentary and interview sources can build a solid and detailed picture of his target company, industry, or entrepreneur. His problem is not one of too little but of too much information. He will have a wealth of data that he must sort and pattern into a coherent structure, matching and confirming key points and casting aside extraneous, conflicting, or biased material. Indeed, the material may be so voluminous, and yet so specific, that the reporter may wish to use counter-sorter or computer analysis of the kind Isaacs employed in his Senate committee study (Chapter 6).

WRITING IT

With so much material, it is easy to write dozens of pages of turgid, complex prose. Reeking of bureaucratic jargon, the story can all too readily be one to turn off all but the most technical-minded reader. The reporter, therefore, should spend a good deal of thought on outlining both the verbal and the graphic presentation of his story. Working with his teammates or editor, he should look for the angle that appeals to his specific target audience: the reader as an individual worker, consumer, investor, or local businessman. Bear in mind that the lead aimed at the mass market will not always get the most readership. Many business stories are most effective if written for businessmen and politicians—that is, at a level of sophistication well above the traditional "milkman in Omaha" audience so dear to the editors of United Press in the 1940s.

The choice of approach is not always easy. If you are writing about a blatant and widespread consumer fraud, it is comfortable to open with the case of a senior citizen whose nest egg has been scrambled by the suede-shoe boys. If you are dealing with the equity-capital problems of a company caught in a recession and a general money supply squeeze, your lead will more likely be aimed at businessmen. If it is clear from facts, interviews, and SEC documents that a company has, as a matter of policy, been laundering illegal political contributions through a Swiss or Bahamian bank, that is hard news for the public. But if another company has been collecting an executive slush fund that is technically legal, your approach should be more restrained. There is still the "how things work" story for your mass reader, but the lead should be more carefully qualified. Vide:

> Monsanto Company's lobbyists have channeled thousands of dollars to favored politicians through an "employee voluntary political contribution plan," which at least a few employees say is not voluntary.
>
> More than $1,000,000 has been deducted from the salaries of the 1800 executives in the political program since it was started in 1968. . . .
>
> A few of the 21 Monsanto executives who were willing to talk about the plan have told the Post-Dispatch that they were "coerced" and "pressured" into joining the plan. At least 20 other Monsanto executives . . . refused to discuss any aspect of the program.

John W. Hanley, president of the company, said he was surprised and angered to hear that some employees had been subject to arm twisting. . . . Some of the executives to whom the Post-Dispatch talked said they had joined of their own volition.

Hanley said that an investigation of the program that he ordered in 1973 had concluded that some elements of the program were no longer appropriate under new federal laws . . . For that reason, he says, a new plan is being developed and will be put into effect this fall.[9]

By WILLIAM FRIEVOGEL AND LOUIS J. ROSE
Of the *Post-Dispatch Staff*

Consumer-Employee Stories

Stories about the consumer and the employee are stories about business policies, decisions, machinations, or mistakes that affect the mass of your readers as buyers and workers. Typical subjects include the recall of products, employee health and safety, quality testing (by the reporter) of products and services, corporate policy decisions that eliminate local jobs, environmental impacts, price manipulation, fraud and misrepresentation in sales pitches, overpriced health-care delivery systems, investment of pension funds, rate-making activities by public utilities, and the health of local banks.

If you are going to do a consumer story, do it all the way. Document your facts carefully and have them checked against industry standards and specifications so you can defend what you have written against the inevitable counterattack. Name local names. If you don't, you will be confusing your reader, you may be damaging reputable businesses by innuendo, and you will contribute unnecessarily to consumer doubt.

In the early 1970s the *Minneapolis Star* had a three-person consumer team headed by David Nimmer. Working with a sizable budget to pay for laboratory tests and technical advice, the team methodically examined and compared the quality and price of goods and services ranging from hamburgers through auto and television repairs to martinis. Surveys made weeks after major stories appeared indicated *Star* readers retained specific information from the series and used it gratefully to guide their purchasing.

When writing about employees, don't write generalizations, describe people such as Hal Drenttel:

> Inside his house at 730 Thompson Ravine, Hal Drenttel cracks a broad grin and sticks out a massive, calloused hand. Like the rest of him, the hand is hard and muscular, the result of 20 years of handling steel at the Dotson Company.
>
> The tables and shelves of the living room are cluttered with porcelain and plastic—knick knacks collected by his wife, Gladys. Ashtrays are everywhere.

An elderly television stares out of the corner. An old rust-colored dog, chained outside, barks incessantly.

It is Saturday. For Drenttel, it is a day to relax. Wearing a football jersey, tan fatigue pants, and slippers, Drenttel slides into a reclining chair and leans back. He breathes deeply, and talks about his life and his work.

"It ain't the ideal place to spend your life," he sighs. But he has spent a good deal of his life there—almost 20 years. However, there is no commitment, no loyalty to the company. "If I could find a decent job, I'd walk out of there like that," he says snapping his fingers.

Injuries? Yes, there are injuries. Pinched fingers, burns, sand and dust in the eyes. A mold falls from a crane and drops on his foot. A sliver of metal flies out of his machine and cuts him. His back is eternally sore; he has lifted tons of steel during his years at Dotson.[10]

By HARVEY T. ROCKWOOD

Public-Policy Stories

Business stories dealing with public policy are essentially political in nature. Stories of business's influence on zoning, or transportation, and on other local-government services abound—and most of them are written as stories about the venality by politicians. But what a businessman may call a political shakedown, a politician may describe as a bribe offered by a corrupt developer. Too often, I think, the reporter concentrates on the politician as culprit when he would be wiser to look at the businessman as perpetrator. In their series on corruption of the FHA Section 236 program to offer low-cost inner-city housing to families on welfare, Barlett and Steele documented and interviewed until they could identify several mortgage brokers who lavished favors on salesmen who brought them profitable high-interest mortgages from families that would be expected to default, leaving the FHA to pay off the loan so the whole process could start again.[11]

The operations of a national lobby of supercorporation chief executives working to kill antitrust legislation is a broad story of general interest. A story about a local or regional company influencing rules issued by a state regulatory agency, however, might be written as a consumer story. A piece about a business angling for government subsidies, such as industrial-development bonds backed by the full faith and credit of the state, would fall nearer the middle of the spectrum: it raises a question of basic governmental policy about subsidizing private business ventures.

There are many other subjects to explore in the public-policy category of business stories. One might be on the use of special commissions and nonprofit corporations to do public business outside constitutional and statutory lines. Another might describe the use of public funds to provide risk capital for private business. The creation of "front" companies, like the construction-contract broker who starts to erect a public building with minimum capital and has to be bailed out with public funds, is yet another.

Many public-policy business stories present difficult judgment problems for the reporter. They may be "how things work" stories, not uncovering blatantly illegal practices. They come to light because an enterprising corporation or individual is pushing an idea to gain a favored position or a windfall profit (as in the case of the Omaha State Office Building in Chapter 12). If the enterprising idea is fully presented so that a public decision can be openly arrived at, the reporter's job is simple. But this is seldom the case. Behind the corporation's smoothly prepared presentation to the city council, there is usually a special angle, a tacit understanding with the political leaders. The reporter cannot expect the business promoter to volunteer arguments against his own case. So, as Jim O'Shea of the *Des Moines Register* puts it, "we have to be a sort of devil's advocate toward every idea that comes along."

Another, broader type of public-policy story relates to the influence of business on the customs, mores, and attitudes of the community. Stories about business effects on society often get into "power structure" politics (Chapter 11) and rarely present clear-cut issues. Nonetheless, the reporter has the opportunity and, in my view, the duty to tell his readers who, how, and when business has influenced community leaders in their civic planning. Decisions to embark on new programs like building projects, or making zoning changes may be doing more to line business pockets than to benefit the public. One of the more interesting efforts in this genre was done by Dick Gibson in the Twin Cities in 1971. In a series entitled "In the Board Room," Gibson presented profiles of the chief executives and board chairmen of a dozen national companies based in the Minneapolis-St. Paul area, and it brought out clearly the reasons for the swapping of directorships among a small circle of business leaders. Although Gibson found it was fairly standard procedure for bankers to want to be on company boards to keep an eye on their investments, he also found an improvement in the quality of membership on boards of directors. The old good-buddy system had begun to change, as directors were expected to assume major responsibilities involving more work than some wished to take on.[12]

In writing stories about the pressures business sometimes places on decisions of public policy, the reporter cannot fall back on a handy good guy-bad guy formula. He faces special challenges in defining the issues—the new shopping center vs. increased traffic and noise, the new school building program vs. increased taxes and segregation patterns, the new freeway vs. the demolition of beloved old neighborhoods. He must build his base, collect precedents and expert opinions, and then construct a story which touches the lives of his readers. Business does not always turn out to be the villain in these pieces, but sometimes business works too quietly for the public good its wonders to perform.

THE BUSINESS AUDIENCE

There is plenty of evidence that business executives may be the most influential audience you write for in these visual-news days. Your selection of topics and approaches should include stories that you know will not reach a broad audience but will be read avidly by the business community. This audience includes people who, though they may not manage or wholly own a business, own stock or manage investments in one or more companies. The members of your business audience are interested in systematic investigative reporting for several reasons:

1. They want intelligence. They want "inside information" about individuals or companies, particularly those that seek special or illegal advantage from the system.
2. They want to know the standards by which the total business community is operating. Their interest may be highly moral or it may be entirely venal, but it is certainly intense.
3. They want to know how the public feels. Good reporting helps them learn, explicitly or implicitly.
4. They have their own axes to grind. A man who operates a car-rental business, for instance, has a special interest in how the police and courts enforce traffic and parking laws. His customers leave him with a lot of unpaid tickets.

Ideas and facts in these categories are important to decision-makers in business and investment fields. Profit dollars, personal security, the delicate balance of the economic system are at stake.

The top business executive has still another, special problem: he wants independent sources of local information. The people he sees and talks to tend either to say yes a lot, to discuss only parochial affairs, or to view the world from an unrealistically elevated position. So the business executive values good reporting from independent sources. He would prefer that you select your targets outside his own company, but at times he will accept a public airing of his problems if it tells him something his own associates won't. I remember a story Wes Iversen did about an efficiency study in the headquarters of the Union Pacific Railroad. It was causing much dissension at the third and fourth levels. The day after we published the story, Iversen got a call from the UP president who wished we hadn't done the story, but ruefully admitted it told him things he needed to know.

Story Projects

So you should not automatically blanch when your editor suggests you research a hard or technical story that you know will be read by nobody but businessmen. Think of projects like these:

Shaky pyramids. In the tight-money era of the mid-1970s, stories began cropping up about promoters who borrowed too much money and tried to launch overvalued and underfinanced corporations to build anything from business centers and apartments to housing developments and franchise empires. Pyramid-type corporations are layered on top of each other with only a minimum of equity. Identifying and tracing one of these enterprises before it gets to bankruptcy court is a challenge. If you do, your story will be appreciated by financial analysts, securities-law enforcers, bankers, contractors, and suppliers of the subject company—and just about everyone else in business. It may influence standard business practice, the applicatin of existing law, and perhaps the creation of new laws or regulations to forestall future catastrophes. Your story's most important effect may not be measurable: it may cause bankers or prospective promoters to shy away from other ill-timed projects they have on the drawing boards.

Fake pyramids. Ponzi-type schemes that depend on high-pressure salesmanship applied to inexperienced investors rather than sophisticated financiers are known as fake pyramids. In these swindles, handsome payouts are made to some early investors, who are encouraged to increase their stakes unaware that most of the money really is coming from their own or other investors' funds rather than from legitimate business activity. (They are named after Charles Ponzi, a Boston confidence man active in 1919 and 1920, who promised $1.40 in 90 days for every $1 invested and, for a while, delivered. He took in $10 million before he was arrested.) Stories about them are particularly interesting to the business community because the tarnish of this kind of operation rubs off on ever business, and because it represents a diversion of risk capital.

The money market. Probably the single most important factor affecting business decisions is the availability of money. If it is easy to get, most businesses will borrow, expand their operations, and perhaps hire more people. If money is tight, businesses will cut down, delay capital expenditures and perhaps raise prices in order to obtain operating capital. The competition for working capital—bank loans, common stock corporate bonds, convertible debentures, publicly subsidized loans—at favorable rates is heavy. Any story that traces the influences on your local or regional money supply, particularly if it identifies factors that discriminate against local interests, will make you more friends than you might lose in the business community.

Public regulators. Not always white knights, public regulators are usually an interesting story subject. They may lose sight of their goals, yield to political pressure, or be subverted by inside shakedown artists. The aftermath of Watergate has given us some understanding of how government agencies can squeeze people seen by a public executive as enemies. The reporter's challenge in working on such stories is to separate the wheat of truth from the chaff of charges that businessmen throw out about unreasonable inspections, arbitrary administrative findings, and veiled threats. Few businessmen are willing to be quoted on such charges, particularly if they believe they are alone. In recording the shakedown of builders in the Westhaven, Ill., area by Mayor Curtis Whitaker, Rick Friedman and his *Star-Tribune* staff heard from dozens of contractors before they could convince one to give them and the United States attorney's office enough information for a documented, provable case.

Concentrations of business power are anathema to more business readers than you may think. The hundreds of thousands of small retailers, manufacturers, wholesalers, bankers—yes, even publishers—are concerned about facts like these: less than 1 per cent of manufacturing businesses collects more than 80 per cent of the profits and is owned by less than 2 per cent of the adult population; approximately 500 corporations dominate virtually all of the basic markets. Half a dozen chains control nearly 15 per cent of all daily newspaper circulation in the United States.[13]

Securities laws and regulatory agencies affect the ability of small businesses to raise necessary capital. The complexity of forms and record-keeping required by these agencies, product liability, set-asides on payment in government contracts are all subjects in which small business owners are particularly interested.

The heads of regulatory agencies, usually political appointees, are often stories in themselves. They may make appointments, control promotions, and spend money. Some are survivors, continuing in office through changes of administrations, and building almost impregnable empires.

The hundreds of thousand of businessmen who are outside this concentration of power are sensitive to—and many are highly critical of—its influences. Hence, the thoughtful reporter who writes accurately and authoritatively about these influences and how regulatory agencies deal with them will find a ready and perceptive audience in local business and political circles. The Barlett and Steele series on the "created crisis" in oil in 1973 was more than most daily newspaper readers cared to follow, but it had strong acceptance in business and political circles.

The politics of business. Businessmen want candidates elected to office who are favorable to themselves and their interests. They want to know who is exercising or trying to exercise influence over whom. Thus, they are interested in stories that deal in the rise and fall of local political leadership. Because they are contributors to political campaigns, businessmen can be valuable sources to reporters for political stories.

Management of public funds. Even though their philosophical bases may be different from yours, most businessmen will read and respond to stories on questionable fiscal policy long before the public realizes there is a problem. They will quickly comprehend the perils of investing state employees' pension money in speculative ventures. They will smell the political links involved in selecting investment counselors for public bond issues. They will react to stories about the avoidance of open bidding on public purchases. Bankers will read each others' condition statements and note possible variations from law, administrative regulations, or prudent practice.

LABOR

From the 1930s to about the middle '50s, most reporters had rather romantic views of the American labor movement. They saw it as pitted against Big Business in the true tradition of Marxist class war. Things have changed.

The labor movement itself has grown big and institutional (see Chapter 10). Some national unions (which often call themselves international) have amassed such piles of assets, particularly pension funds, that they themselves are targets of corruption. And as in any institution, many have passed into a stage of conservatism in which the preservation of the structure and of thousands of staff and executive jobs becomes more important than the welfare of individual members. Today, the big unions have become potent political forces whose influence and financial support are sought by party leaders.

Covering the labor movement these days is not much different from covering business. Within the national and international unions there are "ins" and "outs" who become sources of information about each other. The hierarchy of a major union may be smaller than the hierarchy of a major corporation, but it is still big enough to contain sources for the enterprising reporter. Unions are required to make financial reports under the Taft-Hartley law. They sue and are sued. They maintain lobbies and technical staffs, much the same as business organizations do. They publish newspapers, legislative reports, and other data for their members. They operate their own business ventures (insurance companies seem to be a favorite), which are incorporated, licensed, regulated, and inspected like any other business venture. And sometimes they even have dissident employees.

In summary, the investigative reporter must not adopt a narrow, stereotypical view of all businessmen as natural enemies and all labor leaders as philosophical soulmates. If he explores carefully, builds his own independent base of knowledge, exercises his own judgment in the interests of his readers, he will learn to ask informed questions about these two vital sectors of the community. He will get better stories, professional recognition and, in some cases, direct and visible support from community leaders.

BECAUSE IT'S RIGHT: A NOTE IN CONCLUSION

Investigative journalism is right for many people in many ways at many levels.

For the concerned reader it is right because it provides new, significant, and useful information that he cannot obtain elsewhere.

For the reporter it is right because it gives new value to his efforts. It frees him to pursue the truth with more intellectual independence. It also restores much of the fun to reporting.

For the conscientious editor it is right because it gives meaning to the craft of journalism. It provides a socially important role for the editor.

And for the thinking publisher it is right because it can make a worthy service a profitable one. It gives him new stature in his own community and fills a vital need of society.

Chapter Notes

CHAPTER 1: *WINNERS AND LOSERS*

1. Walter Lippmann, "syndicated," column, May 27, 1965 (part of an address he gave that day to the International Press Institute in London).

2. Robert Daley, "Super-Reporter: The Missing American Hero . . .," *New York,* September 16, 1973, pp. 42-48.

3. "Detroit Free Press Sued for $60 Million," *Editor & Publisher,* June 23, 1973, p. 42.

4. Richard Pollak, "Column Two: The Firing of Denny Walsh," (*MORE*), September, 1974, p. 2.

CHAPTER 2: *THINKING ABOUT IT*

1. Charles C. Hill, "Such Trying Times to be Raking Muck," *Quill,* December, 1974, p. 22.

2. Ibid., p. 23.

3. "Missing Witness Living in W. Indies," *Milwaukee Journal,* December 25, 1972, and "Nowakowski Traced. . . .," January 3, 1973.

4. Knight News Wire as published in *Columbus Dispatch,* September 10, 1974.

5. *Des Moines Register,* November 10, 1974, et seq.

6. "Medicaid Probe 'Was Justified,' " *Sun Newspapers of Omaha.* January 7, 1971.

7. "Watergate: Tracking It Down," *Quill,* June, 1973, p. 6.

8. *Chicago Sun-Times,* May 13, 1973, et seq.

9. "Auditing the IRS," *The Philadelphia Inquirer,* April 14, 1974.

10. David Kraslow and Stuart H. Loory, *The Secret Search for Peace in Vietnam* (New York: Random House, 1968).

CHAPTER 3: *NEEDLES AND HAYSTACKS*

1. Robert Daley, "Super-Reporter: The Missing American Hero . . .," *New York,* September 16, 1973, pp. 42-48.

2. *Orange County Investigative Reporting Seminar* (Los Angeles: Urban Policy Research Institute, 1975), pp. 6-7.

3. Address to Suburban Newspapers of America editorial seminar, Northwestern University, October 23, 1974.

4. *Orange County,* p. 29.

5. Leonard Downie, *The New Muckrakers* (Washington, D.C.: The New Republic Book Co., 1976), p. 117.

6. Carl Bernstein and Bob Woodward, *All the President's Men* (New York: Warner Paperback Library, 1975), p. 60.

7. *Orange County,* p. 19.

8. "Influence and the Legislature," *Minneapolis Star,* July 6-17, 1970.

CHAPTER 4: *TALKING AND LISTENING*

1. *Orange County Investigative Reporting Seminar* (Los Angeles: Urban Policy Research Institute, 1975), p. 28.

2. "Pallotine Informer Fired, Tells of Role," *Washington Post,* February 3, 1976, p. 1.

3. Leonard Downie, *The New Muckrakers* (Washington, D.C.: The New Republic Book Co., 1976), p. 152.

4. Carl Bernstein and Bob Woodward, *All the President's Men* (New York: Warner Paperback Library, 1975), pp. 140–41 and 180.

5. Dave O'Brian, "Spotlighting the Boston Globe's Investigative Team," *Boston Phoenix,* January 14, 1973.

6. Bernstein and Woodward, *All the President's Men,* chap. 3.

7. "Mayor's Ally Got $83,000 in City Land Deal," *St. Louis Post-Dispatch,* September 10, 1972, p. 1.

8. 1974 APME-PRSA survey, released through APME, 1975, n. p.

CHAPTER 5: *INSIDE AND UNDER COVER*

1. "Two Investigative Reporters for the Star . . .," *Indianapolis Star,* September 13, 1974, p. 1.

2. Lisa Bercovici, "The Road to Hong Kong," (*MORE*), August, 1975, p. 20.

3. "Combustion Engineering's Order Surge . . .," *Wall Street Journal,* May 7, 1974, p. 40.

4. *Editor & Publisher,* December 13, 1975, p. 47.

5. "Detective Spied on Dita Beard . . .," *Rocky Mountain News,* October 6, 1973, p. 1.

6. *Chicago Tribune,* September 7-10 and 14, 1975.

7. "Deadly Drug Easy to Get Here," *Cleveland Plain Dealer,* January 27, 1974, p. 1.

8. *Orange County Investigative Reporting Seminar* (Los Angeles: Urban Policy Research Institute, 1975), p. 16.

9. "Police Involved With Pawnbroker," *Indianapolis Star,* March 3, 1974, p. 1.

CHAPTER 6: *WORKING WITH NUMBERS*

1. Jay Harris, unpublished memorandum to I. W. Cole, August, 1973; cited hereafter as Harris memo.

2. Frederick O'Reilly Hayes, "How to Read a Budget," *Columbia Journalism Review,* January-February, 1976, p. 21.

3. Harris memo.

4. *Orange County Investigative Reporting Seminar* (Los Angeles: Urban Policy Research Institute, 1975), p. 14.

5. "Nixon's Questionable Gift of Papers," *Oakland Tribune,* September 3, 1973, p. 1.

6. "Crime and Justice," *Philadelphia Inquirer,* February 18-25, 1973.

7. "Justice and the Drunken Driver," *Paddock Publications* (Arlington Heights, Ill.), July 28-August 2, 1975.

8. Stephen Isaacs, letter to author, February 15, 1976.

9. *Washington Post,* February 16-22, 1975.

10. *Editor & Publisher,* November 25, 1972, p. 14.

11. *Wilmington Evening Journal,* June 27-29, 1972.

12. David J. Armor and Arthur S. Couch, *Data-Text Primer* (New York: The Free Press, 1972).

13. Philip E. Meyer, *Precision Journalism* (Bloomington, Ind.: Indiana University Press, 1973). Maxwell McCombs, Donald Leslie Shaw, and David Grey, *Handbook of Reporting Methods* (Boston: Houghton Mifflin, 1976).

14. "Inequality Marks Sales-Assessment Ratios," *Sun Newspapers of Omaha,* June 18, 1971.

15. "Our Doctors: A Self-Examination," *Dubuque Telegraph-Herald,* August 17-24, 1975.

16. *Des Moines Sunday Register,* November 10, 1974, et seq.

17. Philip E. Meyer, letter to author, February 20, 1976.

18. "Over 100 False Arrests Bared," *Cincinnati Enquirer,* June 7, 1975.

19. "Plea Bargaining" series, *Minneapolis Tribune,* October 14-18, 1973.

20. "'73 Campaign Floated on a Sea of Cash," *Roanoke Times.* February 10, 1974.

21. *Orange County,* p. 32.

22. "Will Washington Be a Supersnoop?" *Detroit News,* April 28, 1974, p. 1.

23. Harris memo.

24. *Precision Journalism,* p. 113.

25. Harris memo.

26. *The People Beyond 12th Street* (Detroit, Mich.: Detroit Urban League, 1967).

27. *Return to 12th Street* (Detroit, Mich.: *Detroit Free Press,* 1968).

28. Philip E. Meyer, *Miami Negroes: A Study in Depth* (Miami, Fla.: Miami Herald, 1968). Previously published in the *Miami Herald,* April 28-May 2, 1968).

29. "Sanilac County Loyal to the GOP Even Unto Defeat," *Detroit Free Press,* April 21, 1974.

30. "Clouds Remain Over G.O.P.," *Chicago Tribune,* August 26, 1974.

31. "Our Doctors: A Self-Examination."

32. Harris memo.

33. "Incomplete Data Contaminated Poll," *Columbus Citizen-Journal,* October 24, 1975.

34. Meyer letter to author.

CHAPTER 7: *GETTING THE MESSAGE ACROSS*

1. "Discrimination Found in Congressional Job Orders," *Fort Worth Star-Telegram,* August 18, 1974, p. 1.

2. "Report U.S. Grants Went to Help Nixon," *St. Louis Post-Dispatch,* January 14, 1974, p. 1.

3. *Police Brutality.* (Chicago, Ill.: *Chicago Tribune*). The articles were originally published in the *Chicago Tribune*, November 4-11, 1974.

4. "Crime and Injustice," *Philadelphia Inquirer,* February 18-25, 1973.

5. "Few Duties Involved for Many . . .," *Wall Street Journal,* June 30, 1976, p. 1.

6. "Boeing Sold 11 Jets to Pakistan . . .," *Wall Street Journal,* June 15, 1976, p. 2.

7. "Kings, Princes, Foreign States . . .," *Washington Post,* May 14, 1974, p. C-1.

8. "Boys Town: America's Wealthiest City?" *Sun Newspapers of Omaha,* March 30, 1972, Sec. C.

9. "Will Washington Be a Supersnoop?" *Detroit News,* April 28, 1974, p. 1.

10. *Wall Street Journal,* June 30, 1976, p. 1.

11. "The Farview Findings," *The Philadelphia Inquirer,* June-July 1976.

CHAPTER 8: MEMOS TO THE EDITOR

1. Neale Copple, *Depth Reporting* (Englewood Cliffs, N.J.: Prentice-Hall, 1964).

CHAPTER 9: *THE BOYS TOWN STORY*

This chapter is a slightly expanded version of "Boys Town: An Exposé Without Bad Guys," in the January-February, 1975, issue of the *Columbia Journalism Review,* p. 30, reprinted by permission of the *CJR.*

CHAPTER 10: *THE INSTITUTIONS OF OUR SOCIETY*

1. Wes Gallagher, "A Nation Best Informed or Most Disillusioned. . .," speech to APME, October 18, 1975.

2. "New Stock Manipulation Controls Needed," *Rocky Mountain News,* October 24, 1971.

3. "The Claim Jumpers," *Oakland Tribune,* February 25-28, 1973.

4. *Philadelphia Bulletin,* September 22, 1975, p. 4.

5. "Judge Contributed Illegally. . .," *Boston Globe,* November 26, 1974, p. 1.

6. "Influence and the Legislature," *Minneapolis Star,* July 6-17, 1970.

7. *Riverside Press-Enterprise,* May 12-18, 1971.

8. *Minnesota Daily,* May 21-25, 1973.

9. "The News Machines," *Minneapolis Star,* August 25-September 6, 1975.

10. *The News Machines* (reprint ed., Minneapolis, Minn.: *Minneapolis Star,* 1975), p.

11. *New York Times,* June 27-30, 1976.

12. *Nashville Banner,* March 13-April 22, 1975.

13. *Nashville Banner,* March 29, 1975, and *Gannetteer,* July, 1975, p. 12.

CHAPTER 11: *WEBS AND SHADOWS*

1. "Twenty Top Omaha's Power Structure," *Sun Newspapers of Omaha,* April 7, 1966, p. 1.

2. "Nason's pitch renewed. . .," *Minneapolis Star,* June 10, 1969.

3. "Smalltown traits abound in St. Paul," *Minneapolis Star,* June 20, 1969.

4. *Maine Times,* February 15, 1974.

5. "C. Arnholt Smith: The Man, The Myth. . .," *Chula Vista Star-News,* April 20, 1972, p. 1.

6. "The Smith Saga: Who Pays?" *Chula Vista Star-News,* May 4, 1972, p. 1.

7. *Gannetteer,* July, 1975, p. 12.

CHAPTER 12: *BUYING AND SELLING GOVERNMENT*

1. Kenneth B. Clark, "The American Dilemma," *New York Times,* February 16, 1975, p. E-15.

2. Clark R. Mollenhoff, "What Every Courthouse Reporter Should Know," lecture to API seminars.

3. "Land Use," *Minneapolis Sun Newspapers,* April 11 and 25 and May 9, 1974.

4. Ibid.

5. "Boston the Loser in $2 Million Land Deal," *Boston Globe,* July 9, 1971, p. 1.

6. "Will the City Have to Give Away. . .," *Sun Newspapers of Omaha,* June 12, 1969, p. 9-A.

7. "Contracts, Contributions: A Way of Life in Nassau," *Newsday,* September 28, 1974, p. 1.

8. "William J. Ronan: Makings of a Czar," *Newsday,* March 29, 1972, p. 16-R.

9. "Firefighters Tell of Pressure. . .," *Boston Globe,* April 17, 1975, p. 1.

10. In its various community editions, the *Star-Tribune* papers carried on investigations of the three communities for more than a year. Typical of a story on one of them: "Probe Indicates Orland Officials Violated Statutes. . .," *Tinley Park Star-Tribune,* April 26, 1973.

11. *Dayton Journal Herald,* April 10-21, 1972.

12. The *Minneapolis Tribune* stories ran for five months. The heart of the project was stated in "Study Shows Light Sentences," the first of the series which appeared August 22-25, 1973.

13. "The Greening of the Legislature" appeared as a *Miami Herald* series from March 25 to March 30, 1973, and was reissued as a reprint booklet, which is my source.

14. "Retirement Fund Lends. . .," *New Orleans States-Item,* September 16, 1974.

15. "Proposal for 'New' Offices. . .," Sun Newspapers of Omaha, August 2, 1973, p. 1-B.

16. Martin Dyckman, Letter to author.

17. The *St. Petersburg Times* series, which began December, 1970, included some fifty articles over a three-month period.

18. "What Makes a Newshound Sniff," *Village Voice,* January 27, 1975, p. 16.

19. "Huge C.I.A. Operation Reported. . .," *New York Times,* December 22, 1974, p. 1.

20. "What Makes a Newshound Sniff."

21. "The Silent Partner of Howard Hughes," *Philadelphia Inquirer,* December 14-20, 1975.

CHAPTER 13: *THE BUSINESS OF BUSINESS*

1. Paul Gruchow and Paul Berg, "Coverage of a Scandal," *Twin Cities Journalism Review,* August, 1975, p. 14.

2. As quoted by Michael Moffitt in a UPI dispatch, *Columbus Dispatch,* November 11, 1975, p. A-6.

3. Kenneth B. Clark, "The American Dilemma," *New York Times,* February 16, 1975, p. E-15. ©1975 by the New York Times Company. Reprinted by permission.

4. "The Dotson Company: bosses, workers and the art of surviving to forge another day," *Medicine Jug* (Mankato, Minn., State College), spring, 1975.

5. Gene S. Anderson, Fraud Division, County Prosecutor's Office, Seattle, Wash.

6. "The Silent Partner of Howard Hughes," *Philadelphia Inquirer,* December 15, 1975.

7. San Diego Investigative Reporting Seminar (Los Angeles: Urban Policy Research Institute, 1976), pp. 1-12.

8. Ibid., p. 2.

9. "Monsanto Lobbyists Direct Political Fund," *St. Louis Post-Dispatch,* August 24, 1975.

10. *Medicine Jug,* p. 3.

11. This Barlett and Steele project ran intermittently from August, 1971, to April, 1972. A highlight: "Real Estate Brokers Sail South. . .," *Philadelphia Sunday Inquirer,* December 12, 1971.

12. "In the Board Room," *Minneapolis Star,* January 18-21, 1971.

13. *Editor & Publisher,* August 17, 1974.

Index